CHILD SEXUAL ABUSE

Child Sexual Abuse

A Feminist Reader

Edited by
Emily Driver and
Audrey Droisen

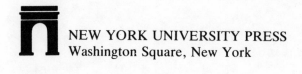

NEW YORK UNIVERSITY PRESS
Washington Square, New York

Printed in the People's Republic of China

First published in the U.S.A. in 1989 by
NEW YORK UNIVERSITY PRESS
Washington Square
New York, NY 10003

Library of Congress Cataloging-in-Publication Data

Child sexual abuse: a feminist reader/edited by Emily Driver
  and Audrey Droisen.
    p. cm.
  Bibliography: p.
  ISBN 0–8147–1815–9
  ISBN 0–8147–1818–3 (pbk.)
  1. Child molesting. 2. Child molesting—Great Britain. 3. Feminism. I. Driver,
Emily. II. Droisen, Audrey.
HQ71.C557 1989   88–39886
362.7′044   CIP

Man to man is so unjust
Children
Don't know who to trust
Your worst enemy could be your best friend
And your best friend, your worst enemy
Some will eat and drink with you
Then behind, them suss upon you . . .
. . . So who the cap fit, let them wear it.

Bob Marley, *Who the Cap Fits*

The right to affection, love and understanding
The right to adequate nutrition and medical care
The right to full opportunity for play and recreation
The right to a name and nationality
The right to special care, if handicapped
The right to be among the first to receive relief in times of disaster
The right to learn to be a useful member of society and to develop
  individual abilities
The right to be brought up in a spirit of peace and universal
  brotherhood
The right to enjoy these rights, regardless of race, colour, sex,
  religion, national or social origin

UN Declaration of the Rights of the Child

Contents

Acknowledgements

This book evolved over a two-year period during which the editors gained invaluable help and inspiration from several groups and individuals. We would like to thank women's groups such as A Woman's Place, the London women's centre; the Child Sexual Abuse Preventive Education Project, London; the Incest Survivors' Campaign, UK; and TABOO, the Manchester refuge for girls. Emily Driver is grateful for advice from Tabitha, Benedict and Felix Driver; Jane Fleming; Liz Hunter; Hilary Kelly; Kim Porter; Isabelle Postill; and workers at the Camden Community Law Centre, especially Russell Campbell. Audrey Droisen is grateful to Aqeela, Ann, Debbie, Diane, Effie, Elizabeth, Ellen, Kris and Leah.

We wish to dedicate this book to Anne Driver and Paula Bartley, in gratitude for their support.

EMILY DRIVER
AUDREY DROISEN

Notes on the contributors

Emily Driver recently qualified as a barrister. She graduated with a degree in Russian and Ancient Greek from Oxford University in 1980 and went on to complete a Diploma in Comparative Slavonic Studies (specialising in linguistics). She then worked as a lexicographer, with a particular interest in learners' dictionaries, for seven years, during which time she was actively involved in the British women's movement and helped to found both the Incest Survivors' Campaign and the Child Sexual Abuse Preventive Education Project in the UK. She has trained professionals in the field and counselled abused children. She worked as a play therapy consultant to Social Services Departments in London until recently and is now embarking on a legal practice in London, concentrating on criminal and family law.

Audrey Droisen is an independent film producer and director. Her work included *Redundant Women, A Crime of Violence* (a programme on child sexual abuse) and *Bitter Wages*. She is also a member of the Advisory Group for the Child Abuse Studies Unit at the Polytechnic of North London and a member of the Feminist Coalition Against Child Sexual Abuse.

Dympna House is a feminist incest counselling centre in Sydney, Australia. The Centre, which is community- and not government-based, was set up in December 1983 by Sydney Women Against Incest. These women, from both non-government and government services, ran a three-day telephone incest survey from Dympna House in February 1984. The publicity and awareness generated by this phone-in led to the establishment, by the State government, of the New South Wales Child Sexual Assault Taskforce. Its recommendations are now being implemented by the NSW Child

Protection Council, and include legal reforms, development of counselling services, training, and a multi-lingual community education campaign. Part of this campaign is aimed at men, with huge billboards all over New South Wales saying 'Child sexual assault offenders – no excuses, never ever'.

Simmy Viinikka is a solicitor living and working in south-east London specialising in family law. Over the past ten years she has been actively involved in a number of feminist campaigns and organisations, particularly around the issue of sexual violence. She has been a member of two Rape Crisis Centres and a Women's Aid Refuge. Professionally, she acts in many cases where the sexual abuse of children is an issue, and is trying to develop a feminist approach to legal practice.

Introduction

EMILY DRIVER

'Then there was the astonishing thing that in every case, blame was laid
on perverse acts by the father . . . though it was hardly credible that perverted acts against children were so general.'
(Freud)[1]

'The widespread reality of incestuous abuse has been repeatedly un-
earthed in the past hundred years, and just as repeatedly buried.
Any serious investigation of the emotional and sexual lives of women
leads eventually to the discovery of the facts of incest. But until recently,
each investigator who has made this discovery has ended by suppressing
it. The information was simply too threatening to be maintained in public
consciousness.'
(Judith Herman)[2]

What is child sexual abuse? Why is it so widespread? Why has its
influence on us, our families and our societies been almost entirely
hidden? This book attempts to answer those questions from
the female point of view.

Judith Herman and other feminists have suggested that it is
women who have the answer to the riddle of incest. They argue that
it is largely an expression of male dominance over women and
children, ensuring silence and submission by enforcing the
institution of heterosexuality on young girls[3] in order to prepare
them for a powerless role in the family and society as adults.

But before looking more closely at the feminist response to child
sexual abuse, one must consider the facts. Certainly, there is a
gender bias to the phenomenon: the American Humane Association Children's Division in a publication of 1969[4] found that 92 per
cent of sexually abused children in their survey were girls, and 97
per cent of child-molesters were heterosexual men. Our contributors reflect this survey in the language of their chapters, by referring

1

to child-molesters with the male pronoun and to abused children
either with the female or with both. This usage may be deterministic
and indeed offensive to some, but readers who dislike such
grammar may if necessary treat it simply as a convention for ease of
style, comparable to the convention by which 'he' usually represents
both genders. The fact remains that gender-neutral language
has for too long disguised the realities of child sexual abuse.[5]

Definitions

Historically, women have only been able to break their collective
silence on incest after gaining strength through other forms of
emancipation struggle. Throughout the twentieth century, women's
causes as varied as the fight for votes, the right to work, housing,
health care, contraception, protection from rape and domestic
violence, and initiatives against colonialism and nuclear war, have
all contributed to their liberation. This book is a product of that
progress in that it was inspired by the work of thousands who are
themselves survivors of sexual abuse. By breaking the silence
imposed by the abusers, these women have managed to extend
networks of support throughout the world, which in turn create the
opportunity to begin our own analysis of our experience and use it
to help others. Whilst not all the contributors to this book would
claim to be survivors of sexual abuse, each believes that any analysis
and treatment of the subject must be firmly founded on the experience of survivors themselves. Hence Chapter 1 is dedicated to
the biographical accounts of those who were sexually abused as
children. The writers do not present themselves as the doomed
'victims' that one is accustomed to see in the traditional incest
literature; instead they speak for the resilience and creativity that all
of us can share in overcoming the cruelty of sexual abuse.

So how representative are these women? Over recent years,
research has projected an increasing percentage of children within
the population who are being subjected to sexual abuse, usually by
reference to questionnaires completed by adult respondents. At
present, sexual abuse of children in Britain is seen as affecting as
many as one in eight girls and one in twelve boys.[6] This increasing
percentage reflects not so much a real historical increase in the
sexual abuse of children, as greater openness in society and more
permission for women and children to come forward and name their

abuse. Reports increase in geometrical progression as soon as there is an an established base, group or crisis centre set up for survivors to report to. It is important to acknowledge the input of informal women's networks in exposing the extent of child sexual abuse, since as Sarah Nelson states:

> If we rely on criminal statistics, as many researchers and professionals have done, we will indeed see incest as a minuscule social problem . . . If estimates are based on conviction rates, figures are lower still – because police discretion, and problems about getting corroborative evidence for child witnesses, produce a low rate of prosecutions . . . Till all the taboos on reporting are eased we cannot gauge the exact frequency, nor 'prove' that 4 per cent or 9 per cent of British women have an incest history. What we can do is look at various clues which suggest that incest is widespread, and infinitely more common than statistics indicate . . . the traditional estimate of one in a million is no more than a wish.[7]

Many feminists have suggested that child sexual abuse is not only more widespread than present research reflects, but that it is experienced by all women:

> I hope your questionnaire takes into account the 'normal' experiences of all of us in the family as well as actual 'incest' as so defined. I mean adult males exposing themselves/touching us up/bouncing us on them with sexual motives etc. It's not rare. I wonder if any woman has not gone through it in some form.[8]

The comment suggests that defining child sexual abuse and incest can be problematic. In this book we take child sexual abuse to be any sexual behaviour directed at a person under 16[9] without that person's consent. Sexual behaviour may involve touching parts of the child or requesting the child to touch oneself, itself, or others; ogling the child in a sexual manner, taking pornographic photographs, or requiring the child to look at parts of the body, sexual acts or other material in a way which is arousing to oneself[10]; and verbal suggestions or comments to the child which are intended to threaten the child sexually or otherwise to provide sexual gratification for oneself. It must be defined by every circumstance in which it occurs: in families representative of all classes, races and social strata; in state-run and private institutions; on the street; in classrooms; in pornography, advertising and films.

With growing concern about corporal punishment in schools and legal sanctions against it in Europe,[11] physical abuse of children is perhaps becoming confined to the privacy of the home, residential establishment or hospital. Sexual abuse, however, has no boundaries. A stranger who walks up to a 6 year old in the street and punches her on the nose might be immediately stopped by passers-by; but if that same stranger quietly pinches a child's bottom or perhaps simply leers at her in an offensive way, we might hardly notice. Yet for a child, the effect will be the same: regardless of the act, the message is that s/he is not safe, not protected, not liked and not respected.

But however we empathise with a child's sense of hurt or violation, this is not the sole measure by which we can define the harmfulness of sexual assault against children. We must recognise that the abusiveness of child-molesters is a part of their make-up which exists regardless of the availability of child objects and regardless of the reactions of individual children whom they assault. We need an ethical approach which does not victimise the child further by refusing to protect her rights in those situations where s/he may by chance derive physiological pleasure from molestation by a person who does not care for or respect her.

Consent

Absence of consent is therefore crucial to our definition of child sexual abuse, because it allows us to take a clear stand on the exploitation of the child without requiring the degree of harm experienced by each individual child to define our attitude to each individual offender. The lack of consent stems from the child's relative ignorance of the implications of adult sexuality and from absence of any real choice in a relationship where a child is forced to rely on adults for her well-being. Some adults argue that the child is making a choice. But in effect there is no choice open to the child other than to say 'Yes'. Children lack the knowledge and experience to make a properly informed decision about the subject, and they do not have the freedom, legal or psychological, to give or refuse their consent in a truly independent manner.

As David Finkelhor claims,[12] many arguments against sexual use by adults of children are too 'intuitive' and complacent. He illustrates three such arguments. The most simple says that such sex is intrinsically wrong, both physically and psychologically. This is weak because it is fuelled by prejudice against any perceived 'deviation', such as homosexuality. A second argument rejects adult-child sex because it entails a premature sexualisation of the child. This is naive in that it regards children as 'naturally' asexual beings. A final argument holds that sexual encounters with adults are clearly damaging to children. But as Finkelhor concludes:

> The [favoured] proposition . . . is that adult-child sex is wrong because the fundamental conditions of consent cannot prevail in the relationship between an adult and a child. The proposition seems to be a great improvement over other arguments, particularly the argument that such acts are wrong solely because they harm the child. It puts the argument on a moral, rather than an empirical, footing.
>
> Thus, even if someone could demonstrate many cases where children enjoyed such experiences and were not harmed by them, one could still argue that it was wrong because children could not consent. The wrong here is not contingent upon proof of a harmful outcome.

Some suggest that a child's consent *can* be ascertained and that this exonerates the offender from responsibility for his assault. Paedophiles are notable for their arguments to this effect. As one pro-paedophile group wrote to a British national journal: 'We reject the definition of a paedophile as a child-molester. A paedophile seeks the consent of the young person before sex takes place. A child-molester does not'.[13] Their letter received a swift reply from another reader:

> Nearly 30 years ago, as an 8-year-old girl, I was the recipient of the affection of a gentleman who would probably now belong to the Paedophile Information Exchange. He was my school-teacher's husband and a respected friend of my parents. It is true that he did not physically harm me but he inveigled me by subtlety and persuasion into sexual contact with him. Any attempt I made to tell him I did not like it led to gentle pleading. 'Don't you love uncle?' . . . There is an imbalance of judgement, emotional

maturity and plain factual knowledge. The child is far too vulnerable to be considered capable of consent.[14]

Sexual abuse by boys

Finkelhor admits that the notion that children are incapable of consent to sexual activity might cause us wrongly to define mutual sexuality between children as abuse, but concludes that sex between one child and another need not be defined as abusive because 'by contrast, in relationships with peers, children are uninformed, but at least there is no inherent power differential'. Many other researchers have treated the abuse of children by each other as unimportant. For example: 'Only sexual abuse by adults was included in [this] study. Therefore, the cases which respondents included in their returned questionnaires regarding sexual abuse by adolescents to each other or to younger children and cases of sibling incest (unless one of the siblings was an adult) were excluded'.[15]

One wonders why such assaults by boys against girls should have been glossed over. A feminist explanation of this lacuna in the research might be that boys' assaults make clear the true dynamics of sexual abuse – that it is not based on an adult-child power imbalance, which is a familiar and unthreatening concept for most of us, but a male-female power imbalance, which is frightening for both sexes to expose.

It is mostly through field work in agencies like rape crisis centres that feminists have begun to gain some understanding of the high proportion of assaults committed by boys:

> We've had to examine the problem of young boys who are all under the age of 15 who are abusing very small children in [Eire]. I imagine it is a worldwide problem but it certainly was startling for us to find out how widespread this is. Very often the boys are coming to the home as babysitters, but very often they are related or well known to the children. Children are abused by boys outside the home, sometimes on the way home from school, fairly relentlessly.[16]

Boys may assault not only children, but adult women, and as they grow older sometimes their own mothers are thus victimised:

He can be very nice one minute, then hating the next. He went for me with a carving knife because he said I was a bad cook. He said, 'You're not bad looking, but you'd look better if I took a hammer to your head.' The attacks started because he did not want me to remarry.

He came in drunk once and I asked him to leave. He called me a 'shitcunt' and beat me up as I phoned for a taxi to escape.

My son beat me up and sexually assaulted me. I broke links with him and went to a priest, for advice. He told me how dare I try to talk to God about this.

I discovered my older son was raping my little boy. He was also dressing up in my clothes and underwear. Now we are getting help for the little one, but nobody's helped me with my own feelings. I find myself checking my cupboards and constantly cleaning out the bath . . . it leaves me feeling so dirtied.[17]

A second reason why sexual assault by boys has been glossed over in the traditional research is because it sheds light on the inadequacies of the 'family dysfunction' analysis, whereby sexual abuse occurring within a group is seen not as an assault by an attacker who has exploited his socially sanctioned access via his dominant position within the group, but as a subtly collusive group dynamic. One of the favourite themes of family dysfunction ideology is that men turn to children for sex because the adult women whom they live with will not provide it. When we expose the sexual violence of young boys who are not in a position to expect any sexual servicing from wives or girlfriends, we have to question our analysis of the adult offender's motivations too: 'These young boys are going to grow up to be very skilled abusers, and to go on abusing both within their family and outside their family. There's no question of a dysfunction within their home as triggering this. They have found a source of pleasure. They have found that male power gives them access to this pleasure and to break the habit is going to be very difficult.'[18]

It is a pity that sexual abuse by boys is not taken seriously as yet, because studying boys' behaviour and working to block their developing patterns of re-offence would be a far more effective preventive measure than attempting to help adult men or to teach children how to defend themselves from such men. Clodagh Corcoran, who headed the Irish Council of Civil Liberties Working Party on Child Sexual Abuse, conducted some interesting research in this area:

> One of the problems which the working party are currently addressing themselves to is the question of young offenders. What we're trying to find out is why are they abusing – is it learned behaviour? Are they copying something that they've seen on video nasties? Are they copying something they're seeing in pornographic pictures, or are they looking at inappropriate sexual behaviour at home? Another possibility is that they may themselves be being sexually abused.[19]

Sexual abuse by females

So far we have discussed sexual abuse of children by males. What of abuse committed by women and girls? It is obviously much rarer, and this contrast with male behaviour has been ascribed to

> the historic experience of women both as sexual property and as the primary caretakers of children. Having been frequently obliged to exchange sexual services for protection and care, women are in a position to understand the harmful effects of introducing sex into a relationship where there is a vast inequality of power. And, having throughout history been assigned the primary responsibility for the care of children, women may be in a position to understand more fully the needs of children, the difference between affectionate and erotic contact, and the appropriate limits of parental love.[20]

Many researchers are keen to present their findings in a gender-balanced way and therefore, whilst their articles abound in empirical data and direct quotations from clients about the sexual abuse of children by men, their insistence on the frequency of abuse by women is backed up only by vague generalisations: 'While most attention is directed toward the male "abuser" and the female child [survivor], there are instances in which the mother overstimulates a male child, especially when the father is absent from the family.'[21] In some cases it may be asserted or implied that women's pleasure in physical interactions with children is comparable to exploitative sexual abuse by men: 'Several mothers have told us of their erotic or orgasmic response to breast feeding.'[22] Whilst any suggestion that these responses are analogous to the criminally assaultive behaviour of the child-molester is laughable, it is of great concern that ordinary women may well internalise such professional prejudice, and this will be particularly destructive for them if they themselves have experienced real sexual abuse as children.

Women rarely sexually abuse children and yet, in the few cases that have come to light, public outrage against female abusers reflects society's contradictory expectations of women. Take the case of Myra Hindley, whose part in the 'Moors murders'[23] was that of colluder rather than initiator. The press attention she has received as a failed mother-figure has been far worse than that directed at Ian Brady, who actually staged the murders. Almost without thinking, we calmly accept his violence as part of the continuum of male aggression, whilst saving our rage for Myra's refusal to nurture and protect. The assignment of such roles to these strangers is symptomatic of our expectations of family life. Mothers who are living unawares with child-abusers may be being physically or sexually abused also. We often see these women as colluders, forgetting that collusion implies equal access to information and power. And when a mother is plainly guilty of neglect, our angry response can prevent us from noticing that we are operating a sexual double-standard – we take it for granted that men abuse, and yet expect women to refuse to accept this. Psychiatrists and social workers in particular hold women responsible in families where men are abusing children. As the public is aware, professionals often refuse to use their own powers to protect children in such situations.[24]

The characteristics of a sex offender

Can we identify the child-molester any more precisely than by stating that he is usually male? Is there any abnormality of make-up that would distinguish him from others? Does he belong to a recognisable social group? One study of father rapists was carried out in 1965 by Gebhard *et al.*[25] This study found nothing at all special about father rapists when compared with the rest of the prison population. They were not psychopaths or inadequate personalities. Maisch came to the same conclusion, claiming that men who sexually abuse children form a 'completely heterogeneous picture'.[26] Given the fact that research has failed to disclose any fundamental differences between the make-up of child-molesters and that of ordinary men, the sexual abuse of children is seen by some as an extension of normal male sexuality. Indeed, appropriate sex partners for men are generally considered to be women younger and smaller than themselves. Sexual prowess is an important part of male self-image and by tradition involves conquest, domination and taking the initiative, all of which are easier with children than with adult women.

In examining the identity of the abuser, we often ask ourselves what motivates his behaviour. I will first consider the emotional motivation of the abuser, and then the sexual and social implications of his behaviour. Chapter 6 covers this area in more detail.

Emotional motivation

The child-abuser is someone who, for whatever reason, refuses to love or respect children. This refusal is the lowest common denominator, marking 'monsters' – the sex killers – and 'normal family men' – the incest offenders – alike. To label child-abusers as 'monsters' is to put them at a safe distance from the so-called normal people who, it is assumed, would never do such a thing. This false distinction does nothing to help us identify the occurrence of child abuse, which is so widespread precisely because it is frequently disguised by 'respectable' circumstances. On the other hand, to treat child abuse as part of a routine emotional normality – which is therefore acceptable – is to distance oneself unforgivably from the rights and interests of children. Unfortunately, this attitude – that two broken bones are part of the rough and tumble of family life, but three are a social problem – is deep-rooted in all of us.

Sexual motivation

A common analysis of the sexual behaviour of the offender is manifested by the 'thin line theory': according to this the offender, confusing love and sexuality, accidentally slips into molestation whilst cuddling the child in the ordinary way:

> Just as there is a shifting and invisible line between constructive discipline and dehumanizing punishment, there is a vague borderline between loving sensuality and abusive sexuality.[27]

> It is helpful to establish clearly that thin line between what are desirable acts of affection and warmth between adults and children and what is unacceptable conduct.[28]

> Incest slips over the boundary from loving cuddles to abuse.[29]

Of course it is an aspect of male socialisation in some cultures that physical affection be confined to sexual encounters. But does this really mean that no male can be affectionate without getting sexual? Such an analysis is an insult to men as individuals with freedom of choice. Moreover, the 'thin line theory' suggests that women are subject to the same socialisation, which is not necessarily so. It implies that anyone might cross such a boundary by mistake. In reality, according to the testimony of children, the offender is knowingly and deliberately committing a sexual assault. The assault may well be presented in public in the guise of loving cuddles, as in one case I observed where a grandfather at a family gathering pulled his unwilling granddaughter towards him wheedling, 'Don't you want to give your granddad a kiss then?' It was only when she resisted further that he gripped her by the waist and continued sharply: 'Come here when I tell you to', that the assaultive nature of his behaviour was exposed. Even so, of the adults who witnessed this behaviour I was the only one who knew that he had a moment before sexually assaulted the child outside the room. Since they had assumed that the man was merely showing gentle affection, the other adults were shocked and embarrassed when I chose to intervene on the girl's behalf.

The assault may also be perpetrated on the child in such a way that exploitative behaviour is interspersed with gentle caresses.

Again, the 'thin line theory' misinterprets the offender's motivation, since his *motives* are not at all confused: he is simply alternating his *conduct* in order to entrap the child into physical contact for his own benefit. One survivor wrote a poem describing the child's appreciation of the selfishness and abuse which the offender seeks to disguise by his 'gentleness':

> I wake to find him next to me, and he whispers, I love you,
> You're such a pretty girl, I love you more than Jill or Joan . . .
> His big thick fidgety hands are touching me.
> His breath smells of stale beer . . .
> I'm so tired now I could sleep, but he wants me
> To wake and touch him, I don't know why . . .
> Why now does he wake me up, I will kill him when I get big.[30]

Another fashionable analysis of the sexual motivation of the offender is that he is not seeking sexual gratification at all, but committing an act of aggression or violence against the child. This interpretation was originally put forward by feminists who aimed to expose the connections between abusive sexuality and physical violence, as shown by the following report from a battered women's refuge: 'A recent study from Edmonton WIN House states that 87% of children who accompanied their mothers to the shelter over a nine-month period had, themselves, been abused physically and sexually.'[31] In 1978 the US Feminist Alliance Against Rape interviewed a women's project combating child sexual abuse whose representative stated:

> People look at sexual assault as a sexual act and it's not. It's a violent attack. It's made up of anger, emotional pain and immaturity . . . Most sex offenders will tell you that 90% of their needs were for sex, which is not true. They turn all their emotional needs into sexual needs.[32]

The theory has now been taken up by the establishment for quite different purposes. In arguing that the offender is motivated by aggression, it is implied that he is not really interested in sexual gratification as such. The idea then develops that his behaviour is not *sexually* oriented at all. This allows us to avoid looking at any connections between male aggression and male sexual pleasure, and to avoid the uncomfortable thought that male sexuality in general may be implicated in his acts. Yet it is plain from pornography that for many traditionally 'normal' men, sex and violence are inextricably interlinked. If we say that sex offenders are violent but that males with traditonally male sexuality are not, we are lying to ourselves. We have drawn a false distinction which prevents us from recognising sexual abuse when it occurs and which exonerates the many by stigmatising the few. For all of us, sex may be used to express an infinite variety of moods. If, say, we have sex in a gentle romantic mood, we are still 'getting our oats'. And the same aim is achieved by those who enjoy violent, aggressive sex – it is done for pleasure. Those who molest children do so for many reasons, but the immediate and primary goal is sex.

Some child-molesters are quite open and unashamed about the sexual gratification that they derive from using children:

She was just there and I helped myself.[33]

This whole damn society is built around youth and nothing but. Look at all the millions of dollars that are being spent by old bags trying to make themselves look young – why should I feel like a pervert for going for somebody who really is young?[34]

Until we acknowledge that many men will choose to abuse children for amusement, we will collude in the pretences by which these men disguise their fun.

Social motivation

Turning to the social motivation of the offender, we can observe that some child-molesters actively identify themselves as paedophiles whose chosen sexual preference is for children rather than for adults. In recent years, paedophiles have made attempts to justify their activities by grouping together and fighting for their interests as a 'politically oppressed minority'.

In Britain, the Paedophile Information Exchange was set up in 1974 to enable those who are sexually attracted to children to get in touch with each other for mutual support and to campaign for the legal and social acceptance of paedophilia. Not surprisingly, its membership [is made up] almost entirely of adult males (97%). In a skilful tactic towards the end of the 1970s PIE changed direction, and instead of campaigning for the right of adult men to have sex with children, it now campaigned for the right of *children* to have sex with *them*. This was to prove a shrewd move because it enabled PIE to present its case under a banner of children's rights and to accuse all those who opposed its aims of being moralists out to control or crush childhood sexuality.[35]

Paedophiles may well make attempts to 'convert' children to their cause, as illustrated by the Edinburgh group, 'Minor Problems'. On one of its leaflets children are encouraged, 'if you think kids should be both seen and heard . . . that "childhood" is an adult myth . . . that we need to facilitate children's *liberation*, not a false bunch of "rights", [then subscribe to the magazine and] support the kids' lib youth communes sex freedom'. The fact that this publication represents the interests of adult paedophiles and not of young people is evidenced by its somewhat opaque subtitle, 'Review for Free Intergenerational and Childhood Relations'. Even so, membership of such groups may well be influential:

> Idealization is institutionalized by radical groups such as the René Guyon Society . . . the society claims that children need sex with compassionate adults to reduce violent antagonisms supposedly aroused by societal repression and guilt. Sexual repression is advanced as the cause of depression, suicide, delinquency, gang warfare, assault, and a host of other social problems. Under the slogan 'Sex by year eight or else it's too late', the group advocates sexual rights for children, including abolition of laws restricting incest and sexual abuse. The Guyon Society claims a membership of '2000 parents and psychiatrists'.[36]

Much of paedophile argument is presented as though it sprang from a broad-based sexual politics encompassing the women's movement, the gay liberation movement and the left. Feminists, however, have rejected this claim[37] and insisted that these issues 'be discussed and understood within the framework of a society where men have power over women and children'.

The paedophile is a quite specialised version of the child-molester. What about the man who uses children whilst continuing sexual involvement with adults? What are his characteristics? Rich Snowdon ran a counselling group for incest offenders in San Francisco in 1981. In his report[38] he compares the child-molester to the 'normal' man:

> I considered myself a 'nice guy' who 'could never do such a thing'. I wanted these men to be monsters. I wanted them to be different from me, as different as possible. Yet as I heard them talking about childhood and their early teens, I was less and less able to deny how much we had in common. We grew up learning the same things about how to be men . . . We were taught that privilege is our birthright and aggression is our nature, so we learned to take but not to give. We learned to get affection . . . mainly through sex. We expected to marry a woman who would provide for us like a mother, but obey us like a daughter. And we learned that women and children belong to men, that there is nothing to keep us from using their labour for our benefit and their bodies for our pleasure and anger.

Many men, like Snowdon, have tried to disassociate themselves from rape and sexual abuse, partly because some are indeed innocent of it, but mostly in order to side-step the question of their benefit as a social group. Women's economic oppression is undoubtedly linked to sexual violence. The control and fear it imposes on women can cause them to lose confidence and self-esteem, to mistrust their own judgements, to avoid risk-taking or any idea of competition with men. Being molested as a child may well affect your status and job prospects as an adult. For a start, your schooling may have been severely disrupted in various ways. Your medical records may have been influenced and could be used to your detriment. Your working life may suffer while you battle with the depression or breakdowns that can occur as a result of incest. Thus some women have lost on the job market before they have even begun to compete. This means that many of their male competitors will benefit from their violation on a practical economic level.

The motive of the individual man may also be part of a larger desire amongst men as a group to maintain sexual control over women.

Major theorists in the disciplines of both psychology and anthropology explain the importance of the incest taboo by placing it at the centre of an agreement to control warfare among men. It represents the first and most basic peace treaty. An essential element of the agreement is the concept that women are the possessions of men; the incest taboo represents an agreement as to how women shall be shared. Since virtually all known societies are dominated by men, all versions of the incest taboo are agreements among men regarding sexual access to women. As Mitchell points out,[39] men create rules governing the exchange of women; women do not create rules governing the exchange of men. Because the taboo is created and enforced by men, we argue that it may also be more easily and frequently violated by men.[40]

The male bonding described above may be illustrated by the collusion that sometimes takes place between sex offenders and agency workers or the authorities. The bonding is clearly more likely to occur when the men involved are of the same social status: for example, a paediatrician found guilty of procuring and peddling child pornography in London gained sympathy from the Lord Chief Justice, who compared his obsession to that of a schoolboy collecting cigarette cards.[41] But it may also cross class boundaries: a Berkshire probation officer knowingly concealed a lorry-driver ex-prisoner's long record of child molestation when recommending him for volunteer babysitting work with the council. This babysitter later assaulted and murdered a little girl.[42] As pointed out in the nineteenth century: 'It may be argued [by middle-class people] that men who physically assault women are mostly of the lower and uneducated classes, but the inadequate prison sentences are passed by judges and magistrates who occupy a high position in society, and who profess to be chivalric gentlemen.'[43]

Thus, even when the child-molester is exposed and punished or medically treated, he may manage to retain power, authority and attention in a way that is not open to women and children. Currently this opportunity is being afforded to him by those who suggest that he has expertise on sexual abuse. As argued in the US journal, *off our backs*,

Rather than offering testimony from survivors, offenders are being cited as 'experts' on child sexual assault. One recent TV show featured a convicted offender who revealed ways in which he tricked children so that parents could learn to take better care . . . Molesters' stories only reinforce a child's position as powerless and increase the fear for both children and adults . . . [presumably] it is important for men to remain in positions of authority, even if that means we must depend on child-molesters to tell us the 'truth' about child sexual assault.[44]

Familial v. non-familial abuse?

So far I have defined child sexual abuse by examining the relation between attacker and attacked without considering the difference between assault by strangers, assault by family members, and child prostitution. From extensive interviewing of both children and adult women, I would argue that incest offenders and strangers who molest children on the street are not distinct groups, although the child's emotional experience of molestation may certainly vary according to circumstances. Physiological data show that both offender groups have the same arousal levels to children.[45] Attempts by researchers to categorise the offenders separately manifestly fail when increasing exposure begins to show that many of them are indiscriminate in their preference for family members or strangers, choosing one or the other simply because of considerations of access or avoidance of detection. Furthermore, our attempts to define child-molesters by confining them to one or other group is an expression of our fears as a society that the phenomenon cannot be contained or controlled. Until recently the assumption was that sexual abuse of children was committed by dirty old men in parks. On recognising that sexual abuse is very likely to occur within families as well,[46] we have swung to the opposite extreme and are now asserting that the majority of abuse is committed by men who know the child,[47] especially fathers or stepfathers.[48] I would suggest that neither of these perspectives is accurate in gauging the risk to children. Admittedly, a longstanding series of assaults committed by a family member will be perhaps the single major experience of abuse in a child's life. On the other hand, children have reported that they are daily molested in minor ways by strangers who may have less constant access, but whose motives are no different from that of the incest offender. We do not make a habit of counting up such disagreeable incidents because they are so common – even for adult women, they are such a regular part of our everyday lives that we learn to ignore them.

Many feminists reject the theoretical distinction between familial and stranger assault, considering that incest is simply another name for child sexual abuse. Some women's groups, however, prefer to retain the concept of 'incest' in their analysis, albeit defined in very wide terms in order to avoid the artificial kinship categorisations posited in patriarchal law or religion:

> We use the term to cover the sexual molestation of a child by any person whom that child sees as a figure of trust or authority – parents, relatives (whether natural or adoptive), family friends, babysitters, youth leaders, social workers, teachers, church officials, priests etc. We see the questions of blood-relationship and taboo as red herrings which obscure the central issue: the irresponsible exploitation of children's ignorance, trust and obedience. Incest is the sexual abuse of power.[49]

The above group believed that 'incest' should be retained as a useful shorthand term to describe the experience of women who felt that sexual abuse had influenced their concerns in family, emotional and domestic relationships as well as their general sexual safety as females. They added:

> We choose to retain the title 'incest' since this word has been censored by a taboo which shocks the outsider into inaction, protects the aggressor and silences the child. Even on an impersonal level, we find our campaign's name [Incest Survivors] is often abbreviated or whispered, so as not to shock the sensibilities of ourselves and others. This is an illustration of the horror that the word evokes: but we are not freaks – our experience is common. We must expose incest for the reality it is and rid this word of its false shame.

Although groups like these wish to distinguish the experience of stranger assault from that of assault by friends and family members, most survivors are strongly critical of the use of jargon (such as 'incest victim', 'incestuous family', 'incestuous relationship') that frequently crops up in the academic literature. These phrases suggest that incest is a two-way phenomenon in which the child participates. The word 'relationship' alone is so often used in colloquial language, to mean a chosen sexual liaison between adults, that this is bound to colour our thinking if we refer to incest with the same word. 'Implying that survivors shared in the responsibility for what happened can serve to discredit them. This can be as subtle as the consistent use of the word 'relationship' when referring to incest. We don't talk about a rape relationship.'[50] The media also misrepresent survivors' experience of assault by sensationalising the family aspect in phrases such as 'A family affair', 'Behind closed doors', etc.

Child prostitution and pornography are, like incest, often considered separately from child sexual abuse in general. They have been a part of many cultures for centuries,[51] but have only recently begun to be studied widely. The rape of children, like that of women, has been shown to be fuelled by the use of readily available child pornography.[52] The year 1981 saw the publication of Abdelwahab Boudhiba's report on child labour to the United Nations Sub-Commission on Prevention of Discrimination and Protection of Minorities, which singled out child prostitution as one of the 'most sickening' forms of economic exploitation of children. In response to this, Rädda Barnen (the Swedish 'Save the Children' campaign), the Anti-Slavery Society and Defence for Children International decided to conduct a study into the sexual exploitation of children which concentrated on child prostitution, child pornography, sex tourism, and the sale of children for sexual purposes. This study is reported as follows:

There is no doubt that children are being sexually exploited outside their families on a large scale. The most conservative estimates are that these practices today involve hundreds of thousands of children and there are indications that the numbers are much higher and not only increasing but also involving younger children, even as low as five years of age . . . One popular misconception is that only children of the developing world are involved, but the phenomenon occurs worldwide, and it cannot be asserted that the problem is greater in one continent than another. In the United States alone it has been estimated that more than 300 000 boys are sexually exploited outside their families, and the total of both sexes is likely to be more than twice as high. The practice is known to be widespread among Latin American street children . . . Many of the most publicised child sex stories are associated with South East Asia, and it is estimated that there are 30 000 prostitutes under the age of 16 in Bangkok alone . . . A further type of traffic in children involves the sale of a child's body for pornographic photographs and films. The Netherlands is the only Western European country where the sale of child pornography is not prohibited, but it is possible to buy the products easily in many other Western and non-Western countries . . . Perhaps one of the most disturbing factors in the sexual exploitation of children is its association with tourism which is blamed on increased international travel over the past forty years . . . Attempts to eradicate these forms of exploitation will fail unless changes in attitudes to sex can be effected which will no longer make it possible for large economic gains to be made in these illegal activities.[53]

Even without changing our attitudes to sex there are many methods available to governments of preventing the commercial exploitation of child sexual abuse. Yet in 1984, Interpol noted the 'lack of interest on the part of governments to communicate information on prostitution . . . to international organisations such as the United Nations and Interpol', stating that 'such reticence is unwarranted when the matter at stake is the dignity and fundamental rights of persons'.[54]

The politics of child abuse

Sexual abuse of children, whether conducted inside the family or outside it, must be contextualised within two broader perspectives, that of child abuse in general and that of sexual violence against women.

The age perspective

Analyses of child abuse often highlight the powerlessness of children, not only as a class of people who are younger, smaller, and in the physical and legal control of adults, but also as people who are almost universally treated as the possessions and servants of adults, especially within the family. For example, one incest survivor describes her experience of powerlessness as follows:

> Most kids have somewhere they can go for privacy – you have things you can call your own . . . I had nothing – presents were given to me by my father, and taken back the next day. My bedroom was no sanctuary, letters were opened . . . phone calls were listened in on – every minute of the day and night he wanted to know where I was going, who I was seeing, what I had done . . . I always felt like I had no identity of my own, save that which was allowed me by my father.[55]

Frederick Powell has done extensive research into injuries caused to young Northern Irish people by police and British Army violence. As he has argued, the power dynamic behind child abuse by adults is a much more broad-based problem than would appear from the current studies on specific categories of violence against children such as abuse within the family:

> It is contended that in post-war society the general focus on the family in child care policy and the specific attention given to family violence . . . has resulted in an unduly restrictive definition of the problem . . . Political violence [such as killing, brutality, detention and separation] vented against children is becoming an increasingly disturbing phenomenon in contemporary society. Politically-associated child abuse cannot be attributed to psychologically disordered individuals or the effects of personal stress; it is the product of the systematic utilisation of violence against children for political ends . . .[56]

Joscelyn Boyden echoes this broader political analysis:

> [In Oxfam's work], conserving health and an adequate level of nutrition is only part of the story. Many children are at risk primarily because of their political, social or religious status or because they are forced to assume adult responsibilities at a very early age. Others are made vulnerable because of a breakdown in the relationship with their parents . . . The evidence is that not only are large numbers of children maltreated by their so-called

adult 'protectors', but also thousands are victims [sic] of violence, persecution, involuntary disappearance, detention, torture and capital punishment perpetrated by governments. Many governments are not simply failing to act as custodians of children's rights, but are actually abusing them.[57]

She extends her criticism to the neo-colonialist exploitation of children as representative images of third-world suffering in the Western media: 'Images of the frail and starving children in Ethiopia's feeding camps have become very familiar to us all over the past 18 months. Aid agencies like Save the Children Fund, Oxfam and UNICEF rely heavily on media coverage in emergencies and photographs of children are used all the time in campaigning and fundraising efforts . . .'

These images are in some ways similar to the images of physically and sexually abused children exploited by Western childcare charities and agencies to raise funds in aid of their work.[58] One such picture was even accompanied by the caption: 'Four years old. Seriously underweight for her age. Scavenging for food where she can find it. And she's English.'[59]

The gender perspective

A second dynamic in which we may contextualise child sexual abuse is that of male violence against females. The continuum of male violence has often been an object of feminist concern. Florence Rush places her experience of child sexual assault in this context:

It never occurred to us to hold the man responsible for what he had done. This was our problem, not his, and we handled it as best we could. In subsequent years, Jane and I reported regularly to each other on the number of exposed men we had seen, how we handled attempts to be touched, and how we escaped from what might develop into something violent and dangerous. After a while, we became rather casual about our experiences, rarely outraged, but simply tried to develop greater skills in avoiding and extricating ourselves from the sexual aggression of men without embarrassing the offender. This was excellent training and prepared me in later years for the breast-grabbers, the bottom-pinchers, the body-rubbers. The horror, the shame, and the humiliation never left me, but until recently I never knew I had the right to be outraged and fight back. I was, after all, trained to be a woman . . . That sexual abuse of children is permitted because it is an unspoken but prominent factor in socialising and preparing the female to accept a subordinate role; to feel guilty, ashamed, and to tolerate, through fear, the power exercised over her by men. That the female's early sexual experiences prepare her to submit in later life to the adult forms of sexual abuse heaped on her by her boyfriend, her lover, and her husband. In short, the sexual abuse of female children is a process of education that prepares them to become the wives and mothers of America.[60]

Attitudes to the sexualisation of girl children by men have perhaps always been strangely contradictory: on the one hand, it provokes such a sense of outraged taboo that it continues to be unmentionable; on the other, it is such an everyday part of our lives that we hardly notice it – in a Shirley Temple or Marilyn Monroe film, or an adult woman's baby doll nightgown, for example, or the absurd coyness of those bikinis designed for toddlers. In a year when the media had been overflowing with outrage at the subject of child sexual abuse, a film critic and television presenter could still refer to a scene in a film as 'a tasteful bit of incest'.[61]

Examples from popular culture can easily be found to illustrate the gender stereotyping and consequent sexual coercion of girls by men, and the collusion in this by the rest of society. The following extracts reflect every age at which a girl is conditioned for sexual abuse as an adult, and demonstrate the manner in which the child is made to look or act like a woman, and the woman made to look or act like a child, in order to cater to the requirements of a paedophiliac society.

Caption to tabloid pin-up of small girl: The loveliest ladies are always in the *Record*. Thank heaven for little girls. Page three girls are always stunners. And today's is no exception . . . even though she's only four. This little smasher is Danielle . . . [Her mother] has tried to keep her out of the limelight. But there is a problem. Danielle loves getting her picture taken. And the results speak for themselves.[62]

Caption to popular magazine advertisement featuring small girl:
There are no rules in the 80s – well, maybe one . . . indulge
yourself.[63]

*Popular poster on sale in London newsagents, from a series
featuring small children's conversations:* Boy: 'I've got *three*
sweets.' Girl: 'I've *four* sweets.' B: 'I've got *five* pence.' G: 'But
I've *six* pence.' B (pointing to penis): 'Bet you don't have one of
these.' G (pointing to vulva): 'No . . . but with one of *these* I can
have as many of *those* as I want!'[64]

Film Poster: This film makes Emmanuelle look ten years old.
Alba Valeria is . . . Giselle. Barely a woman.[65]

Letter to national Agony Aunt on problem-page: I am 12 years of
age and have a problem with my father. He turns everyone in the
family against me by treating me as his favourite, calling me
princess and lovey, and so on. He only calls my mother by her
name. I hate being favoured, and my brother teases me. I feel it is
not fair for my dad to make out he loves me more than the others.
Please could you give me some hints on how to tell him, as I do
love him but don't like being spoiled? *Answer*: It's often a fact
that girls are Dads' favourites because they love their femininity.
They take pride in a son's achievements, but a daughter has a
special place. Mums often favour sons, and I hope yours is
especially loving to your brother to even things out. If I were you I
should snuggle up to Pa and say you are glad to be called princess,
but that makes your mum his queen, and she should have a special
loving name, too. He should recognise your young woman's
intuition and realise you are growing up. As you do get older, I
am sure that this family 'problem' will be put into perspective.
How nice, though, if you could use your special influence to get
your dad to call your mum by a loving nickname.[66]

*Telephone call by adult woman seeking male partner on
'Dial-a-Date' radio chat show:* The DJ asked for details about her
children, aged 13 and 14, and then commented, 'Little Crackers.
He'll need to get on with your two stunning daughters . . .'[67]

Newspaper interview with artist on general relationship with her father: We really came together when I was adolescent. He liked taking me to the theatre and hearing the gossip that Louis had this nubile girlfriend.[68]

Women's magazine reportage of marriage between a stepfather and his legally adopted stepchild: The girl: 'There were some difficulties in switching roles from daughter to wife of course. For starters, I had to behave a lot more sensibly, more grown-up, and be an equal to Dave. I was so used to him telling me what to do that the habit hasn't left me, even to this day.' The father: 'When I came into the family they took to me straight away and they never had any problems calling me Dad, or treating me as such, and they were extraordinary kids. Now, with their mother [dead], they needed me more than ever. I was the only person they had, really . . . Suddenly I noticed through my grief that Kay was no longer a child but a responsible, caring young lady. It was a little bit frightening . . . I felt [the 25-year age gap] was morally wrong although, once she passed the legal age of 16 and told me she loved me, that made it right in my eyes . . .'[69]

Feminist writers have documented the way in which sexual abuse of children prepares them for sexual exploitation as adult women. According to Phyllis Chesler: 'Women are encouraged to commit incest as a way of life . . . As opposed to marrying our fathers, we marry men like our fathers . . . Men who are older than us, have more money than us, more power than us, are taller than us, are stronger than us: —our fathers.'[70]

Some theorists have even gone so far as to suggest that incest imposed on a girl is a preparation for a life of 'compulsory heterosexuality'.[71] They would see the incest attacker as deliberately breaking the girl's spirit in order to prepare the ground for future submission to other men. The institutions of society are seen as colluding in this attempt to subjugate women as a class. Thus if an adult woman, whether she is an incest survivor or not, rejects abusive male sexuality, society's assumption is that she 'just needs a good screw' to cure her. The ancient superstitious belief underlying this assumption is that the Good Penis, like a magic wand, can counteract the effects of the Bad Penis. The belief may be superstitious, but it is widespread and deep-rooted, as Martina Navratilova illustrates in her autobiography. She informed her father that she was having a lesbian relationship, to be told: 'I'd rather you slept with a different man every night than sleep with a woman . . . There must be something wrong with you physically . . . The reason you don't like it with men is because you didn't enjoy it the first time you were with a man . . . It's too bad I wasn't the first man with you, because then you would have enjoyed it more.'[72] Navratilova dismisses the possibility that this comment may be incestuous, considering it simply to be the personal retaliation of a man whose 'male pride was injured by having his daughter turn out in a way he couldn't accept', with a 'macho, fifty-years-behind the times Czech view'. However, similar views on the therapeutic equivalent of the 'good screw' form the basis of much psychological theory (classically, Freud's notion of 'penis envy') and professional treatment of incest survivors today. Agencies may insist that male offenders continue to have access to children they have abused, as if the offender alone can 'cure' the child; that abused girls be treated by male therapists or in groups including males, as if women alone cannot 'cure' each other; or they may view their adult female clients as suffering from pathological man-hatred. Lesbianism amongst incest survivors is commonly treated professionally as a mental health problem rather than a positive adult choice.

The traditional Western mythology of child sexual abuse

Chapter 2 looks further at some of the ways in which the male-female sexual exploitation continuum has been categorised by the theoretical and ideological models of the Western establishment. Psychologists' explanations of incest tend to mystify. Common-sense considerations about disparities of age, power and resources between abuser and child are lost in the search for complex causes. Families are studied in isolation from their social, economic, political and cultural context.

Until recently the most common reaction to allegations of child sexual assault was disbelief. The denial of incest survivors' experience has been maintained not only by society at large, but also by those academics and theorists who have attempted to study the subject dispassionately. As Rasjidah St John comments:

It is not as if [psychologists] can claim any special knowledge or expertise in this field. If it were not for the unpaid, voluntary work of thousands of women in many countries over the past fifteen years, the women on Rape Crisis lines and the women working in refuges for battered wives, and incest support groups, [psychologists] would still be assuring us that incest never happens, that the girl just imagines it. This is Freud's teaching. In the Child Sexual Abuse Preventive Education Project we still get young women coming to us, today, who are told by their psychiatrist that it never happened.[73]

The occurrence of incest may not be overtly denied, but it may be minimised at a more subtle level even when it is admitted to have taken place, by the acceptance of various incest myths. Incest denial and incest myths seem to have three purposes: (a) to silence the survivor; (b) to protect the attacker; and (c) to comfort the community member or professional worker with the idea that she or he is totally removed from the experience of the people in the 'case', and free from any implication of responsibility or collusion; thereby to reinforce the illusion that incest is an isolated aberration rather than a fundamental pattern of societal abuse.

In the following examples, professional and academic myths are sometimes juxtaposed with stereotypes created by the lay community, thus exposing their non-scientific origin.

Myth no. 1: Children and women lie

This is an ancient myth which has particular implications for allegations of sexual abuse made by children and their mothers. There follow several subcategories of this myth: (a) children invent accusations; (b) adult women fantasise about childhood experiences; (c) vindictive mothers for their own purposes cook up stories of abuse to their children.

(a) *children*

The child's allegations of sexual abuse are based upon sexual fantasies rather than on reality . . . Fantasied incest is more common in preadolescent or adolescent girls, who project their own sexual wishes onto the parent. They also exhibit hysterical personality traits; more rarely, they are frankly delusional and paranoid.[74]

This myth is counteracted by Roland Summit's research:

> Rather than being calculating or practiced, the child is most often fearful, tentative and confused . . . If a respectable, reasonable adult is accused of perverse, assaultive behaviour by an uncertain, emotionally distraught child, most adults who hear the accusation will fault the child . . . Of the children who were found to have misrepresented their complaints, most had sought to *understate* the frequency or duration of sexual experiences . . . Very few children, no more than two or three per *thousand*, have ever been found to exaggerate or to invent claims of sexual molestation.[75]

In public opinion on child sexual abuse, if any one group of people is to be classified as likely by definition to be dishonest, it does seem remarkable that *children* should be the group to be so designated. Is dishonesty not the hallmark of the sex offender?

(b) *adult women*

> Almost all of my women patients told me that they had been seduced by their father. I was *driven* [editor's italics] to recognise in the end that these reports were untrue and so came to understand that the hysterical symptoms are derived from phantasies and not from real occurrences . . . It was only later that I was able to recognise in this phantasy of being seduced by the father the expression of the typical Oedipus complex in women.[76]

> Though they all insisted that what they were recalling did happen, I was doubtful . . . they seemed to be groping in a twilight of half-truths and wished-for fulfilments. The question of truth was indeed perpetually begged . . . These quasi-pornographic scenarios suggest the correctness of Freud's hypotheses . . . 'Reaching out': according to the solicitous shrinks, that's what the

incest victims [sic] are doing when they blurt out their dubious tales.[77]

(c) *mothers*

These women bombard their children with incessant interrogations about the alleged sexual contact, and pressure them to accept their delusions, creating a 'folie à deux' . . . These women foster abnormal dependency in the children to enhance their own narcissism and to compensate for their unsatisfactory love relationships . . .[78]

The author of the above opinion, Arthur Green, attempts to show the ways in which lying mothers can be detected. He believes that where the child is fearful in the man's presence, this is congruent with sexual abuse. If, however, the child is either affectionate towards the man or needs prompting by making frequent eye-contact with the mother instead of the man, then the mother is likely to have indoctrinated the child into complying with her story. These arguments are a paltry substitute for rigorous thinking. Not only is it obvious why a child might need eye contact with its own mother in the presence of an abuser, but as Jean Moore reports:

People who have experienced being raped, held hostage, or mugged, have reported how, much to their surprise – and later guilt – they have behaved in a clinging, ingratiating way towards their victimiser. It is just this clinging, ingratiating behaviour . . . which can be mistaken for affection. Add to this that the child builds up a feeling of gratitude towards the [offender], sees positives, and accepts his or her behaviour as normal, which is confusing for the worker.[79]

Compare the effects of terrorism on passengers hijacked on a jumbo jet in April 1988. Describing the well-known 'Stockholm syndrome' they suffered, a psychologist commented:

All proper contact is cut off for the passengers. It is like solitary confinement. The average citizen who is dealt with in a cold manner becomes very susceptible and will do just about anything he [sic] is told to do. Under these circumstances captives instinctively try to establish a rapport with their captors . . . It works like an encounter group. The people who are hijacked may come on to the phone and swear at the authorities because they have come to believe that it is the outsiders who are to blame. This is why the passengers say when they come off the plane that the hijackers treated them well.[80]

Myth no. 2: Children are seductive

For example:

These children undoubtedly do not deserve completely the cloak of innocence with which they have been endowed by moralists, social reformers, and legislators. The history of the relationship in our cases usually suggests at least some cooperation of the child in the activity, and in some cases the child assumed an active role in initiating the relationship . . . It is true that the child often rationalised with excuses of fear of physical harm or the enticement of gifts, but these were obviously secondary reasons. Even in the cases where physical force may have been applied by the adults, this did not wholly account for the frequent repetition of the practice. Finally, a most striking feature was that these children were distinguished as unusually charming and attractive in their outward personalities. Thus it was not remarkable that frequently we considered the possibility that the child might have been the actual seducer, rather than the one innocently seduced.[81]

The third corner of the incestuous triangle is, of course, the daughter . . . She radiates the fragile innocence of a child mixed with the vaguely destructive allure of the temptress.[82]

Frigid gentlewomen of the jury! I had thought that months, perhaps years, would elapse before I dared to reveal myself to Dolores Haze, but by six she was wide awake, and by six fifteen we were technically lovers. I am going to tell you something very strange; it was she who seduced me.[83]

The myth that children are seductive is the commonest device by which a defensive society can rationalise the occurrence of child sexual abuse, and operates in much the same way as the notion that adults who get harassed must have 'asked for it'. Interesting logical problems can occur when people attempt to define an age at which it is acceptable to see children as seductive for the purposes of this myth. Some assume that only older children are sexually attractive to abusers. This means that use of younger children goes unsuspected; use of older children is seen as more understandable and thus goes unchecked; and those children who happen to have an 'age-inappropriate' appearance or demeanour go unprotected. In one textbook for students of forensic medicine, the author advises doctors who are about to examine survivors of alleged sexual offences: 'While taking the history, note the general appearance and behaviour of the girl, [her] apparent age and physique, and whether she dresses or looks older than her age'.[84] Presumably this last impression will be interpreted by the doctor as discrediting the rape allegation, since the same author warns us: 'Such allegations may be from spite, jealousy, [or] in order to precipitate marriage . . .'

Myth no. 3: Sexual involvement with adults does children good

The judicial inquiry into the Cleveland child abuse cases in the North of England was told in 1987 that one of a team of psychiatrists at one northern hospital considered that the experience 'probably enriched the lives of the children [they] had seen'.[85]

Myth no. 4: Children are responsible for the dynamics of sexual abuse – the offender is the real victim

One family therapist asserts: 'People always think of the father as an aggressive autocrat, but in many cases, he's like a child . . . He has an adolescent romance with his daughter.'[86]

An academic journalist claims:

For incest to be harmless, there has to be an equal balance of emotional maturity and power between the participants. For children often have power over adults. Some from an early age exploit their elders if the proposition is put in acceptable ways. An old man, living alone, deprived of any human contact, may offer local children 50p to touch his penis. Usually it will involve no more than that, and although a number of children may be involved, the whole affair is kept from adults . . .[87]

Elizabeth Brown explodes this myth for the projection that it is: 'After therapists began to believe that on occasion, incest happened, the question became not, 'why didn't he keep it in his pants?', but 'why didn't *she* keep it in his pants?'.[88]

Myth no. 5: Sexual abuse committed by boys is not as serious as that committed by adult men

The harmful effect that this myth can have on children is illustrated by Quentin Bell's biography of Virginia Woolf. Here he describes the experiences of Virginia and her sister Vanessa:

To the sisters it simply appeared that their loving brother was transformed before their eyes into a monster, a tyrant against whom they had no defence, for how could they speak out or take action against a treachery so covert? Trained as they were to preserve a condition of ignorant purity they must at first have been unaware that affection was turning to concupiscence and were warned only by their growing sense of disgust . . . It would have been hard for his half-sisters to know at what point to draw a line, to voice objections, to risk evoking a painful and embarrassing scandal – harder still to find someone to whom they could speak at all . . . Their only course seemed to be one of silent evasion; but even this was denied them; they must join in praising their persecutor, for his advances were conducted to an accompaniment of enthusiastic applause in which the girls could hear the repeated hope that 'dear George' could not find them ungrateful.[89]

Myth no. 6: Sexual abuse is mainly confined to ethnic minorities

For example, one magazine article states: 'Black [male] sexual bravado leads frequently to abuse of women.'[90] This myth not only bolsters society's general racism against all individuals belonging to an ethnic minority group, but also ensures that any abused children within that group are not afforded the same protective and preventive services as other children. Even when they reach adulthood, there will be more penalties for them when they wish to disclose their experiences. Mothers too are penalised:

> Black women, in trying to protect their own children, face racism from the police which compounds the abuse already suffered by the children. Black mothers do not want to put their children through this, yet they wish to get justice for [them]. They find themselves in a cleft stick, wondering whether to go for police involvement or not. The social services are often not sympathetic to the quandary that mothers and children feel on this question.[91]

A common racist stereotype is that males of the stigmatised cultural or racial group are bent on undermining the authority of the dominant group by, for example, seducing and raping the dominant men's women or stealing and murdering their children. This myth is a bitter irony in the light of everyday abuse of ethnic minority women and children by males from the dominant group:

> There's a particular fear of white men that Black girls grow up with. We know that they think we are sexual animals, that we're always available. It goes back to slavery.[92]

The fact that here sexual and racial abuse are combined, far from being acknowledged by the authorities, is exploited by them as an excuse for inaction:

> Police deliberately attempt to keep racial violence and sexual violence separate when incidents are recorded . . . Part of the reason for keeping such rigid artificial boundaries is to try and hide the fact that racial or sexual violence takes place on such a wide scale and thereby justify lack of action on the part of the authorities. This also has the effect of further denying the

experience of Black women. In Bradford two years ago when fascists carved NF ['National Front'] into an Asian woman's breast, the attack was not classified by police as either a racial or a sexual attack despite demands for recognition by the Asian Youth Movement.[93]

Myth no. 7: Sexual abuse is a predominantly working-class phenomenon

or, as one British doctor described his survivor client: 'She is an anxious, low-grade young lady'.

A British study of Irish working-class people[94] claims that father-daughter incest, which occurred in 4 per cent of an unselected outpatient clinic population, was 'the expression of a type of sexual behaviour accepted by the particular sub-culture of their social group'; and that where other types of incest were concerned,

> in most cases the incestuous relations were a cultural (or, more correctly, a sub-cultural) phenomenon, and in many cases they were precipitated by overcrowding, or on the contrary, by social isolation . . . In children the incestuous activities seem to have been only a transitory, culturally permissible, phase in the process of their normal psychosexual development, and as such did not result in any bad effects.

Why is it that incest is considered to be a working-class phenomenon? The fact is that ruling-class men have the wherewithal with which to hide their crimes – and, of course, a greater source of potential targets amongst people less powerful than themselves. It is in the interests of middle-class molesters to perpetuate this myth.

Myth no. 8: Children with disabilities do not get sexually assaulted

On the contrary, they frequently do. Disabled children are a neglected group in the diagnosis and treatment of sexual abuse. First, social prejudices about the supposed sexual unattractiveness of disabled people lead those who believe that sexual abuse is caused by the attractiveness of the child to discount disabled children as targets for abuse. Secondly, abuse of these children goes undetected where family or workers cannot distinguish symptoms of abuse from symptoms of disability (especially where a post-traumatic emotional reaction is misdiagnosed as, for example, brain damage or autism). Third, few resources are channelled into preventive education for disabled children, and those techniques that are taught may be useless to a disabled child (for example, advising a child to 'run away and shout as loud as you can').

A great deal of molestation of disabled children occurs in Children's Homes and day care centres; when parents protest they find that their child's report is doubly discredited. For example, the Director of Lambeth Social Services stated of one child whose parents claimed he had been molested in a home under her authority: 'The doctor who did the examination is not familiar with mentally retarded children. What looked to her like abuse could be the result of normal treatment.' Yet evidence of abuse was as follows: 'His bottom was all split and there was loose skin and dried blood around it, and when I asked him about it he was very frightened'.[95]

Myth no. 9: Men who work professionally or therapeutically with children and women, do not molest them

The concept of 'class' is being deployed anew by professionals in the child sexual abuse industry. The cohesion of this group is increasingly threatened by exposures of molesters who are in positions of trust as social workers, teachers, child counsellors, and so on.[96] These men cast doubts on every member of the profession – and as such are protected by that profession to the hilt. Instead of admitting that they, like the rest of us, are fallible, or that they too cannot tell a child-molester from an innocent man, professionals have opted to create a new class of riff-raff: their clients, the 'dysfunctional families'. And to ensure that these families stick together in their separate social class, they keep the women feeling guilty by deployment of Myth no. 10. If the family refuses to submit to the group treatment posited as the solution to such 'dysfunction', it may then be labelled as a 'problem family' and therefore any allegations members may make of abuse by professionals will automatically be discounted. Professionals in this way retain their false position as experts who can do no wrong.

Myth no. 10: Sexual abuse is caused not by male violence, but by family dynamics

Today sociologists may not dare openly to suggest that incest is a peculiarly working-class phenomenon, or that it is confined to particular regions, races or subcultures. Yet the old 'subculture' myth persists throughout professional thinking, in a disguised form. As in the CIBA report of 1984 on 'Child Sexual Abuse Within the Family',[97] it is now argued that incest is a 'manifestation of family pathology',[98] unique to 'dysfunctional' families (as opposed, presumably, to 'functional' ones) and passes from generation to generation like some leprous disease or Oedipal curse. The theory is that a victimised and passive man, whose mother or even grandmother[99] was domineering, falls into the hands of a passive but scheming wife who is deliberately cold towards her children. He becomes frustrated because she will not give him sex (to quote the CIBA report, 'conjugal rights') – or maybe because she wants too much sex. She, meanwhile, either wilfully falls ill,[100] dares to give birth to a new child,[101] has the audacity to go out to work,[102] or commits the sacrilege of filing for divorce,[103] thus throwing him and the children together. What then more natural than that they should take advantage of this access to their father and initiate sexual relations?

Writers such as Forward and Buck[104] insist that the mother not only condones, but actually sets up and participates in the incest on an 'unconscious' or 'preconscious' level (they never at any point define what this level of awareness actually is). For example:

We were *impressed* with [the fathers'] psychological passivity in the transactions leading to incest. The mother appeared the cornerstone in the pathological family system.[105] [editor's italics]

But:

Contrary to popular myth most mothers are not aware of ongoing sexual abuse. Marriage demands considerable blind trust and denial for survival. A woman does not commit her life and security to a man she believes capable of molesting his own children. The 'obvious' clues to sexual abuse are usually obvious only in retrospect. Our assumption that the mother 'must have known' merely parallels the demand of the child that the mother must be in touch intuitively with invisible and even deliberately concealed family discomfort.[106]

As Lucy Berliner has remarked,

In hindsight, many women can look back and see some signs. Signs that at the time didn't mean anything or weren't significant. But the kinds of signs they are talking about are things like being asked to go to the store all the time. Or the husband getting out of bed to see if everything is OK in the house; if these things happened in my family, I would not immediately assume that my husband is diddling my kid.[107]

Blame of mothers is central to the family dysfunction analysis and the gender-bias inherent in such blame is amply demonstrated by asking ourselves whether a father whose son was sexually abused by his wife would be castigated in the same manner for failing in his role as a parent. No one would deny a man's right to social and work commitments outside the home. The expectation that mothers should serve as an emotional safety net for the entire family ('Because of her illness and preoccupations, she was unable to meet her family's dependency needs'[108]) is one which society imposes on women alone. If mothers are 'neglecting' their families every time they go out anywhere leaving father and daughter together, then ultimately they can only prevent abuse by watching their husband's every move. The logical conclusion to this chain of thought, which is obviously never expressed in the literature, would be that women and children should not live with men at all, since men are apparently not to be trusted. Again, it demonstrates the double standards inherent in the family dysfunction approach: opinions which if attributed to ordinary women would be classed as paranoid are, when issued from the pens of psychiatrists, authoritative.

The varied experiences of any group of women who care to come together to discuss them will belie the theory that sexual abuse is caused by family dynamics, specifically marital problems. It says nothing for the child who is used by her uncle, grandfather or brother. It does not explain the fact that many men who molest children within their family will also molest outside it. Most importantly, it obscures the whole aetiology of the offender himself. The majority of child-molesters are 'repeaters',[109] who start their career of abuse in childhood or adolescence and continue against fresh targets, through every changing family circumstance, until they are caught and controlled.[110] The idea that a man will suddenly become a child-molester when under stress is one favoured by professionals, quite simply because it is less frightening than the thought of a man who carefully plans and prepares the ground for his activities, and yet passes for Mr Average. But boys as young as 5 years old have been known to molest other children and babies. It is usually only at adolescence that their behaviour may be detected by concerned adults, since it is at this point that the choice of more powerless or helpless targets becomes apparent as the age gap between offender and target widens.

> Therapists who work with members of violent families should read the range of political perspectives on the roots of violence and come to a personal resolution about the societal causes of family violence. Most counsellors are well-schooled in humanistic thought and have embraced an understanding of family systems theory. However, they are too often ignorant of the feminist literature, sometimes lacking in clinical precision, which has been the keystone in exposing family violence as a social problem in our time . . . Yet therapists who have accepted – even expressed – other theories ignore the rage and pain of those who have known victimization. To accept an 'incest-triad' theory, to say that children invite sexual exploitation; to continue to work with battering men and their partners as if their family has a unique dysfunction is to abet, not treat, the problem . . . Most people now acknowledge that family violence exists. The task, today, is to convince those who want to work against family violence that the problem is pervasive. The theory that a small number of families fail to function well is potentially dangerous.[111]

Of course, the 'dysfunctional family' interpretation of incest is not just another instance of theoretical mumbo-jumbo. It has its roots in a real live phenomenon – the dishonesty of the incest offender himself.

> Emlyn Jones made the choice to disclose publicly that he sexually abused his children . . . It made me angry that he could write an article entitled 'Help for the Incestuous Family' when in fact all he talks about is fathers who abuse and how they get help to share the blame and guilt around, when the ultimate responsibility is their own. Emlyn Jones, how are your children?[112]

Myth no. 11: Sexual abuse is not caused by abusive sexuality, but by other factors

or, in the words of a treatment paper published by the Harborview Sexual Assault Centre in Seattle,[113] 'The problem is not the problem'.

> Harborview cite the mental health myths that sexual abuse is 'only a symptom of something else'. For example, the notion that 'it is not a sexual deviance problem' but is caused by low self-esteem, insecurity/inadequacy, confusion of affection with sex, etc. Or, that 'it is situational' (it is stress-related or spontaneous). They assert that clearly it is also a planned, premeditated act by virtue of efforts made to conceal it and to keep children from telling. A third myth mentioned is that sexual abuse is caused by alchoholism – but they found that although frequently present as an issue with the offender, this was not always the case or necessarily event-related. They had no evidence that treatment for alchoholism reduces the incidence of antisocial behaviour. Finally, they point out that 'there is no evidence that treatment for other problems is effective in reducing sexual molesting behaviour'.

Myth no. 12: Sexual abuse causes permanent damage to children

On one level this is a circular development of Myth no. 1. The assumption is that if a child is not lying about the sexual abuse, then the sexual abuse has made her a liar. Thus survivors are often by definition assumed to be biased or paranoiac, not only in their attitude to their abuse, but also in other areas of their lives. In one newspaper counselling column, a mother requesting advice on how to support a sexually abused daughter (whilst giving no details either of the abuse of the girl's reactions to it), was advised: 'As her parent you have an important role in correcting her distorted view of things.'[114]

Most survivors testify to the 'freak' status that has been imposed on them at the disclosure of their own sexual abuse. The freak incest survivor is almost a Jungian archetype, which has taken many guises throughout history, for example as the village idiot, the witch, or the teenager who brings forth poltergeists. She can be seen in ancient myth and religion as the psychic, the clairvoyant, or the oracle of the gods,[115] the child or woman 'possessed' by the devil, and her archetype is reflected in many horror films to this day.[116] Romantic as this may sound, the day-to-day experience of being treated as a monster is extremely painful for many women. We are to some people almost 'untouchables':

> Both religion and literature decided a long time ago that the act of incest constitutes a curse that dooms all participants [sic], no matter how innocent, no matter how unaware they were of being related to their incestuous partner. The myth has been widely spread from generation to generation that calamities of such enormity befall incestuous unions [sic] that even to speak of the subject is enough to strike fear and repulsion in people's hearts.[117]

The current fashion is to regard abused children as so sexually damaged that they will inevitably communicate that harm to others in various sexual ways. The 'promiscuous' survivor is ascribed almost magical sexual powers:

> Within six months of Keith's reception into care the young residential social worker . . . was forced to resign following allegations of sexual relationship between him and Keith . . . there is no doubt in my mind that Keith's heightened awareness, his detailed knowledge of sexual activities and his particular state of adolescent development combined to give him unnatural powers of seduction vis-à-vis the young worker.[118]

In other cases the survivor is projected as causing sexual damage – through frigidity: 'Effects vary but a childhood experience could cause a mother to be prudish about the way her children behave . . . She might tend to shun close physical contact. Sexual relationships with her husband might prove difficult';[119] or through sexual practices which are even today condemned by the psychiatric profession as 'perversions':

> Child victims [sic] of sexual abuse often exhibit hypersexual behaviour . . . this active repetition . . . is distinctly maladaptive in a normal environment . . . While sexually abused boys often become homosexually eroticized, sexually abused girls may engage in homosexual activity in order to avoid sexual conflicts with males.[120]

Far from attempting to dismantle this myth of the survivor as communicating some kind of sexual infection, many agencies contribute to it further. A newspaper advertisement placed by a fostering agency ran: 'Vicky is 9 years old and a strikingly pretty child, with brown hair and big brown eyes. Her looks belie the deep pain that she has experienced in her past and she needs a family with the strength and patience to deal with the provocative behaviour that she often displays.'[121] The potential for further molesters to respond to this advertisement, safe in the knowledge that the child would be branded as a liar if she disclosed their abuse, is plain.

One is never allowed to forget the 'family curse' through the popular 'cycle of violence' theory; reference is constantly made to

> the long-term harmful effects emotionally and physically and other adverse consequences on future child-rearing ability including the high incidence of sexual abuse in children of those who were themselves sexually abused.[122]

> Just as abused children are at risk of becoming abusing parents, sexually abused girls are at risk of selecting an abusing partner and failing to protect their children from intrusion.[123]

The determinism of such theories is not only painful to many adult survivors who work actively against child sexual abuse and are most concerned that the 'sins of the fathers' should never be revisited upon anyone, let alone their own children. It is also used highly destructively in work with very young children, actually playing a part in moulding the pattern of their upbringing. For example, I once attended a case conference where a child of 4 who had possibly been molested was pronounced therefore to have 'potentially severe problems in her later mothering capacity'. If social workers and psychiatrists already saw a toddler through such a negative filter, what hope was there that she might escape the unspoken injunctives that she live up to their preconceived stereotype? Why is it that when faced with the suffering of a real 4-year-old, workers prefer to consider a hypothetical problem 20 years away rather than to give their client immediate help?

On another occasion, a young single mother had summoned up the courage to telephone a hotline that was in temporary operation after a television screening of a fictional incest drama.[124] The first advice that the psychiatrist on the end of the line gave her was that she was bound to abuse her own children. This diagnosis was not merely unprofessional, it amounted to an unfounded accusation, which fed into her already well-developed sense of irrational guilt. Far from being of use, it simply oppressed her further. Although there may be some evidence that molested children can become molesters, this is based to a large extent on studies made on selections of convicted male criminals.[125] Since these men would have an understandable urge to deny personal responsibility in the belief that this will save them from punishment, they will speedily pick up on the researcher's own quest for external causation. They will then highlight their previous victimisation in an attempt to parrot the researcher, and both sides will be lost in a circle of collusion.

A person's urge to dominate may well be reactive, rather than innate, as Alice Miller argues[126], and therefore reflect a childhood influenced by domineering and punitive figures. However, the fact that one has been abused as a child is not a reliable indicator that one will become an abuser. A more useful indicator of potential abusiveness would be the survivor's attitude to her or his experience of abuse. Here the difference between the sexes can be marked. John Mortimer, in interviewing James Anderton, Chief Constable of Greater Manchester, remarks on grown men's apparent acceptance of abuse dealt out to them as boys, as part of a rationale for their own right to abuse as adults:

'As for young people convicted of violence, I would be in favour of punishment with a medically approved cane . . . I'd do it [myself]. My father beat me.' The chief constable sat back, still smiling . . . He had the look of deep and complacent satisfaction which men assume when they speak of having been beaten in childhood.[127]

Compare this to a typically female response from Charlotte Bronte:

Next morning [the teacher] wrote in conspicuous characters on a piece of pasteboard the word 'Slattern', and bound it . . . round Helen's . . . forehead. She wore it till evening . . . The moment [the teacher] withdrew, after afternoon school, I ran to Helen, tore it off, and thrust it into the fire. The fury of which she was incapable had been burning in my soul all day, and tears, hot and large, had continually been scalding my cheek; for the spectacle of her sad resignation gave me an intolerable pain at the heart.[128]

Chapter 3 provides some ideas on why the traditional male response to being abused should differ so markedly from the traditionally female. But to abuse children is a choice we all have, male or female; and we can all choose not to if we so wish. To claim that even boy survivors will invariably become abusing men is an insult to those men who have learnt to reject rather than to mimic the role models of their childhood.

In Britain, such stereotypes are already having a concrete effect in the management of families where incest has occurred or where there are custody and access disputes. In the first type of case, where sexual exploitation of a child of the family is disclosed, social workers often home in on analysing the parents' past experience, usually as a form of mother-blame, instead of concentrating on the needs of the child herself. In the second, cases have been documented where, regardless of the absence of current sexual abuse, mothers have lost custody battles over their children simply on the grounds of psychiatric reports stating that they are incest survivors and that their parenting abilities are therefore permanently damaged.

It is unpleasant enough for a woman to endure a childhood of sexual abuse; let alone to come to realise that society discards her as an adult and that the state is prepared to collude with her assailant to the extent of depriving her of ordinary civil liberties. Are we really to be punished in our abusers' stead for the rest of our lives?

Myth no. 13: Intervention or preventive education causes more harm than the abuse itself

For example: 'The most damaging experience may be during professional intervention or the exaggerated reactions of family, friends, neighbours or teachers.'[129] Alfred Kinsey's study of sexual behaviour in the human female[130] is a typical expression of this notion:

> It is difficult to understand why a child, except for its cultural conditioning, should be disturbed by having its genitalia touched . . . Some of the more experienced students of juvenile problems have come to believe that the emotional reactions of the parents, police and other adults . . . may disturb the child more seriously than the contacts themselves . . . many small girls reflect the public hysteria over 'being touched' by a strange person, and many a child who has no idea at all of the mechanics of intercourse will [therefore] interpret affection and simple caressing . . . as attempts at rape.

Undoubtedly, a bad experience on disclosing sexual abuse increases a child's suffering. But the effect of this myth is to suggest that child sexual abuse is really not all that important a crime; or is more a fantasy in the child's head than a fact.

Professional treatment of child sexual abuse

Chapter 3 deals with some of the professional practice corresponding to the models of analysis outlined above. It might be useful here to define the notion of 'secondary abuse', that is, depersonalising, punitive, or collusive treatment from doctors, social workers, schools, etc., which compounds the ill effects of the primary sexual abuse on the child.

Depersonalisation

An example of the depersonalising approach to sexual abuse which may prove offensive or hurtful to children is that of the police surgeon who treats the patient as an unfeeling piece of meat. The practitioner's approach is reflected in this article, designed to give guidelines on the medical examination of sexually assaulted children: 'Healed fissures with an associated skin tag may be seen, and easy acceptance of three or four fingers into the anus may be demonstrated. The "funnel-shaped" anus, so beloved by the forensic pathologist, is rarely seen in the living . . .'[131]

Punishment

The punitive approach may well be endemic to the professional-client relationship. Those whose job is to help others from a position of patronage rather than solidarity will often find that their very livelihood depends upon keeping the client population under. Clients are therefore seen as permanent 'victims' having 'problems' that set them apart from the 'normal' population, and especially from psychiatrists, social workers and the like. British psychiatrists in particular sometimes treat abused children as an inferior breed without ordinary human rights. This disrespect takes different guises depending upon the analysis and practice in fashion at the time. Decades ago, the tiny minority of women and children who were not disbelieved or told that they were fantasising, were simply silenced with chemical or electroconvulsive treatment. Nowadays these methods continue, but more fashionable treatment is family therapy combined with the use of anatomical dolls and video. The punitive effect on the child of many such methods is summed up by Sylvia Plath:

'Don't worry,' the nurse grinned down at me. 'Their first time everybody's scared to death.' . . . Doctor Gordon was fitting two metal plates on either side of my head. He buckled them into place with a strap that dented my forehead, and gave me a wire to bite. I shut my eyes. There was a brief silence, like an indrawn breath. Then something bent down and took hold of me and shook me like the end of the world. Whee-ee-ee-ee-ee, it shrilled, through an air crackling with blue light, and with each flash a great jolt drubbed me until I thought my bones would break and the sap fly out of me like a split plant.

I wondered what terrible thing it was I had done.[132]

Collusion

Collusion with sexual abuse is common amongst professionals. At an inaugural conference held by the British Association for the Study and Prevention of Child Abuse and Neglect, in April 1982, one American guest speaker described how in therapy with a girls' group he ran, he would roleplay strangers who had approached the girls sexually in a café. He told the audience how he had pressed his groin against one girl in a manner similar to that of the stranger, in order to make her more assertive. At this point he added: 'But without the pelvic thrust'. The professional audience found this heartily amusing. The speaker went on to play a tape-recording of a teenage survivor being raped, which he had managed to obtain from a rape crisis centre who had advocated the tape as an evidence-gathering exercise. We were not told whether the survivor had given her permission for her screams and protestations to be repeatedly replayed for the benefit of an audience of hundreds.

The area in which professional collusion with child sexual abuse is most evident is that of treatment for the offender. This is often primitive in the extreme and almost an insult to the name of science, as illustrated by the case of a child-molester presented on British television in 1984.[133]

The first attention this man received was aversion therapy via electric shock treatment, which would be given to him as he watched slides of child pornography. (Nowadays the effects of the treatment are recognised to be shortlived, and it has also been acknowledged that the treatment may have the unfortunate but predictable effect of providing the sex offender with a new fantasy, this time about giving electric shocks to children.[134]) This was replaced by 'covert sensitisation' – the patient was asked to indulge in pleasant sexual fantasies which he would then be required to replace with unpleasant ones at the tap of a pencil. The patient filmed chose to replace his fantasy of little girls in a playground with that of little girls covered in excrement, which the psychiatrist involved considered to be curative. No mention was made on the programme of the fact that this particular man regularly visited parks where he urinated on little boys. Even apart from this fact, coprophilia is a well-known perversion and could hardly be discounted in this case. Thirdly, the patient was treated for his 'anxiety about relationships with adult women' by being given a jar containing some female pubic hair to carry around in his pocket. It was suggested that he wear a rubber band on his wrist, which he was to flick whenever he had an inappropriate fantasy. If this failed, he was to carry pornography featuring adult women in his wallet and to paper his bedroom walls with the same material, in the hope that upon masturbating he could replace the fantasy image of children with these adult pictures ('orgasmic conditioning'). Finally, upon his marriage to a woman who had three children, the whole family group was placed in family therapy in order to forestall any question of abuse of the new stepchildren. Needless to say, one of these children was subsequently molested by the patient.

In the light of the recidivism admitted by professionals in all such cases, it is surprising that these ineffectual therapeutic techniques continue. Yet it seems that many people who work with sex offenders find the techniques valuable in that they allow us to deny that the man himself is the problem. We constantly submit to the urge to displace his problems onto women within his environment, and consequently we also collude in his future abuses of children:

> Frank raped and killed a two-year-old California girl in 1978, just a few weeks after he was released from a state mental hospital. Irving Prager, a law professor who prosecuted Frank, says that as part of his treatment, 'Frank's wife . . . was asked to dress up as a child. She and Frank . . . were then supposed to have sex together so that he could work out his fantasies.'[135]

One approach to offender therapy which attempts to deal with the offender alone involves treatment with synthetic hormones, usually of the type that is used as a contraceptive in women, which are supposed to reduce the sex-drive in men. The main disadvantage of this treatment is that it is based on the notion that only the penis can cause danger to children. As proved by a tragic West German case in 1980, castrated offenders can still sexually assault and murder children.[136] However efficient or inefficient hormone treatment is in preventing sexual abuse, it is usually rejected as an option on the grounds of hardship to the patient. It appears that the main concern for professionals is that the hormone encourages the development of breasts in men. This is one of the reasons why the National Council for Civil Liberties campaigns against such treatment in Britain.[137]

As for the clinical approach to the offender, many have shown that the manipulativeness of this particular type of client is not necessarily amenable to therapy, which depends on client and professional having a shared goal which they work towards in an atmosphere of trust. Too many who work with sex offenders are as yet unaware of their capacity to abuse the trust even of the professional and to dupe the therapist that one is 'cured' simply by making excuses –

> The clinical interview is open to the the fallacy of 'false cause' or 'post hoc propter hoc'. The patient's explanation of his present condition is taken too easily as the only valid one rather than standing as just one unvalidated hypothesis . . . 'The offender's crime was a sick act, alien to his own better judgment and conscious ideals to which he had been driven by emotional urges that he could not at the time fully comprehend or control',[138]

or by parroting the therapist's analysis of one's problems in a flattering manner – 'The molester knows that if he sings the right song and dances the right dance, he'll be out a lot quicker.'[139] As Ray Wyre, who runs a voluntary centre for child-attackers released from gaol, concludes:

> Present treatment of these men is patchy and inadequate. Often they are either given 'social skills' training or psychotherapy. Both, if given alone, may be useless, or even dangerous. 'Educate a devil and you get a clever devil.' They may give a man more seductive power to use against children. As for psychotherapy, you are talking about a very obsessive, powerful behaviour pattern. Merely understanding why they do it won't stop them doing it again . . . [I feel] strongly that the present system [in Britain] is totally inadequate. We're talking nonsense when we release a child sex offender from prison without supervision.[140]

So what of group work? Family therapy is the group therapy solution corresponding to the family dysfunction analysis of sexual abuse outlined earlier. It was first designed for working with children to protect the child but is now, ironically, often more useful for the protection of the adult offender. It serves to blur the issues of power and responsibility within the group: 'My own very early work with the families where sexual abuse has occurred is to help all members of the family to share responsibility, but with the primary task to ensure that the adults take prime responsibility . . .'[141] As usual, 'adults' in this sense means primarily mothers. The mother must admit that she has precipitated the incest: '[in Giaretto's therapy at the Child Sexual Abuse Treatment Project in California] the mother must also state her responsibility for not protecting her daughter and for her part in the failure of the marital relationship'.[142] She must then take sole responsibility for preventing it from recurring:

> During family therapy, the mother is brought quickly from isolation to a central position, and focus given to her relationship with the child. The hypothesis is that a strong mother-daughter relationship blocks incest.[143]

Therapeutic success is considered to occur where sexual relations are re-established between parents and the family is a reunited self-contained group, highlighting the fact that family therapy has an ideological as well as a therapeutic purpose. There is great reluctance to admit that anything might be fundamentally wrong with the nuclear family as an institution. The taboo on speaking about incest prevents us from realising that it is in fact integral to patriarchal family life; that a man's position in the family (as head of the household, with unquestioned rights of access to other family members) produces a situation where incestuous assaults can continue to occur.

Family therapy for sexual abuse is innately hypocritical. To blame a woman who unknowingly remains with her husband while he molests her children and yet require her to stand by him, have sex with him, and allow him access to her children when this is sanctioned by professional 'guidance', is plainly illogical. But then such illogicality is more and more the order of the day. Family therapy used to be an option offered to incarcerated offenders only and was sometimes even carried out in prisons,[144] disregarding entirely the unjustified stigmatisation that this would create for mother and children. It is now extended to those who are on probation and even to those who have not been formally prosecuted but are simply filing for greater access after a divorce. Social workers on hearing allegations of sexual abuse from a child's mother (mothers make up the vast majority of adults who report and prevent child sexual assault[145]) have to date been officially required to pass this report on to the police. In Cardiff, Wales, the National Society for the Prevention of Cruelty to Children has launched a programme[146] where, conversely, the police are duty bound to involve the social services in any case concerning assault. Social services then press for family conciliation work. This means that women on the run from violent men can no longer find protection. Even if they choose to live rough in a refuge, they live in the knowledge that seeking assured state protection for their children will simply result in these children being coerced all over again.

No child can recover her physical and mental health whilst that health is still under threat. To keep a child under the same roof as a sex offender and to treat them jointly for incest is like attempting to cure a major gumboil by chewing a clove. Certainly, the clove oil may anaesthetise the gum temporarily. But meanwhile the boil flourishes undetected, doing yet more damage. Until the tooth itself is removed, the gum will continue to be infected and the infection may well spread to the rest of the mouth. Remove the tooth and only then can the gum at last begin to heal. A similar solution is appropriate for therapeutic work with families. Only once the offender is removed can the child find peace, and experience enough psychic space for the healing process to begin.

Not only are abused children under increasing threat of being used as guinea-pigs in the professional zoo. I was chilled to hear an eminent family therapist state recently that he thought it was never too late for even adult incest survivors to go for therapy with their abusers. One fears for any survivor with fewer civil rights than the average citizen – for example, a woman in prison or in a mental hospital – whose therapists hold such views. She will not escape their experimentation.

Powerful as they are, professionals would not be permitted thus to insult the women and children in their trust if this were against the interests of governments. But the capitalist state has a vested interest in the continued privatisation of women within the nuclear family. Such families provide at low cost a male worker who is serviced, fed and cleaned at home by unpaid females. Childcare is free – and so is healthcare for older family members. The state sees to it that women's work is never done; a policy that dovetails beautifully with that of the wife-beater or the incest offender, who sees to it that she is kept even busier simply staying alive and maintaining her sanity. For the incest survivor or the battered wife, stipulations made by agencies offering social security and other benefits may add to the pressure to remain at home, glue the broken family together, and accept abuse in return for survival. For them, from a cynical point of view, these government policies may amount to state-run prostitution. And for those who are not forced back into the home by economic strictures, current media coverage of and professional response to child molestation cases will be enough psychological pressure to push some mothers out of the job market as they guiltily strive for 100% supervision of their children. Mothers will be racking themselves over whether they 'sacrifice' their children to their career, or 'sacrifice' their career to their children, their guilt again, as so often before, preventing many from realising that child-molesters and their friends will profit either way.

Education

The nuclear family is glorified ideologically as a safe haven for women and children. In reality, it can be quite the opposite. Schools are another social institution in which children are supposed to be nourished and protected. Yet much research has exposed the ways in which the education system institutionalises sexism; the methods by which male pupils can silence and verbally harass females; the fact that some male staff not only assault girls, but encourage boys to exploit their own position of male privilege; and finally, the problems in the education system even for adult female staff, who may be subjected to this continuum of abuse.[147] Sexual abuse within the education system has grave implications for the intellectual and career development of those who are subjected to it. It is therefore important to reconsider the equal opportunities policies that are currently in operation within schools. Usually these concentrate on enabling particular groups of pupils to gain access to subjects or courses in which they have traditionally experienced discrimination. We might query an 'equal opportunities' analysis which ignores the brutality and violence underlying the relative subtlety of educational discrimination. Without having to debate whether institutional ideology is the cause of personal abuse or vice versa, it must be plain that as yet society has not acknowledged the great extent of direct racial and sexual harassment that occurs in schools. Individual incidents when exposed are often neutralised as 'bullying', without considering the underlying power relations between social groups which children are acting out. Furthermore, in dealing with these incidents on a piecemeal basis, teachers have no way of combating the parental values which may be reflected by their children's violence in school. Thus, racist and sexist attacks committed by schoolchildren upon each other can be viewed as the domination of one social group by another, using child abuse as its primary tool of indoctrination. The surface structure of this model would involve child-on-child violence. The deep structure, however, would be adult violence against children, using one's own children as tools for manipulating the children of the subordinated social group, in order to ensure that subordination continues smoothly from generation to generation. By this model, we cannot dismantle racial or sexual oppression in society at large unless we stop parents from using their children to perpetuate it within schools. Any equal opportunities policy must accordingly take account of the deep structure of school violence.

Increased access to sex education, with information about both homosexual and heterosexual relationships, is to be welcomed in schools. However, as with equal opportunities policies, the thinking behind it must be revised to take account of the fact that abuse does not start to occur at the point when the child is actually assaulted. It starts in the mind of the abuser and can only be effectively prevented at that point. Hence, current preventive education programmes which address mainly children should really be termed 'protective' programmes. Whilst it is of immediate practical use to teach children how to say 'no' or to get help, we should be accepting that abused children have all along been saying 'no', whether in words or otherwise, and that many offenders are hardly likely to be intimidated by the mere verbalisation of this refusal. To effect genuine prevention, what we have to teach long-term is not so much how to say 'no' as how to accept it from others. There is more benefit to be derived from a sex education approach which challenges power relations in society and which views sex not as sets of individual acts which are seen as 'acceptable' or 'taboo', but as part of relationships between people, with discussion of issues such as trust, pleasure, discomfort, and so on. As adults we tend to forget just how knowledgeable children can be of the various sexual acts.

What we do need to educate them about is the contexts in which those acts can take place in a fulfilling manner without hurting ourselves and others. There is no need to fear that children will lose their 'innocence' in the process. If anyone is shockable, it is often the adult!

The placing of sex education on the curriculum may be of vital importance. It must not be a one-off session, but a regular course for all ages, supplemented by discussions in other classes such as those covering current affairs, ethics, history, religious education, literature, drama, and life sciences. The suggestion that parents have a right to opt their child out of such sessions is defensive and should not be countenanced, unless the sex education class is simply a disguised form of cultural indoctrination, conveying, for example, that sex is only pure when consummated in a Christian marriage, or that homosexuality is a sickness and causes people to catch the HIV virus. Where children are prevented from attending classes, we must ensure that they receive sex education elsewhere, preferably in a group setting where no adult can take advantage of the educational materials in order to inveigle the child into a one-to-one, 'secret' relationship. The most important aim of sex education is to share and make public our knowledge, and to discourage any secretiveness or exploitation of privacy.

The law

Chapter 4 tackles another major institution within society, that of the legal system. It is mainly concerned with a critique of the criminal law. We have learnt both from 19th-century female activists and from the experience of present day women's campaigns that violence within the family, which is a nightmare for women and children alike, is not seen as a 'real' crime. The state will not defend the individual when that individual is a woman or child within the family with the same protection that it affords to people assaulted by strangers. British caselaw still upholds the prejudice in favour of child-molesters who stick to their own families, as against offenders who stray beyond the confines of their homes. In a wardship case of 1987, it was held that a 'more stringent degree of probability' is required to satisfy the courts that a father is guilty of sexual misconduct with his daughter than would be needed to justify the conclusion that there had been sexual abuse by a stranger.[148] This problem dates back to medieval law which designated rape as the stealing of another man's possession – the logic being that you cannot steal what is already your own:

> In the Middle Ages the law was preoccupied on the one hand with the preservation of virginity and the provision of legitimate heirs, and on the other with the protection of family interests and the succession to landed property. The evil that the law tried to prevent [by penalising rape] was the abduction of propertied virgins who, to the detriment of family rights in their disposal, were thus compromised into marriage.[149]

The essence of the crime was theft of another man's property. Male ownership of women continues to this day both in its public version where prostitutes are managed by one group of men and hired to another, and in marriage where women's domestic and sexual services may be privately owned. The medieval sexual economy was enshrined in modern British tax law and in the Department of Health and Social Security's policy on welfare benefit for cohabitees. The modern state had a vested interest in the continued privatisation of women within nuclear families.

It is well known that the British laws for the prevention of cruelty to animals were passed before those protecting children were enacted. The suspended sentences often dealt out to offenders for crimes of sexual or physical assault against children can be compared unfavourably with the response of the judiciary to assaults on animals: 'A man who beat his 10-week-old . . . puppy after having a row with his wife was gaoled for three months by Newcastle upon Tyne magistrates . . . [he] was also barred from owning a dog for 10 years.'[150] Animals even get more credibility as witnesses in court:

> The [English] rules [on evidence, especially the hearsay rule] seem completely irrational. If a tracker dog recognises a scent and tracks the suspect this fact can be put before a court and presumably also the fact that a dog recognised a person it knew if it was relevant. Yet a court cannot be told that a child of three or four has recognised or described or identified an attacker. The law seems to rate the evidence of little children lower than that of dogs.[151]

Much attention has been devoted of late to the harrowing experience of children being interrogated in the courtroom:

> The ordeal for the children giving evidence has been so acute, that many parents have withdrawn their children from it, for fear of what the defence lawyers were doing to them. The trial started with 42 child witnesses and now there are only 16 . . . One little boy was confronted by a threatening lawyer who used the word 'kill' 27 times in four minutes . . . In one case a boy was asked how old he was and he said four. The lawyer asked, 'Four days, four weeks, or four months?' The boy thought he had to choose so he said 'Four months' and the lawyer tried to claim it proved his evidence was worthless.[152]

Even as adults, survivors do not escape this courtroom abuse:

> During the civil suit Anna [filed as an adult], Judge Milton Pollack called [her] a liar because when she was a child she had not informed the [welfare] agency of the rapes . . . [he] was also hostile to Anna's attorney, saying 'The problem with you girls is that you don't know how to practise law in federal court the way men do.'[153]

The chapter comments on the assault on children in our courts and suggests guidelines for its reduction. It suggests that if present court practices are oppressive to children, then the solution is not to remove children from the legal process altogether but to provide services that cater more to children's needs and requirements. So often the law has been a tool in the hands of the child-molester, used to punish children further for disclosing their abuse; and yet it may be the sole forum in which the child's rights and interests are completely respected:

> Of all the systems marshalling support for the sexually victimized child, the justice system alone has the unique and primary mandate of searching out the truth. The process may be lengthy, and complex. At times bewildering to all except its practitioners, it is certainly only clumsily adapted to familial crimes. The law, nevertheless, holds the most powerful tools to seek out the truth. By its nature, it can overcome the secrecy, confusion, and guilt

that have allowed the abuse to occur. With the exception of infants and toddlers, young [survivors] in the courtroom for the first time are close to being on a par with the offender. While the court proceedings create a crisis, they also can blow away the mists that made the child vulnerable.[154]

Indeed, a Swedish appeal case that recently came before the European Court of Human Rights[155] has now shown that the justice system is clearly capable not only of searching out the truth, but also of dealing adequately with the civil liberties issues that may arise in the conflict between parental and children's rights. The applicants, a married couple, complained about a decision of the Swedish social authorities, confirmed by the courts, placing their children (who were incest survivors) in public care. They based their appeal for the return of the children on Article 8 of the European Convention on Human Rights ('Everyone has the right to respect for his private and family life, his home and his correspondence'). The Commission in fact found that the decisions in question, although interfering with the applicants' right to family life, had a basis in law and were necessary in a democratic society for the protection of the children. It held that the complaint was manifestly ill-founded. We may well expect further cases to consider the potential conflict of interest between child, family and state, and Chapter 4 attempts to outline the legal developments in this area.

Some interesting legal changes that may be of help to survivors of sexual abuse are the institution of all-women police stations, as in Barcelona, Spain;[156] the introduction of special advocates who appear in court to represent the concerns of raped women and children, as opposed to those of the state, pioneered in the Danish legal system;[157] the use of civil suits to seek damages against the offender;[158] legislative measures to ensure that suspected child abusers, rather than children, be removed from their family home;[159] and retrospective prosecutions, which may entail criminal injuries compensation, and can be commenced as late as twenty years after the last assault took place.[160]

Racism and anti-Semitism

Chapter 5 addresses the issues of racism and anti-Semitism and how they interact with sexual abuse. It examines the ways in which the mythology of racism is bolstered by negative sexual stereotypes which have a direct impact on the sexually abused child. Both personal and institutional racism may often cause situations in which the child is further isolated, silenced, or prevented from seeking help from people outside her family. The chapter suggests that even in cases where the child has managed to ask for help, those professionals with misguided notions of 'anti-racist' practice may well refuse to act on her behalf either because they assume that sexual abuse is a cultural norm within certain communities, or because they do not dare to challenge her abuser. Some guidelines are given on training for workers, with the strong recommendation that children have adequate access to professionals from their own communities and backgrounds.

Positive action

Chapter 6, the last chapter in this book, is intended to counteract any sense of despair that the reader may encounter in dwelling on the painful and panic-laden topic of child sexual abuse. It pays tribute to the survival powers both of abused children themselves, and of the women who have campaigned on their behalf for over a century. It attempts to empower the reader, not by addressing every issue of detection, intervention and treatment, but by focusing on one issue: that of recognition of distress signals from the child which may indicate that she or he is being sexually assaulted. The booklist following should provide a short guide for those who wish to raise their awareness further on methods of combating, treating or preventing child sexual abuse.

In editing a book subtitled, *'Feminist Perspectives'*, we are aware that we cannot represent every radical female viewpoint on the subject of child sexual abuse, but wish to emphasise that all contributions to the collection of essays have arisen from work and experience in the women's movement. Whilst this introduction may have gone some way towards describing a female response to child abuse, it does not claim that that response provides the full solution to the problem. What it does argue is that just as children have been silenced by abuse, so women's points of view have been ignored and must now be taken into account. Until they are, a true understanding of human history and psychology will never be developed. We would hope that this book has something to offer women and men, ordinary readers, students and professionals alike. Most of all, we hope it is of use to those readers who have themselves experienced sexual assault. So often we see a mirror of our abuse on the pages of academic books, which reduce us to a set of depersonalised statistics or sensationalise the outer aspects of our experience whilst ignoring the complexity of feeling within. If this book leaves one incest survivor free of the sense that she or he is mere sociological material to be analysed, pilloried, and finally discarded, then it will have achieved a vital aim.

Notes and references

1. Sigmund Freud, *The Origins of Psychoanalysis: Letter to Wilhelm Fliess, Drafts and Notes 1887–1902*, ed. by M. Bonaparte, A. Freud and E. Kris, translated by E. Mosbacher and J. Strachey (New York: Basic Books, 1954).
2. Judith Herman, *Father-Daughter Incest* (Cambridge, Mass: Harvard University Press, 1981).
3. For example, Carol Jones, 'Sexual Tyranny: Male Violence in a Mixed Secondary School', in G. Weiner (ed.) *Just A Bunch of Girls* (Milton Keynes: Open University Press, 1985).
4. Vincent DeFrancis, *Child Abuse Legislation in the 1970s: Protecting the Child Victim of Sex Crimes Committed by Adults* (Denver, Col.: American Humane Association, Children's Division, 1969).
5. The pronoun 's/he', used in this Introduction, is an abbreviation for 'she or he'. I have used 'her' meaning 'her or him' for the sake of brevity.
6. MORI Report, *Childhood*, September 1984.
7. Sarah Nelson, *Incest: Fact and Myth* (Edinburgh: Stramullion, 1981).
8. Sandra McNeill, letter to Incest Survivors' Campaign, London 1981. See also Leeds Revolutionary Feminist Group, 'Incest as an Everyday Event in the Normal Family' (eds Dusty Rhodes and Sandra McNeill, *Women Against Violence Against Women* (London: Onlywomen Press, 1985.)
9. The age at which a child becomes an adult is obviously a matter of cultural convention, not to mention philosophical dispute. Since the definition of child abuse given depends upon a rights perspective, we have adhered to a legal framework and accepted the legal age of heterosexual consent in Britain as a convenient dividing-line. According to the new United Nations Convention on the Rights of the Child, a child is 'every human being to the age of 18 years unless,

under the law of his/her state he/she has reached his/her age of majority earlier'.

10. For a serious analysis of the assaultive nature of exhibitionism, see David Finkelhor, 'Risk Factors in the Sexual Victimization of Children', *Child Abuse and Neglect*, vol. 4, 1980. Sexual abuse is being more narrowly defined in the panic reaction to the controversial Cleveland inquiry in Britain, 1987–8. Exhibitionism is therefore amongst the types of assault which are being trivialised. See *The Independent*, 27 November 1987: 'a child psychiatrist from the Hospital for Sick Children, Great Ormond Street, said that the much-quoted figure that one in ten children are sexually abused should be subject to scrutiny. Half these cases of abuse involved "flashers" and did not involve physical contact.'

11. See, for example, direction to UK government by European Commission to pay £3 000 damages to a boy who refused to be caned as a school punishment and was consequently suspended from classes. According to press reports there may be as many as thirty complaints against the UK involving corporal punishment waiting to be considered by the Commission. Reported in *Interights Bulletin*, vol. 2, no. 1, spring 1987; *New Law Journal*, vol. 137, 13 February 1987. In the USA, whilst noting equally encouraging developments, the End Violence Against the Next Generation group points out with disbelief that 'special education' for children with all forms of physical, mental and emotional handicaps included 43 360 instances of physical punishment in 1982. See *International Children's Rights Monitor*, vol. 1, no. 4, spring 1984.

12. David Finkelhor, 'What's Wrong with Sex between Adults and Children?', *American Journal of Orthopsychiatry*, vol. 49, no. 4, 1979.

13. Jeff Vernon, 'Defend the Right to Free Discussion', *The Observer*, 11 September 1983. This letter was written on behalf of the Campaign for Homosexual Equality. It is a shame that a group campaigning for adult male homosexual rights should ally itself with the interests of paedophiles. However, as Vernon points out in his letter, 'From the available figures it seems that heterosexuals are more likely than homosexuals to be child-molesters.'

14. 'My Gentleman Pal', *The Observer*, 18 September 1983.

15. Patricia Beezley Mrazek, Margaret Lynch and Arnon Bentovim, 'Sexual Abuse of Children in the UK', in P. B. Mrazek and C. H. Kempe (eds), *Sexually Abused Children and Their Families* (Oxford: Pergamon, 1981).

16. Clodagh Corcoran, Irish Council for Civil Liberties, from an interview for the film *Crime of Violence*, by A. Droisen (Channel 4 Television, 1986), July 1985.

17. Women callers to television hotline, London Weekend Television, 29 March 1985.

18. Anne O'Connell, Dublin Rape Crisis Centre, from an interview for the film *Crime of Violence* (Channel 4 Television, 1986), 9 July 1985.

19. Ibid.
20. I. Herman and L. Hirschman, 'Father-Daughter Incest', *Signs*, Journal of Women in Culture and Society, summer 1977.
21. R. Brant and V. Tisza, 'The Sexually Misused Child', *American Journal of Orthopsychiatry*, vol. 47 (1), January 1977.
22. Roland Summit and JoAnn Kryso, 'Sexual Abuse of Children: A Clinical Spectrum', *American Journal of Orthopsychiatry*, vol. 48(2), April 1978.
23. Myra Hindley was present when Ian Brady captured, tortured and murdered several children from the Manchester area in the early 1960s.
24. Three British examples from the 1980s:
    – Jasmine Beckford, died at the hands of her stepfather whilst legally in the care of Brent Social Services, London, 1984 (see *Child in Trust: The Protection of Children in a Responsible Society*, ed. by Louis Blom-Cooper, 1985, Greenwich Borough Council).
    – Tyra Henry, died at the hands of her father while in the care of Lambeth Council, London, 1984 (see *Whose Child?*, ed. Stephen Sedley, 1987, Lambeth Council).
    – Kimberley Carlile, died at the hands of her father whilst in the care of Greenwich Social Services, London, 1987 (see *A Child in Mind*, ed. by Louis Blom-Cooper, 1987).
25. P. Gebhard *et al.*, *Sexual Offenders* (New York: Bantam, 1965).
26. Herbert Maisch, *Incest* (London: Andre Deutsch, 1973).
27. Roland Summit and JoAnn Kryso, 'Sexual Abuse of Children: A Clinical Spectrum', *American Journal of Orthopsychiatry*, vol. 48(2), April 1978.
28. Derek Heptinstall, 'Sexual Abuse of Children', *Community Care*, December 1984.
29. Dr Robin Skinner, interviewed by Jean LaFontaine on 'Thinking Out Loud', October television programme, 1985.
30. Incest Survivors' Campaign newsletter, London 1984.
31. *Vis-à-Vis*, Newsletter of National Clearinghouse on Family Violence, Canada, vol. 4, no. 2, spring 1986.
32. 'Daddy Said Not to Tell', *Aegis*, September/October 1978.
33. Quoted by Gerald Lubenow, 'A Troubling Family Affair', *Newsweek*, 14 May 1984.
34. Quoted by Elizabeth Matz, 'In My Opinion', *Milwaukee Journal*, 7 March 1983.
35. Romi Bowen and Angela Hamblin, 'Sexual Abuse of Children', *Spare Rib*, no. 106, May 1981.
36. Roland Summit and JoAnn Kryso, 'Sexual Abuse of Children: A Clinical Spectrum', *American Journal of Orthopsychiatry*, vol. 48(2), April 1978.
37. Romi Bowen and Angela Hamblin, 'Sexual Abuse of Children', *Spare Rib*, no. 106, May 1981.
38. Rich Snowdon, 'Working with Incest Offenders: Excuses, Excuses, Excuses', *Aegis*, no. 29, autumn 1980.

39. J. Mitchell, *Psychoanalysis and Feminism* (New York: Pantheon Books, 1974).
40. J. Herman and L. Hirschman, 'Father-Daughter Incest', *Signs*, Journal of Women in Culture and Society, summer 1977.
41. See note (88) on Dr Oliver Brooke. The comment was made by Lord Chief Justice Lane, according to *Streatham and Tooting News*, 10 and 24 July 1987.
42. Colin Evans killed Marie Payne in 1984. He had been introduced to Toc H, a Christian voluntary organisation, by his probation officer Peter Southerton, who did not reveal Evans's criminal background either to the organisation or to the Council. See *Community Care*, 3 January 1985.
43. Matilda Blake, 'Are Women Protected?', *Westminster Review*, no. 137, 1892. Quoted by Susan Edwards, *Female Sexuality and the Law* (Edinburgh: Martin Robertson, 1981).
44. 'Media Attention to Child Sexual Assault – A Good Thing?', *off our backs*, January 1985.
45. Gene Abel, 'The Components of Rapists' Sexual Arousal', *Archive of General Psychiatry*, vol. 34, 1977.
46. According to research, offences against boys are mostly committed by men known to them, but less often by actual family members than are offences against girls. See David Finkelhor, 'Risk Factors in the Sexual Victimization of Children', *Child Abuse and Neglect*, vol. 4, 1980; Roland Summit, 'The Child Sexual Abuse Accommodation Syndrome', *Child Abuse and Neglect*, vol. 7, 1983.
47. For example, Derek Heptinstall, 'Sexual Abuse of Children', *Community Care*, December 1984; Doris Stevens and Lucy Berliner, 'Special Techniques for Child Witnesses', in L. Schultz and C. Thomas (eds), *The Sexual Victimology of Youth* (Springfield, Ill.: 1980).
48. For example, David Finkelhor, 'Risk Factors in the Sexual Victimization of Children', *Child Abuse and Neglect*, vol. 4, 1980; National Children's Bureau, UK, *Highlight on Child Sexual Abuse and Incest*, July 1982.
49. Incest Survivors' Campaign, 'Breaking the Silence', in Dusty Rhodes and Sandra McNeill (eds), *Women Against Violence Against Women* (London: Onlywomen Press, 1981).
50. 'Media Attention to Child Sexual Assault – A Good Thing?, *off our backs*, January 1985.
51. Blair Justice and Rita Justice, *The Broken Taboo* (New York: Human Science Press, 1979).
52. See, for example, Florence Rush, 'Pornography: Who is Hurt', in *Take Back the Night: Women on Pornography* (ed Laura Lederer, Bantam Books, 1982).
53. Defence for Children International, 'Sexual Exploitation', *International Children's Rights Monitor*, Special Edition 1984.
54. See M. Kesera Karunatilleke, 'Some Aspects of the Role of Interpol in the Prevention and Suppression of the Traffic in Women and

Children', *Revue Abolitionniste*, no. 5, Premier Semestre 1985, Paris.

55. 'Incest', *Revolutionary and Radical Feminist Newsletter*, no. 10, summer 1982.

56. Frederick Powell, 'Political Violence and Child Abuse', *International Children's Rights Monitor*, vol. 1, no. 4, spring 1984.

57. Jo Boyden, 'Personal View', *Oxfam News*, spring 1986. For a description of political abuse directed against Black children in South Africa, including forced labour, de-education, discriminatory health care, police violence, arbitrary detention, torture and capital punishment, see Glenys Kinnock, 'Suffer Little Children', *Journal of the National Union of Students*, no. 4, February 1988. For a description of violations of Black children's rights in South Africa and elsewhere, see The Minority Rights Group, Report no. 69, *Children: Rights and Responsibilities* (London: 1985).

58. For example, a photograph of a girl, naked except for her knickers, with burns down one arm (NSPCC, *Child's Guardian*, Christmas 1984).

59. NSPCC advertisement, *The Guardian*, 26 September 1986.

60. Florence Rush, 'The Sexual Abuse of Children', *Journal of Child Psychology and Psychiatry*, vol. 21, 1980.

61. This comment was made on the Barry Norman television show in 1985.

62. *Daily Record*, Glasgow, 8 July 1982.

63. *Eve* magazine, quoted by Elizabeth Matz (see note 32 above).

64. Dated 1982, sold in London, no publisher or printer indicated.

65. *Giselle*, distributed by CBS/Fox, 1982.

66. 'Dear Katie', *TV Times*, 30 August – 5 September 1986.

67. BBC Radio London *Dial-a-Date*, 13 August 1986.

68. Corinna MacNeice, interviewed by Alix Coleman, *The Guardian*, 30 July 1986.

69. 'I Married My Father. . . ', *Nineteen* magazine, June 1983.

70. Phyllis Chesler, 'Rape and Psychotherapy', in *Rape: The First Sourcebook* (New York: New American Library).

71. See, for example, Adrienne Rich, *On Lies, Secrets and Silence* (New York: W. N. Norton, 1979; London: Virago, 1980); 'Compulsory Heterosexuality and Lesbian Existence', *Signs: Journal of Women in Culture and Society*, 1980, vol. 5, no. 4.

72. Martina Navratilova, *Being Myself* (London: Collins, 1985).

73. Rasjidah St John, for Child Sexual Abuse Preventive Education Project (independent publication, London, March 1985).

74. Arthur Green, 'True and False Allegations of Sexual Abuse in Child Custody Disputes', *Journal of the American Academy of Child Psychiatrists*, vol. 25, 1986.

75. Roland Summit, 'The Child Sexual Abuse Accommodation Syndrome, *Child Abuse and Neglect*, vol. 7, 1983.

76. Sigmund Freud, *Introductory Lectures on Psychoanalysis*, 1933. See also T. C. N. Gibbens and J. Prince, *Child Victims of Sex Offences* (London Institute for Study and Treatment of Delinquency, 1963).

77. Peter Conrad, 'The Last Taboo', *The Observer*, 1 April 1984.
78. Arthur Green, 'True and False Allegations of Sexual Abuse in Child Custody Disputes', *Journal of the American Academy of Child Psychiatrists*, vol. 25, 1986.
79. Jean Moore, 'Like a Rabbit Caught in the Headlights', *Community Care*, 4 November 1982.
80. Dr James Thompson of the Middlesex Hospital, interviewed in *The Independent*, 14 April 1988.
81. L. Bender and A. Blau, 'The Reaction of Children to Sexual Relations with Adults', *American Journal of Orthopsychiatry*, vol. 7, 1937.
82. Roland Summit and JoAnn Kyrso, 'Sexual Abuse of Children: A Clinical Spectrum', *American Journal of Orthopsychiatry*, vol. 48(2), April 1978.
83. Vladimir Nabokov, *Lolita*, 1955.
84. D. J. Gee, *Lecture Notes on Forensic Medicine* (Oxford: Blackwell Scientific Publications, 1984).
85. See Sandra Barwick, *The Independent*, 4 November 1987.
86. Henry Giaretto, quoted in *Newsweek*, 14 May 1984.
87. Kay Carmichael, 'When Your Father is Your Lover', *The Guardian*, 11 May 1983.
88. Elizabeth Brown, 'Incest: A Child *is* Being Molested', *Maenad: A Women's Literary Journal*, 1981.
89. Quentin Bell, *Virginia Woolf: A Biography* (London: Hogarth, 1972).
90. John Lahr, 'The Experience of Blackness', *New Society*, 18 October 1985.
91. Marlene Bogle, 'Brixton Black Women's Centre', *Feminist Review* no. 18, spring 1988.
92. From Ruth Hall (ed.), *Ask Any Woman — A London Inquiry into Rape* (London: Falling Wall Press, 1985).
93. Anjona Buckman, 'Racial and Sexual Violence', *Women's Health Information Centre Newsletter* no. 9, autumn 1987.
94. N. Lukianowitz, 'Incest', *British Journal of Psychiatry*, vol. 120, 1972.
95. *Streatham & Tooting News*, 1 May 1987.
96. Examples are many, but three will suffice:
   – Michael Waters, who had used a false reference and bogus employment record to get a job with Bradford Council managing workshops for 'educationally subnormal' teenagers. He had served a ten-year sentence for child sexual assault and murder (*The Guardian*, 14 August 1986).
   – Dr Oliver Brooke, Professor of Child Health and head of paediatric medicine at St George's Hospital, Tooting, London, accused of seven offences of supplying child pornography, soliciting, counselling, and aiding and abetting others to take indecent photographs of children under the age of 16; he was sentenced to six months' imprisonment. See *The Guardian*, 30 August and 19 December 1986.

– The 'Manhattan Beach' case: in 1983 sixteen adults who ran a private junior school in California were accused of belonging to a sex ring in which they abused more than 100 children in their care over a period of ten years. See *Newsweek*, 14 May 1984.

97. The CIBA Foundation, *Child Sexual Abuse within the Family* (independent publication, 1984).

98. See R. Brant and V. Tisza, 'The Sexually Misused Child', *American Journal of Orthopsychiatry*, vol. 47(1), January 1977.

99. For example, Cavallin feels that incestuous fathers have unconscious homosexual traits, relating to their hostility to their paternal grandmothers.

100. See, for example, British Association for the Study and Prevention of Child Abuse and Neglect, *Child Sexual Abuse* (independent publication, 1981).

101. See, for example, A. Kaufman, Peck and L. Tagiuri, 'The Family Constellation and Overt Incestuous Relations Between Father and Daughter', *American Journal of Orthopsychiatry*, vol. 24, 1954.

102. See, for example, Erin Pizzey and M. Dunne, 'Sexual Abuse Within the Family', *New Society*, 13 November 1980; and comments by Alessandro Vassali, a Milan psychiatrist, in *Newsweek*, 14 May 1984. Esther Rantzen of Britain's help organisation 'Childline' openly endorsed this ignorant prejudice: 'Often in these families, either the woman is employed and the man is not, or the woman goes out to work late at night' (*Any Questions*, BBC Radio 4, 11 July 1987).

103. See, for example, Arthur Green, 'True and False Allegations of Sexual Abuse in Child Custody Disputes', *Journal of the American Academy of Child Pyschiatrists*, vol. 25, 1986.

104. S. Forward and C. Buck, *Betrayal of Innocence* (Harmondsworth: Penguin, 1981).

105. Noel Lustig *et al.*, 'Incest: A Family Group Survival Pattern', *Archives of General Psychiatry*, 14 January 1966.

106. Roland Summit, 'The Child Sexual Abuse Accommodation Syndrome, *Child Abuse and Neglect*, vol. 7, 1983.

107. Lucy Berliner, quoted by Louise Armstrong in *Kiss Daddy Goodnight* (New York: Simon and Schuster, 1979).

108. R. Brant and V. Tisza, 'The Sexually Misused Child', *American Journal of Orthopsychiatry*, vol. 47(1), January 1977.

109. One study of arrest records made by the New York Psychiatric Institute's Sexual Behaviour Clinic indicates that each heterosexual child-molester had assaulted seventy-three children and each homosexual child-molester had assaulted thirty children before being convicted. See *Newsweek*, 14 May 1984.

110. Doris Stevens and Lucy Berliner advise, 'if the offender is not prosecuted for his crime, a series of children will undoubtedly be exposed to his abuse'. See 'Special Techniques for Child Witnesses', in L. Schultz and C. Thomas (eds), *The Sexual Victimology of Youth* (Springfield, Ill.: 1980). Even where child-molesters are prevented from repetition by incarceration, this is often because there have

been concurrent offences committed which to the justice system appear more heinous, such as Geoffrey Prime's crimes of spying against the British state, for which he was sentenced to 35 years' imprisonment in 1982. *The Times* reported on 11 November of that year that in the course of investigating indecent assaults on children who were numbered on a list of 2 287 little girls kept on a private hit list by this man, the police 'began to discover material which suggested that the defendant was involved in activities even more grave than the sexual offences', involving 'irreparable harm to Britain'. He received a 3-year sentence for the crimes against the children. One repeater was gaoled on separate occasions: 30 months for indecent assault committed whilst working at a school for maladjusted children; 3 years' probation for assaulting a neighbour's child; a 3-year conditional discharge for abduction; and 5 years imprisonment — this time for impersonating a police officer in order to perpetrate an assault. It seems the impersonation offended the authorities' sense of justice more weightily than did the assaults themselves. See *Streatham and Lambeth Comet*, 20 November 1987.

111. *Vis-à-Vis*, Newsletter of the National Clearinghouse on Family Violence, Canada, vol. 4, no. 2, spring 1986.
112. Gerrilyn Smith, 'Feedback: Incest and Male Power', *New Forum*, 1981.
113. Harborview Sexual Assault Center, *Mental Health Myths*, undated practice paper.
114. 'Helpline' column, *Streatham Guardian Series* newspaper, 1 October 1987.
115. As was the visionary, Cassandra, who became a seer after her rape by the god Apollo, according to the ancient Greek writer Aeschylus' play, *The Agamemnon*. Other cultures, ancient and modern, share these beliefs: see comments on Navajo Indian recognition of a syndrome including incest, seizures and witchcraft in J. Goodwin, M. Simms and R. Bergman, 'Hysterical Seizures: A Sequel to Incest', *American Journal of Orthopsychiatry*, vol. 49. no. 4, October 1979.
116. For example, in *Rosemary's Baby, The Exorcist, Carrie*.
117. Blair Justice and Rita Justice, *The Broken Taboo* (New York: Human Science Press, 1979).
118. Leonard Davis, 'Without Prejudice', *Social Work Today*, vol. 13, no. 14, 8 December 1981.
119. Derek Heptinstall, 'Sexual Abuse of Children', *Community Care*, December 1984.
120. Arthur Green, 'True and False Allegations of Sexual Abuse in Child Custody Disputes', *Journal of the American Academy of Child Psychiatrists*, vol. 25, 1986.
121. Advertisement placed by Familymakers (Kent) in *The Guardian*, 21 May 1986.
122. Family Planning Association, UK, *Policy Resolution on Child Sexual Assault*, 16 May 1985. The classic 'cycle of violence' book was

written by a thriller novelist, Jean Renvoize (*Incest: A Family Pattern*, London: Routledge & Kegan Paul, 1982).

123. Roland Summit and JoAnn Kryso, 'Sexual Abuse of Children: A Clinical Spectrum', *American Journal of Orthopsychiatry*, vol. 48(2), April 1978.

124. *Something About Amelia*, a film on incest and family therapy, shown on BBC2, March 1984.

125. See, for example, Nicholas Groth, *Men who Rape: The Psychology of the Offender* (New York: Plenum Press, 1979); N. Groth and A. Burgess, 'Sexual Trauma in the Life Histories of Rapists and Child-Molesters', *Victimology*, 4, 1979.

126. See, for example, *For Your Own Good: The Roots of Violence in Child-Rearing* (London: Virago, 1983); *The Drama of Being a Child* (London: Virago, 1986).

127. From 'An Ironside Reborn', in *In Character: Interviews with some of the Most Influential and Remarkable Men and Women of Our Time* (Penguin, 1988).

129. *Jane Eyre* (Penguin, 1971).

129. Leonard Davis, 'Without Prejudice', *Social Work Today*, vol. 13, no. 14, 8 December 1981; see also Donald West's comments to the same effect, *The Guardian*, 21 September 1984.

130. Alfred Kinsey, *Sexual Behaviour in the Human Female* (quoted by Susan Brownmiller, *Against Our Will* (London: Secker & Warburg 1975).

131. D. M. Paul, 'The Medical Examination in Sexual Offences against Children', *Medical Science Law*, vol. 17, no. 4, 1977.

132. Sylvia Plath, *The Bell Jar* (London: Heinemann, 1963).

133. 20/20 Vision, *Child Sex Abuse: The Offender* (Gambles Milne, Channel 4, 12 December 1984). Treatment was supervised by the Bethlem Royal Hospital and the Maudsley Hospital, and Professor Isaac Marks of the Institute of Psychiatrists, London.

134. *The Observer*, 6 July 1986.

135. See report in *Newsweek*, 14 May 1984.

136. Klaus Grabowski was accused in 1981 of strangling Anna Bachmeier after sexually assaulting her. He had been convicted twice for child abuse and was voluntarily castrated after the second offence. He was shot dead at the murder trial by Anna's mother, Marianne Bachmeier.

137. The Howard League also opposes the use of such drugs on the grounds of absence of the choice to consent on the part of the offender (see *Heart of the Matter*, BBC, 3 July 1988). Gerald Silverman, consultant psychiatrist at St Bernard's, Ealing, points out, 'These drugs are only useful for compulsive sexual offenders whose primary problem is sex drive. They are useless for those who are primarily violent and incidentally sexually violent'.

138. Paul Devonshire (of Broadmoor Hospital, UK), 'Sex Offenders: There but for the Grace of God . . .', *Symposium on Violent Crime and Individual Differences*, BPS Annual Conference, 1985.

139. Jay Howell, executive director of the American Justice Department's National Centre for Missing and Exploited Children, interviewed for *Newsweek*, 14 May 1984.

140. *The Observer*, 6 July 1986.

141. Arnon Bentovim (of the Great Ormond Street Hospital for Sick Children, London), letter to journalist researching child sexual abuse for *The Leveller*, 9 March 1982.

142. Jane Lloyd, 'The Management of Incest: An Overview of Three Interrelated Systems – The Family, the Legal and the Therapeutic', *Journal of Social Welfare Law,* January 1982.

143. Sue Higginson and Jean Shaw, 'Child Sexual Abuse — Guidelines for a Social Service Department', Kingston Social Services independent publication, 1985.

144. As reported by Arnon Bentovim, letter to *The Guardian*, 21 March 1984.

145. Seventy-six per cent of complaints to authorities on child sexual abuse 'were made by the parents, primarily the mother': Patricia Beezley Mrazek, Margaret Lynch and Arnon Bentovim, 'Sexual Abuse of Children in the UK' (1981). In the first nine months of a new police scheme for reporting child sexual abuse in Bexley, South East London, it was found that 52 per cent of initial reports were made by mothers (Symposium Report, 21 September 1986).

146. See report in *The Guardian*, 4 December 1984.

147. See, for example, Dale Spender and Elizabeth Sarah (eds), *Learning to Lose: Sexism and Education* (London: Women's Press, 1980); Carol Jones, 'Sexual Tyranny in Mixed Schools', in G. Weiner (ed.) *Just A Bunch of Girls* (Milton Keynes: Open University Press, 1985); Pat Mahony, *Schools for the Boys?* (London: Hutchinson, 1985); Susan Ageton, *Sexual Assault Among Adolescents* (Lexington, Mass.: Lexington Books, 1983).

148. *In Re G*, Family Division, *Times Law Reports*, 30 July 1987. Interestingly, Sheldon J suggested in this case that although any suspicion of abuse or wrongdoing might be incapable of formal proof, yet if the court concludes either that it would be an unacceptable risk to the child's welfare to leave her in her previous environment, or that an older child has made an allegation which in itself suggests that a change of regime would be in her best interests, there might still be a case for wardship.

149. Charlotte Mitra, 'Father–Daughter Incest: A Paradigm of Sexual Exploitation', *Justice of the Peace*, 22 May 1982.

150. See report in *The Guardian*, 10 May 1986.

151. John Spencer, 'Suffer the Little Children: Video Technology and the Evidence of Tiny Children', *Counsel*, The Journal of the Bar of England and Wales, summer/September 1987.

152. The Manhattan Beach case, as reported in *The Observer*. See note 96.

153. 'Child Sexual Abuse in Civil Court', *off our backs*, June 1983.

154. *Vis-à-Vis*, Newsletter of the National Clearinghouse on Family Violence, Canada, vol. 4, no. 2, spring 1986.

155. *Application no. 11630/85 v. Sweden*, European Human Rights Reports vol. 9, 1987.
156. See Tim McGirk, 'A Gentle Touch in Spain's Police Force', *The Independent*, 10 August 1988.
157. See Jennifer Temkin, *Rape and the Legal Process* (London: Sweet and Maxwell, 1987).
158. One 16-year-old incest survivor in South Carolina, USA, was awarded $30 million in a suit against her stepfather, including $15m in punitive damages. Technical grounds for damages in other cases could be breach of contract (where an adoptive parent does not fulfil the adoption agreement requiring him to nurture, educate and protect a young person), although this may raise some privity problems; violation of civil rights (in legislatures which have such provision); and negligence or breach of statutory duty (where childcare and fostering agencies have placed children with foster parents who abuse them), although there may be difficulties where the agency could not reasonably be expected to be aware of abuse. See 'Child Sexual Abuse in Civil Court', *off our backs*, June 1983.
159. See the Report of the Inquiry into Child Abuse in Cleveland (Cmnd 413), HMSO, 1987. This was proposed in the U.K. Parliament by the shadow Social Services spokesman, Robin Cook (*The Independent*, 7 July 1988).
160. See Ole Hansen and Melanie McFadyean, 'Getting Away with Abuse', *The Observer*, 4 October 1987.

1

Some biographies

AUDREY DROISEN (compiler)

These biographies are not confessionals or subjective reveries, but first-hand accounts. Conspicuously missing from this chapter will be the mythologised romances and seduction fantasies that past literature and art have suggested were the arenas for incest.[1] Instead these accounts demonstrate that child sexual abuse is about violence and the abuse of power.

In order to understand child sexual abuse, the reader needs to understand what abuse means to a child. So the accounts chosen for this chapter describe how the situation looked from the child's or mother's point of view and what were the many currents of conflict, confusion and pain. These biographies not only describe how abuse affects one's childhood but how one's adult life is also influenced.

These stories emphasise the importance of self-help groups which have consistently been the most successful route for survivors. Whatever personal counselling can achieve and legal redress can accomplish, nothing can replace for an individual the vital knowledge that however awful the abuse was, it was not uncommon but part of the scheme of their society. This does not absolve each abuser from personal responsibility but does free the survivor from the paralysing fear that it was something she or he individually did that caused the abuse. This loss of fear, the electrifying feeling of finally being able to share and *speak* openly with others who can truly understand, has over and over again been what survivors say has helped the most.

There is a great deal of truth in the saying, 'You never really know something until you have experienced it'. Much of feminist theory is based on the validation of personal experience over received ideas.

In fact, child sexual abuse would never have been taken seriously if feminists had not insisted that it was happening no matter how much it was denied as female fantasy. So the real experts of child sexual abuse are the women and men who went through that abuse as children. Any analysis must begin with what they have to say.

Siân

My daughter would have been about 2½ when I first became suspicious that she was being molested by her father. I noticed a fear in Anita when he came home from work in the evening. She tended to run and hide.

The feeling I had that something was wrong became so strong that I felt I had to do something about it. I had to know one way or the other. For too long I had been pushing my suspicions to the back of my mind. I wasn't able to accept that he would do anything like that to her. But in the end I realised I had to face up to it.

I thought the only way to find out why my daughter was afraid of him was to ask her. By that time she would have been about 3½ years old. I put it very simply because she was so young. I just straightforwardly said to her, 'Why are you afraid of your father?' I then emphasised how much she meant to me and how much I loved her and how much I would take care of her. But I told her that she would have to confide in me. I couldn't help her in this matter if she couldn't tell me.

She thought about it for about twenty four hours, with me prodding every now and again, and decided in the end that she would take me into her confidence. She told me that her father was molesting her. Her own words were, 'He puts his penis all over me.'

I realised from the words she used, her age being only 3½, that she couldn't possibly have learned those words from anyone outside the home. They would have had to come from her father. I chose to believe her and I praised her for having told me.

Even though I thought I was ready to hear the truth, I was deeply shocked. I didn't know what to do about it, who to go to or how to help her. But I knew there and then that I had to act immediately and leave and take her to where she could be safe and lead a normal life.

I didn't have any money so I decided to go to the Citizen's Advice

Bureau for help. They put me in touch with the Incest Survivors' Campaign.[2] The next day I went to see women from the ISC, I explained the situation and within forty-eight hours there was accommodation for me and Anita available in a Women's Aid refuge[3] on the other side of London.

While I was waiting for a place to go to, I continued to live at home and to act normally with my husband. I knew that I had to remain calm so he wouldn't suspect that we were planning to leave. When I learned that room had been found for us, I didn't bother packing, I just went immediately to fetch Anita from playschool. I told her there was no need for us to go home again, that I'd found somewhere new for us to stay for a short period and after that we would find ourselves a new home. I could see the relief on her face. She knew she no longer had to be afraid of her father. She knew she was safe with me and she was safe in my love. When we got on the train to go to the Women's Aid refuge, she was jumping up and down on the train seat really pleased, I knew then I had done the right thing.

We settled into the refuge and over a period of about three months my daughter would wake every evening, crying usually, and would of her own accord relate to me what had gone on between her and her father. Her whole body was racked with sobs as she was reliving the pain she went through and the confusion she felt in her mind, and the pressure that was put on her not to tell. It had to be a big secret.

I don't think I could have gone through it all, if it hadn't been for the support of the Incest Survivors' Campaign and Women's Aid. They also helped me to press charges and to get through the eight-month ordeal of the court case. Each time I had to appear in court, women from ISC came with me.

My husband was convicted and given an eighteen-month sentence. I felt he deserved more for what he had inflicted on my daughter. He had stolen her childhood.

Debbie

The first time I was sexually abused was during the war. I was evacuated from London. I was 4 or 5 years old. The woman I was put with would pull down my pants in front of her boyfriend and beat me with a cane. The last time I was so badly beaten that I couldn't sit properly at school. Fortunately, my teacher asked why and I told her the truth. I remember feeling mortified when my teacher looked at my bottom, then the headmistress and a doctor. Then at the hospital a lot of people came to have a look.

After that I was sent to another woman who took good physical care of me but continually told me I was a heathen for being a Jew. I wasn't sure what that meant but I could tell it wasn't a good thing. Finally, I was sent home.

My father started to sexually abuse me when I was 11 years old. I had started to develop, so I asked my mother if I could have a bra. I felt embarrassed when we did Physical Training at school or I played in the street because my breasts kept shaking about. She said, 'We'll see'. Later that day my father said with a big grin, 'What do you need a bra for, you've only got two pimples, not even fried eggs yet.' Then he and my mother burst out laughing. I was upset that my mother had told him. After that he seemed to keep looking at me. It was the middle of summer. I took to wearing a big jumper to hide my shape. Finally some days later my mother dragged it off me. I couldn't tell her why I wanted to wear it.

The first time it happened, I was in my bedroom. I had been told to tidy it. My mother and the rest of my family were out except for my father. He came into the bedroom and said he wanted to look at something. At first, I didn't understand what he was doing. It reminded me of what happened when the teachers and doctors looked at my backside. But then I thought, 'That happened such a long time ago.'

He made me lie face down on the bed. Then I did understand, when I felt his body on me. It was over quickly. He just said, 'Keep your mouth shut about this', and walked out of the room. My back felt cold and wet. I reached behind and felt my back, it was slimy and horrible. I had slime on my back and now on my hand. I felt sick, I didn't move because I didn't want the slime to get on any other part of me. I lay there until it dried.

I shared the bedroom with my older sister. Sometimes she stayed at a friend's house overnight. When she was away he would come to my bed in the night. Not a word was said – no apologies – no endearments – no kind words. He would just wake me up and push and pull me any way he wanted. On those occasions it would be a quickie, but I would lie awake for a long time afterwards and sometimes I would cry quietly so as not to wake anyone else in the house. On his way back to my mother's bed he would pull the lavatory chain to make her think he had been to the toilet. This action became symbolic to me. I had become his lavatory. He deposited his filth on me then walked away.

Until that summer I loved my dad. I always wanted to please him. He liked his hair brushed. I brushed it. I would buy him little presents like a bar of chocolate and wrap it in many layers of newspaper. He would always pretend surprise. I would sit on his lap and make a fuss of him. I wanted his affection and he was jolly and playful with me.

On the other hand, he demanded respect. His word was law. Our mother could shout at us to get up, go to bed, eat, clear up, etc. and maybe take a swipe at us. But the worst she could do was to say, 'I'll tell your father.' Sometimes we could cheek mother, but we couldn't even disagree with father. He would take the strap to us. He had to be obeyed.

With this conflict of having to obey and wanting to please him, I knew no way of stopping him. He became more strict with me. He tried to stop me going anywhere unless it was with him. I stopped buying him presents and anything he gave me became strictly business.

After that summer when it all started I became like two people. At home I was obedient, passive and more afraid of my father. But I was sulky and bad-tempered with my mother. I started to have rows with her and told her I hated her. My poor mother had done nothing to deserve this treatment from me. I unreasonably thought she should find out and stop him. Yet I couldn't tell her.

At school I became rude, disruptive and a habitual truant. He had turned me into a lavatory, so I was going to be a lavatory that didn't work too well. I thought I could never be clean again, so I was going to make as much of a stink as I could. But I also became withdrawn and lonely.

When I was twelve I was kept in after school for something I'd done. It happened quite often. In the middle of a teacher's lecture about my behaviour I suddenly blurted out, 'Sometimes my dad's dirty.' The teacher went quiet for a few minutes, then she said, 'Well, I expect he does a dirty job, dear.' Not knowing any other words for what I wanted to say, I stayed quiet while she carried on talking about all sorts of dirty jobs men did.

My father was often out of work. He was an upholsterer. He was the only employee of a one man firm, and only went in if there was a job for him. My mother, on the other hand, went out to work every day, so we three younger children, who were still at school, were supposed to come home after school to do a little housework before going out to play. If when I left for school in the morning he was still at home, I guessed he would be there after school. Then I wouldn't go home till I was sure my older siblings had come home from work. But if I didn't see him in the morning and so went home after school, and found he was there, I was trapped. He would then send my two brothers out to play saying, 'Debbie and I will do the jobs'. Then he would push and shove me upstairs and use me for sex. Sometimes it seemed to go on forever, and I'd start to cry.

He didn't want me to see anything. I had to lay face down on the bed and he would shut the curtains and switch out the light. He never tried to give me any pleasure. Afterwards, I would lay on the bed waiting for the sperm to dry. He would leave a shilling or two or some sweets beside the bed and go downstairs to do the housework.

If I stayed away but didn't get home just in time to do my jobs before my mother got home, my plan would also fail. For then my mother would shout and slap me. But I was too filled with fear and shame to tell her why I hadn't come home in time.

Apart from the one attempt of telling my form mistress I didn't know who I could tell. I didn't really want other people to find out. The children at school already taunted me with being a 'dirty jew'. There was a lot of anti-Semitic feeling then. They would get in a circle around me and chant, 'yid, yid, dirty yid', so I thought they would see what my father was doing as part of being a 'dirty jew'.

When I was thirteen or fourteen I plucked up the courage to speak to my father. I told him I didn't like it and someone might find out, so perhaps it would be better if 'we' stopped. I didn't want to make him angry, so by saying it that way I thought I was taking some of the blame myself and that that would make it easier for him.

But he interpreted what I said as a threat. He said if I told anyone he would go to prison, I would break up the family, I would break Mum's heart and she would never forgive me. If he had to go inside he would kill me first and I would be put away till I was 18. It would go on my school records and employers and officials would always know what I had done.

As I grew older, my father didn't want me to have boyfriends. He'd shout and carry on at me and send the boys packing. Once he had me followed by a friend of his who saw me up the West End[4] with a man. I wasn't allowed to go up the West End and so I had my face smacked for that. I said, 'What about you, look what you've done'. He said he hadn't done me any harm because he had left me a virgin, but that he didn't know what I was after going out with these blokes. He said he'd kill me if he found I'd been 'had' by any of them. The fact was that I wanted a boyfriend, not sex, so at the time he didn't have to worry. But I couldn't have explained that to him, I couldn't have explained it to myself.

When I was 17 I met a boy I really liked. Father started his tirade again and the boy fled. I was so upset, I screamed at him in front of my mother that I would and could have him put away for years if he didn't leave me alone. My mother said, 'What's going on, what's she talking about.' But I didn't tell her. He never touched me again.

Shortly after this incident, he became ill, wasted away and died within two years from cancer. I felt I had caused his illness and death. I had a recurring nightmare for years after he died. I dreamt I had killed him, rolled him in a bit of old carpet and buried him in the garden. But I couldn't conceal the patch I put him in, because no matter what I planted on top, it always died. My brother would say he would dig over the bare patch and plant something else. I was afraid my father's body would be discovered. I thought I would have to find another place to bury him. So I'd dig him up and carry him over my shoulder inside a tube of carpet but bits of his dead rotting body kept falling off. I could feel bits of cold and wet on my back. I could feel him slipping out of the carpet roll. I was terrified of seeing him, I mustn't see him. Please don't let me see him. Just before he'd slipped out entirely I would wake up in a sweat with my heart racing.

It wasn't until I was in my forties, that I read an article about other women who had been through similar experiences. It was incredible to learn I was not the only one. I was so relieved. I had always thought that there must have been something wrong with me for all these things to have happened.

As a young woman, I used to be frightened of men. I felt I mustn't displease them or make them angry. And I was supposed to feel gratitude for their attentions. But since meeting and talking with other women about our experiences, I have become much more self-assertive and self-confident.

I've learned about navigation and seawomanship. I have done a single-handed passage to Holland. I am as good as, and better at handling a boat and myself at sea, than a lot of men. I feel now that men aren't superior to me. They merely have more privileges and power which they have bestowed on themselves and then abuse.

Diane

My father was quite well liked and respected outside the family. He was a man's kind of man who was interested in drinking and fishing and shooting and . . . abusing children.

The earliest memories I have of the sexual abuse are of when I was 11. But I'm sure it went on before then. Because even before I was 11, I can remember going round to my grandmother's house and feeling safe and secure there until he'd come and drag me home. Nobody ever questioned why we didn't want to go home.

He drove everyone in the family apart; he had such power over us. It's hard to explain it to anyone unless they've been in that situation themselves. The kind of fear and terror you have as a child. But he had such control over us that he was able to keep us all separate. We weren't allowed to feel love and affection for each other because it threatened his position. There's one night that I can remember, when he called me to his room for the usual thing. I remember coming back and my sister was really upset and she climbed into bed with me. He came in and almost dragged us apart and said that we weren't allowed to sleep with one another.

He also separated us from our mother and would get angry with her or us if she showed us any affection. So we really never got close to her. Maybe he was afraid that we would say something to her. She was completely dominated by him. She's still afraid of him. I think she has suffered as much as we have.

I felt that if I didn't do what he wanted, everyone else would suffer. He would just go on more at my mum or my sister. He would make life unbearable for everybody. So I felt that I had to put up with it. What else could I do? I was a child and I thought like a child. I didn't understand the options.

I thought I was protecting my younger sister from him. It wasn't until we were adults that I plucked up courage to say to her, 'Did Dad do anything to you as well?' When she said, 'Yes', I said, 'Oh God, I thought I was protecting you.' I felt so guilty. That's the feeling you get, guilt. You get thrown right back to your childhood, and you react as you did as a child. You think that something is wrong with you that made it happen. You have to remind yourself, once again, that it wasn't your fault. He knew what he was doing and he alone could have stopped it. He chose to do it.

It was always so carefully planned. He knew when my mother would be out. He knew when I would be alone and when we would have our bath on a Sunday night. The whole thing formed a pattern for a long time.

His attitude was, 'You're going to have to put up with this when you start going out with men, so you can start learning now.' I can remember him walking into the bathroom without any clothes on and saying something like, 'Hi, look at me, some man, hey?' He obviously got off on it, while at the same time claiming that he was educating us on the male body.

I would never bring any friends home because he would grope them as well. It was his way of relating to women: staking his claim; spraying his scent; putting women down; dominating; being a man. He just felt he had the God-given right to treat women that way because he was a man. My mother's friends too stopped coming to the house because of him. So he has successfully isolated her.

When I left home, I had very little trust in anyone and very little confidence in myself. But from the outside it could have looked like I was functioning very normally. The crunch came when my daughter was born, literally the minute she was born, and I saw her and thought, 'Oh my God, it's a girl.'—although we really wanted to have a little girl. But I saw me in her and thought, 'God, are you going to have to go through the same things that I went through? I have to protect you so that doesn't happen.'

I became very depressed and went to see my doctor. From there I went into counselling and then on to a self-help group made up of other women who had also been sexually abused as children. The group was a real turning point for me. Just being with other women who knew what I was talking about, who had been through the same things as me and had the same kind of feelings, was a tremendous relief and release. I feel so much better now. I've started college and

I've left my husband and am living with another woman who also has children.

Mrs Sullivan

I noticed a change in the kids for a few months before I found out what happened. They were wetting the bed and wetting their pants, especially the younger one. Then the older child, who was 6 then, started soiling the bed. They were also showing me how sore they were down there and I would have to put Vaseline on them to get rid of the soreness. Finally I took them to the doctor to have urine samples taken, thinking they had kidney infections. I brought the younger one to a specialist in the hospital and he prescribed tablets to stop the wetting. But they didn't work.

Then I noticed a change in their behaviour with the boys on the street. When they saw the boys coming up to the house, they used to slam the door in their faces. I slapped them for doing that and I told them they were being very bold. The little one actually stuck a knife into one of them and I put her to bed without any supper. I was waiting for the boy's mother to come up and tell me my child was mad. I still didn't suspect anything. I just thought the kids were misbehaving.

Then one night I was in bed and the kids were with me. E, the older one, was asleep and M was awake and she was talking away to me. She heard her father coming down to bed and still talking away she said, 'I know what's inside Daddy's pants,' And I said, 'What do you know?' And she said, 'He has a big Micky.' I said, 'Where did you hear that?' She told me the two boys who told her. I said, 'Why did they tell you that?' And she said, 'I know all about it.' And I said, 'You know all about what?' I kept asking her questions and she started getting upset. She said, 'They put their willies up my wee wee and they put their fingers up my wee wee.'

I thought, God, I'll have to do something about this. I woke E up and asked her if the boys ever touched her there and she said they did. She wouldn't tell me anything more and I let her go back to sleep.

My husband wanted to go down after the two boys then and there. But I held him back. I said, 'No, we'll have to get some more evidence that it was done before we can approach them.' Then one of the boy's sisters came in. She was going to babysit. We asked her if her brother was at home. She said, 'No, why, has he done something wrong? Has he broken the swings or something?' We told her it was much worse than that. And she said, 'He didn't do the other thing, did he?' I said, 'The other thing?' She said, 'Well, I know this other boy does it, and he's his friend, but I didn't think my brother would ever.' I said, 'How do you know?' She said, 'Well, he told me he'd done it to another girl in the area.' I said, 'Fine, that's all I needed to know.' I went down to one of the boys' mothers and told her why I was there. Her son was out. We waited for him but he didn't return by the time I had to go to work. After work I went down to this boy's mother again. She was crying and said that he had admitted doing it. First he had told her that my 6-year-old E had got up on top of him and helped him and was looking for it. But she said that she knew that he was only saying that to put the blame on someone else.

I went home and got my husband and the kids and went to the doctor's. But, at first, E didn't want to leave the house. She was frightened because the boys had told her that they would kill her and burn her and that we would beat her up if she ever told. We had to assure her that nothing would happen to her. When we got to the doctor's, he said he didn't know what to do and he had never heard of anything like it. He wanted to know if it was wise for him to examine the children. As the children knew him, I asked him to go ahead. He examined them and said, 'I don't think anything is broken, do you?' I said, 'I haven't a clue'. He then arranged for a social worker to come and see us.

The next day I went down to the other boy's house. I saw him in front of his mother and father and he admitted doing it three or four times. His father said, 'I expected this, him going around with that other feller. He offered three pounds to a friend of mine's child to go down the field with him and he's doing it to this other girl in the area as well.' He said that he would give his son a beating. I said that I would rather he come up to my house with his son and the other boy and his parents, so we could discuss it and have something done. He never came.

I went down to the first boy's house. His mother had been a friend of mine and that's why I had used her daughter and son to babysit for me. I saw them as friends of the family. I didn't know that when he babysat for me he would bring his friend so that the two of them could molest my little girls. When I got there I went to the boy's room. He was sitting there just smiling at me. I went wild. I got hold of him and slapped him around the face and shook him. I told him I wanted to know how long it had been going on. He said that he couldn't remember. I slapped him again. He said that he had done it nine or ten times. I asked him why he had done it and he said he didn't know.

A few days later the social worker came to see us. Basically she advised us to tell our children the facts of life and to just let the whole thing cool down. She told us that she thought the police would only upset the children more and as it was a small community it would probably only aggravate the situation to bring them in.

I did go to the police but they said there was nothing they could do because the boys were younger than 14 and anyway I had no real evidence. But, at the same time, they told me that this kind of assault by boys was quite common.

I was worried about the kids. They were crying and they were afraid to go out. They said that the boys were going to get them and beat them up. I couldn't get them to school as they had to walk past the boys' houses to get the bus. I had to walk them to the bus every morning.

Then the boys started bragging about what they had done. Some of their friends told me how they were bragging about how far they had it up M, and the things they had done to her. So it became widely known. Taunted by the other children my 5-year-old M tore off all her clothes and said, 'all the boys are going to want to do it to me now'.

People in the community started in on us. They said there was no dirt in the place until we came into it and it was disgraceful the way we were carrying on. They claimed our children were lying and that we must have put them up to it.

One of M's teachers was helpful. She suggested I go to the Rape Crisis Centre and the Rape Crisis Centre sent me to Dr. Marie Woods, a doctor in the area who has worked with other sexually abused children and has helped to establish a sexual assault unit[5] at the hospital. She is now doing therapy with the kids.

The kids still sleep with us, they wouldn't sleep alone now. When we went to the Parents' Group meeting at the Rape Crisis Centre, we left them with a woman. She had to stand out on the road with the kids on her arm till we got home at eleven that night. When we got home they were still crying for us.

Kris

My father started abusing me when I was about 3 or 4. I have memories going back that far. I remember feeling very scared and not quite sure what was going on. I tried to tell my mother once and it resulted in my mother and my father beating me up.

I didn't tell anyone at school about it. First, because I didn't think anyone would believe me. Secondly, I thought I was the only one and so they would think I was weird. Thirdly, I was frightened about being taken away from my family and being totally alone. Fourthly, I thought I didn't want to hurt my family and certainly didn't want to be seen to be doing so. I was Black and my teachers were white. I didn't want to be taken away to a white children's home.

I remember as a child doing things to try to stop him from getting to me when I was in bed. Things like getting into my little brother's bed and sleeping next to the wall in my childish attempt to hide from him. But he would find me and drag me out.

When I think about what I went through, I don't know how anyone can talk about 'incestuous relationships' when a child is involved. The balance of power is so off. A child doesn't have any power in that situation. I never had any power. I couldn't say no.

There is so much emphasis on keeping the family together. What adult would want to live with their rapist? Yet we expect a child to want that. I can remember wanting my father to go, hoping something dreadful would happen to him, dreaming that someone would rescue me and take him away. Could I have told someone that? Could I have coped with the guilt, the confusion and responsibility? But why should I have had the responsibility for deciding that? If I was a child standing close to fire, nobody would have asked me if I wanted to move away.

Why do we let children sacrifice themselves 'for the good of the family'? Why can't we take away the guilt that is not theirs but has been given to them? Most children, particularly those who have been victimised, want to help others. We can appeal to this loving side in a positive way by explaining to them that their telling will help to protect other children that their abuser might hurt. We would be telling them the truth. I think I would have responded to that and felt a tremendous relief. I think part of giving children rights is taking responsibility for what they can't yet understand. I had a right to be rescued.

When I was 16, I was the one to leave home. I was too young and I drifted into a lot of different situations, most of which were not very good for me. I started drinking and quickly became an alchoholic in my attempt to block out the dreams, the nightmares, the pain of remembering.

For a while I managed to block it out and make myself forget. I survived like that for about four or five years and then slowly the drink stopped working. I began to find that something during the day would start a memory and I would be thrown back into my childhood going over and over the events. It was then that I made a determined effort to deal with the abuse and the alchoholism.

As I began to unravel it all, I could see that my problem was not just my drinking but the emotionally abusive relationships I kept finding myself in. I finally began to realize through many discussions with other women, that this was not because I enjoy abuse. Rather it was because the abuse that I received as a child stopped me from figuring out a lot of very important things about relationships and what I could expect from them.

I had become grateful for anything and frightened of losing even that. I hadn't learned that getting my own needs met was not selfish. I hadn't learned that I needn't become for other people the rescuing parent I wanted for myself. By being that rescuing parent for them, I ended up becoming emotionally dependent on people who had nothing to offer me.

It's still an upward struggle but I now hope that I can use what happened to me as a child, productively. It doesn't have to be a total waste in time and pain.

Effie

I was about 3 or 4 years old when my brother started sexually abusing me. I can remember the wallpaper, the bedroom, the house.

I didn't have a clue what was going on. I only knew I didn't like the new game. It's obvious looking back that to my brother it wasn't a game, he knew exactly what he was doing. He planned it all. I was frightened and my brother took advantage of that. He would not hesitate to knock me around. So I kept my mouth shut. I also didn't know how to explain it to anyone. I only knew I didn't want it to happen.

By the time I was 5 I felt like an alien. I was confused and alone. Years later my brother said he remembered seeing me walking around with my head down and knowing that he had done that to me.

When I was 9 a gang of boys tried to rape me. I was rescued by my older brother. That evening over tea my mum yelled out at me, 'Did they rape you?' I sat there frozen, feeling embarrassed, hurt and helpless. The subject was dropped after that. Nobody asked me what I was feeling, so I didn't know that that was a question I could ask myself. I never learned that my feelings were important.

Slowly I began to realise what was happening to me was not what happened to every girl. I can remember one day in school, going to the toilet and finding sperm in my pants and suddenly realising that other 10-year-olds didn't have to go through what I was going through. I remember looking at and studying my best friend and coming to the conclusion that what was happening to me was not normal.

I started to tell people what was going on. I was 10 or 11 when I first wrote off to a popular teenage girls' magazine. I got no response. I told a few friends at school, but they thought it was funny and it became a regular joke with them. Perhaps people sometimes found it difficult to believe because I seemed too calm about it. But that was how I coped. I cut off, shut down all my emotions to survive.

I felt so dirty and isolated and powerless and so implicated in what had been going on for seven years. My image of reality and myself was so distorted that I could only think of survival on the most basic level. I didn't know what my rights were, didn't trust my feelings and didn't believe in my own judgement.

When I was about 11 my mother's lodger started sexually abusing me by touching me. I thought he was repulsive but I also thought that this is what happens if you're a girl. I managed to tell my mother this time because he was an outsider. So I felt more confident about her standing up for me. She spoke to the lodger and told him he had to go but he cried and said he was sorry and would never do it again. My mother believed him. Afterwards, he started abusing me again. I didn't say anything this time. I wondered then if there was something in me that men could pick up on.

I felt I had been told I was a whore and a prostitute all my life and that that was all I was good for. When I was 8 and my brother 15 my brother started initiating me into prostitution. He had started work and he would give me what seemed to be huge amounts of money after he had used me. Later, when I was about thirteen or fourteen, I started going with other men for money.

I thought there was something about being paid as a prostitute that somehow made something positive out of my feelings of worthlessness. I could somehow turn my position around and see myself as the powerful one who was using men. But, of course, it wasn't really that way because they were the ones with the money and I was the one who was risking my life and losing my mind.

Looking back at myself, at my state of mind, I was in deep shock. I was numb. I couldn't grasp what was happening. I have since had nightmares where I am in a river, naked, very young and I have this numb expression on my face. Men are throwing fishing lines at me that hook into my flesh and strip my flesh off. I stand there. I don't scream or cry. I just stand there.

I began cutting my arms with razors sometime in my teens. The 'dirt' I felt had been put inside me was in my blood and, in my worst moments, I felt I could get the dirt out by cutting my arms and letting the blood out. It was also a relief to have physical pain rather than emotional pain.

It gets me angry when people try to minimise my experience just because it was my brother who raped me. They use terms like 'mutual exploration'.

Recently I confronted my brother and asked him, 'Why did you do it?' Oh, there were lots of excuses such as he couldn't get a girlfriend, he had spots, lack of affection, etc. He minimised everything. He lied and said that he never 'made love' to me. He said he was sorry but I was very beautiful when I was younger. He told me I should get myself a man and settle down and stop worrying about the past. He said, 'I would like to love you now like a brother loves his sister. Maybe we could go out for a drink sometime.'

Ellen

My father was a child-molester, but in his spare time he was a lawyer – and a successful one. My mother is a lawyer too.

My mother didn't know that I'd been abused by my father until fifteen years after it happened. Once she was divorced, people began to tell her. 'Oh, we didn't want to send our children to your house because your husband used to do funny things to them, but we didn't like to say anything about it.' If only they had said something, my mother could have known about me too, could have known something that I was afraid to tell her and could have protected me which is what she wanted to do.

Many people, professionals and social workers, say that women who have been abused as children will have a bad relationship with their children or abuse them themselves. But I know from my own experience and from other women who were abused that this is simply not true. We've learned from being abused how awful it is, how much we don't want it to happen to our children, and we would certainly never do it to our own children. It makes me wonder though, knowing this about myself and other survivors, why men who abuse children so often claim that they were abused themselves as children and use that as an excuse for why they have to abuse children. Of course, they don't have to at all. They can choose not to, they can stop it if they want to. They just like doing it.

When I was being abused I just hoped it would end and that everything would be all right, that my father would go back to being a nice Daddy and that he would love me. Now that I'm older, I realise that's impossible. He's a child-molester and he doesn't know how to love children. I don't know if there is any help for him.

When therapists are trying to help a family, most of the time they want to glue it back together and make everyone happy again. But that's impossible, someone who sexually abuses a child doesn't have the capacity to care for children. He would have to psychologically die and be reborn and that is not a process that takes place in group therapy or in a few months or years, if ever.

What has to happen, I think, is that children have to grieve for the loss of a parent, or a brother, an uncle, or a grandfather, and realise that that person doesn't love them and that the reason that they don't love them isn't because the child is unlovable but because the abuser is incapable of loving a child. I think in that way incest in a family is like a suicide in the family. The rest of the family can feel guilty and sad and that they are to blame, when that is really not true. They have to learn how to grieve and not to take responsibility for something that wasn't their fault. They have to learn how to get over it and to survive it and to go on. And I think that in my adult life I have learned how to be a survivor and how to go on.

For a long time I wondered if I was an 'incest survivor', if 'incest' had anything to do with me. Because my father didn't have sexual intercourse with me – he sexually abused me in other ways, by coming into my room at night and touching me. And I think what I've learned is that it doesn't matter what happens physically – the point is that trust has been abused and that power has been abused and that you've been sexually violated. Even if to an outsider it can seem like something minor, to a little child just having her father be sexually excited by touching her breast, is an awful, panic-filled and crushing experience.

Robert

I have a very vivid memory of discreetly trying to ask one of my best friends if his father interfered with him in any way, because I wasn't sure what other people did. I thought it probably wasn't normal, but I wasn't sure. Anyway, I found out that it certainly wasn't.

At first, I didn't mind the fondling. But when he began doing things to me, I found it painful and frightening. Yet because I had allowed him to touch me, somehow I felt implicated.

It really made me feel miserable and angry. I can remember planning to hit him over the head with a hammer. I wanted to kill him to stop it and I didn't know any other way. It wasn't until I was 15 that I was able to stand up to him and it had been going on since I was 4.

I found out later when I was a teenager that he had been abusing my sister as well. My sister and I didn't get on as children but we were a real comfort to each other in our late teens and twenties, when we realised that we had both been through the same thing.

I think my sister suffered more than me. She's been in and out of psychiatric hospital for the past twenty years. I suppose as a man I've been more able to get my anger out. I'm not sure how it has affected me. I suppose I can look at the manual jobs that I have always gone for and wonder if I didn't need to prove my manhood.

I think it's very difficult to know what to do about interference with children by parents. And of course, 99 per cent of it is by men, by fathers or close family. I certainly believe that anything that has to be done has to be from the point of view of understanding what is going on and why. But at the same time I don't think that understanding should be used to excuse what's taking place. I think that there definitely has to be punishment for wrongdoing and abuse of children is definitely wrongdoing.

I know that many men say they abuse children because they were abused. But I have two children and I certainly wouldn't touch them in that way. There must have been some element of choice.

Notes and References

1. Toni A. H. McNaron and Yarrow Morgan (eds.) *Voices in the Night*, (Pittsburgh, Pa.: Cleis Press, 1982) p. 17.
2. Incest Survivors' Campaign was a group started in Britain, in 1981, by women who had been sexually abused as children. They were originally a self-help group but later went on to campaign nationally against child sexual abuse.
3. A Women's Aid refuge is a refuge for battered women which is part of a national British network of refuges.
4. The West End is the centre of London.
5. A sexual assault unit is a special unit, usually inside a hospital, which deals only with victims/survivors of sexual assault. All the doctors and social workers in the unit are women and have been specially trained for this work. It was felt particularly important by those setting up the unit that it be attached to a hospital rather than a police station.

2

Theoretical perspectives on father–daughter incest

CATHY WALDBY, with additions on the Power Theory by
ATOSHA CLANCY, JAN EMETCHI and
CAROLINE SUMMERFIELD[1]

Incest and the incest taboo are topics which have attracted the attention of writers from all areas of the social and medical sciences – anthropology, sociology, psychology, and psychoanalysis have all contributed to a vast body of literature on the subject. It is not within the ambit of this chapter to address all the issues and questions raised by this literature; discussion will necessarily be limited to the professional literature which has a direct bearing on the way that social agencies in the twentieth century have understood and dealt with child sexual abuse.

The therapeutic literature is divided into three major categories; psychiatry, family therapy and psychology. Each of these areas will be dealt with separately, although it should be noted that the boundaries between them are somewhat arbitrary. The historical context and major themes of each paradigm will be critically examined from a feminist viewpoint. A fourth section will review the small amount of feminist literature on the subject and a fifth will explain the implications of the feminist 'Power Theory' for working against incest.

The psychiatric literature

Of all the incest literature, the psychiatric studies owe the most explicit debt to psychoanalytic theory; specifically, to Freud's writings on infantile and childhood sexuality and the Oedipus complex. With a few exceptions though the psychiatric literature has made very selective use of Freud's writings on these matters, to focus attention on the 'seductive child' and the 'pathological mother', or to dismiss reports of incest as infantile fantasy.

Freud in his early therapeutic work found that a startling number of his women patients attributed their neurosis or hysteria to childhood sexual abuse at the hands of an adult. Initially he took them at their word, and in his paper entitled 'The Aetiology of Hysteria' (1896) he proposed a direct causal relationship between actual sexual traumas experienced in childhood and later psychic damage sustained by an adult. In 1905, Freud retracted his theory on the basis that childhood seduction could not be such a common occurrence and was rather a recurrent feminine fantasy. While Freud's original proposition had been received with great hostility by his colleagues, his theory of infantile fantasy of seduction was more acceptable and dominated the psychiatric literature on the subject of incest from the turn of the century until the late 1960s.

This infantile fantasy of being seduced by the father was considered by Freud to be the 'expression of the typical Oedipus complex in women'.[2] The Oedipus complex is his account of female socialisation: of the way that girls become 'feminine', i.e. passive and heterosexual. The female child, according to this theory, initially takes the mother as her love object, a result of the mother's early care and attention. However, when the child catches sight of the male genitals, she realises that neither her mother nor herself possesses the 'superior' penis. According to Freud, this realisation is both instantaneous and wholehearted: '[Little girls, when they] notice the penis of a brother or playmate, strikingly visible and of large proportions, at once recognise it as the superior counterpart of their own small and inconspicuous organ, and from that time forward fall victim to envy for the penis.'[3] Consequently, the girl turns from her mother to her father in the hope of being given a penis; her father becomes her new love object. On this model the women who told Freud about their seduction at the hands of their fathers were reporting a fantasy, the projection of an unusually strong case of 'penis-envy' and love for their fathers. The daughter is cast as the active, desiring agent and the father as passive, innocent object.

Thus in the early psychiatric literature it is commonly asserted that first, actual incest is an extremely rare phenomenon although allegations of incest may be common, and secondly, that where it does occur it is usually at the instigation of the child acting out her desire for the father. For example, the Bender and Blau study of sixteen children, who had verified sexual contact with adults, begins with the assertion that such contact is extremely rare, and goes on to look at the special nature of these children in order to find an explanation for the sexual relations. They concluded:

> Some special factors may predict the retention of overt sex interests into the latency period . . . some children may by constitution be very intolerant of any denial of satisfaction or may possess unusually strong desires; in our material most of the children showed an abnormal interest and desire for adult attention and they were endowed with unusually attractive and charming personalities.[4]

In a study of five cases of incest, Sloane and Karpinski draw a similar conclusion about the 'participants':

> . . . the defective formation of the super-ego undoubtedly played a role. In addition the girl's desires in each case received reinforcement from the fact that the man assumed responsibility by being the aggressor. Another factor was the weakness of the [girl's] ego in association with a possible abnormal craving for sexual excitation which led to submission to the incest in the first place.[5]

Alongside the abnormally seductive child, the psychiatric literature has placed the pathological mother as an explanation for the existence of father-daughter incest. Mother-blame is a consistent feature of all the non-feminist literature on incest; the psychiatric version of this theme describes mothers with an unresolved Oedipus complex, who use their daughters as surrogates to act out their own incestuous wish for their fathers. One author explains a case of incest in the following terms:

> Thus . . . we have a mother who rejected a feminine role for herself as the result of hurt and disappointment at the hands of her father. She acts out her Oedipal wish for father through her

daughter . . . the daughter has learned to turn to men for security and affection because of intense affectional frustration at the hands of her mother. She is placed in a role of surrogate wife in which she can turn to her father to gain satisfaction of her needs. This takes place through a sexual channel.[6]

A variation of this theme revolves around the mother's relationship to her own mother. Kaufman *et al.* develop a complex multigenerational model where incest is virtually passed on from mother to daughter:

These mothers displaced onto the chosen daughter all the hostility really felt for the maternal grandmother. They forced their daughter to become their confidant, helper with other children and adviser. They relinquished their responsibilities as parents so that they, in effect, became daughters again, and the daughter a mother . . . the mothers . . . finally created situations where they deserted the fathers, who then became involved in the incestuous relationship with the daughters.[7]

The incestuous act itself is, in the opinion of these writers, always precipitated by the mothers' 'abandonment' of husband and daughter, described by Kaufman as 'either by giving birth to a new sibling, turning to the maternal grandmother or developing some new interest outside the home'.[8]

These formulations are clearly an attempt to rationalise the adult male's power to elicit and determine the incestuous dynamic. The notion of the 'collusive' mother who manipulates her husband and daughter into incest in order to fulfil her own unconscious desires is merely a mechanism for transferring agency away from the father; the father is rendered inculpable by being made into the passive object of his wife's and daughter's desires. By ignoring the father's desire and, more importantly, his social power to act upon it, the psychiatric literature effectively shifts blame from the perpetrator to the survivors.

While the misogyny of the psychiatric model has provoked many feminists to abandon its theories altogether, others have attempted to reinterpret the notion of the Oedipus complex in the light of the father's active and powerful participation in the process. Chodorow emphasises the father's active sexual desire in the Oedipalisation of female children:

> [Fathers] are usually heterosexual and sexualise their relationships to children of either gender accordingly. A girl's [undifferentiated] relation to her mother motivates her to look elsewhere for other kinds of relationships . . . she is likely to be encouraged to look elsewhere to fulfil these generalised needs by her father, who also lends them a sexualised tone . . . it seems, from [social research] that fathers generally sex-type their children more consciously than mothers along traditional gender-role lines and that they encourage feminine heterosexual behaviour in their young daughters.[9]

Judith Herman, on the other hand, has stressed the way that the feminine Oedipus complex places the daughter in a passive relationship to her father, leaving her vulnerable to incestuous abuse:

> The girl's interest in her father does not develop out of an earlier bond with the father as caretaker. Rather it is a reaction to the girl's discovery that males are everywhere preferred to females . . . She turns to her father in the hope that he will make her an honorary boy . . . By establishing a special and privileged relationship with her father, she seeks to be elevated into the superior company of men . . . the father's behaviour towards his daughter thus assumes immense importance. If the father chooses to eroticise the relationship with his daughter, he will encounter little or no resistance.[10]

This reinterpretation of Oedipal and incestuous dynamics has been largely ignored by the orthodox psychiatric community. However, psychiatry has now begun to revise some of its notions concerning incest, most particularly the assertion that it is a rare phenomenon. The overall effect of these developments on the literature has been a new focus on the medical presentation of incest to promote its recognition by psychiatrists and staff. This acknowledgement of high incidence has not been accompanied by a revision of the broad psychiatric assumptions about the aetiology of incest. The mother and child are still the objects of scrutiny in theoretical studies; it is evident that the literature has perpetuated Freud's unwillingness to examine the drives of incestuous fathers and has found an expedient solution in its preoccupation with the mother and child.

Family dysfunction literature

The notion of the 'dysfunctional family' is a widely accepted explanation for the existence of incest. Variations on the theme of family dysfunction can be found in a wide range of medical, sociological, social work and therapeutic literature both in relation to the causes of incest and to treatment methods.

The theory of family dysfunction developed during the late 1940s as an offshoot of family psychiatry. Family psychiatry is distinguished from classical psychiatry by the fact that it treats the family as a single entity, rather than concentrating on the individual psyches of family members. Instead of a concern for individual pathology it proposes that the family as a unit can be pathological and that abnormal behaviour is a symptom of overall current family maladjustment. So within this framework the occurrence of incest in a family is not regarded as a problem in itself; it is only a problem in so far as it signifies a 'deeper' underlying pathology.

The typical 'dysfunctional family' is one wherein the 'normal' family hierarchies based on age and sex have broken down. This breakdown is attributed almost solely to the mother, who is seen as failing to fulfil her nurturing and protective role. The failure takes a threefold form; first, the mother is dysfunctional as a wife, in that she fails to meet her husband's sexual demands and/or pursues interests outside the home. Secondly, the mother is dysfunctional as a mother; the mother who does not want sex with her husband and pursues interests outside the home is also the mother who fails to give adequate nurturing to her children. Thirdly, the mother is dysfunctional as an adult and as a parent. Both mother and father are accused of seeking to turn their child into their parent and themselves becoming like children. All the family dysfunction literature notes that the daughters seem to have inordinate responsibility for housework, childcare, etc, along with their 'wifely duties' towards their fathers.

The family dysfunction literature regards these pathological family relationships (cold distant mother, infantile father, love-starved daughter) as the therapeutic issue, while the actual occurrence of incest is a secondary manifestation, a symptom. Incest is treated in some of this literature as a functional system serving to hold together a family whose internal relationships are so abnormal as to be otherwise completely unstable.

The titles of several articles demonstrate this notion, e.g. 'Incest as a Family Affair',[11] 'Multiple Overt Incest as a Family Defence Against Loss',[12] 'Incest: A Family Group Survival Pattern'.[13] Each of these articles draws on particular case studies of families which, in the view of the therapist, utilise the incest secret as a rationale for maintaining the family's pathology from the eyes of the world. Lustig states: 'The parents' childhood fears, wishes and fantasies are acted out within the dysfunctional family. Many of these impulses which are unacceptable could not be acted out outside the family without jeopardising its stability and even its existence. Thus we propose that incest is a transaction which serves to protect and maintain the family in which it occurs.'[14]

The main treatment implication which flows from this framework is as follows: If incest is only a symptom of dysfunction rather than the real 'problem', then its occurrence is only of secondary importance. 'The appropriate focus for therapy should be the family dynamics rather than the current or historical fact of sexual activity. The sexual activity may be incidental to inverted and confused relations.'[15]

Within this framework a concentration on the incest is considered to act as a red herring and impede treatment. The first step in this treatment is to persuade all family members to admit to equal responsibility in the participation in 'age and sex inappropriate roles'. A concentration on the act of incest is thought to lead to an 'unfair' emphasis upon the father's responsibility. This is one reason why any criminal proceedings against the father in such cases are felt to be anathema: Machotka condemns the prosecution of incestuous fathers as a 'somewhat inappropriate assignment of legal guilt which allows other family members to maintain a destructive denial of their own responsibility'.[16] Correct treatment is believed to involve all family members acknowledging their responsibility and with the help of the therapist realigning their behaviour into more appropriate 'gender and generational roles', and thus becoming the functional family. The mother is here instructed to become a 'perfect' mother, the provider of sexual satisfaction to her husband, watchful protector of her children and full-time housewife. On the other hand, the father is encouraged to reinstate the authority he has supposedly lost in his 'inappropriate transaction' with his daughter. One therapist warns that, during treatment, 'all family members may act to perpetrate an aura of fear and a myth that the father is dangerous . . . ways must be developed to bolster the father's status through these difficult times'.[17]

Although family dysfunction theory maintains that it is concerned to realign all family roles, it effectively concentrates on the positions of mother and daughter, leaving that of the father intact. The father's right to demand sexual servicing and nurture from females is never questioned; the problem arises when he demands it from the 'wrong' female. Given the normative concerns of this form of therapy, the 'cured' or 'functional' family is one where the man retains the same authority, the woman is concerned only with her maternal, domestic and sexual duties, and the child's welfare is still accepted as being the sole responsibility of the mother.

The psychological literature

The psychological literature differs from the psychoanalytic and family dysfunctional perspectives in that it tends to take the father, rather than the mother and daughter, as its object of study. There is a simple reason for this difference; psychologists encounter incest mostly when performing compulsory evaluations on convicted offenders, either at the point of prosecution or during imprisonment. The purpose of such evaluations is to supply court, prison or psychiatric institutions with a 'profile' of the offender for the purposes of classification and treatment. Hence the psychological literature adopts one of two approaches; either it is concerned to demonstrate the existence of a specific 'incestuous personality', i.e. a series of fixed personality traits in the offender that explain his actions and that differentiate him from other types of sex offender; or it attempts to find subclassifications within the group of incestuous fathers that indicate a variety of motives.

The first approach proceeds via comparative studies of incest offenders with other types of sex offenders, e.g. paedophiles, exhibitionists or rapists, and occasional comparisons between incestuous and 'normal' fathers. Among the studies that have made use of personality tests and personal histories, a fairly strong agreement emerges on several characteristics. Groth,[18] Meiselman[19] and Gebhard *et al.*[20] corroborate a background of chaotic family life and emotional deprivation, possibly including sexual abuse. Meiselman and several other studies describe the outstanding characteristic of incestuous fathers as their tendency to exercise an unusual degree of dominance over their families. Meiselman outlines 'a range of domination patterns. At the one extreme is the father who is sociopathic and is . . . treating his family . . . as objects to fulfil his desires. At the other extreme is the father who seems to be overinvested in his family and seeks to control all aspects of their lives.'[21] Another commonly reported personality trait is that of paranoic rationalisation and the attribution of blame to others rather than self.[22]

As previously noted, the psychological literature also differentiates between types of incestuous father.[23] Groth distinguishes two major types of offender, the fixated and the regressive. He argues that the fixated offender, due to abnormal psychological development, has from adolescence been sexually attracted primarily or exclusively to significantly younger persons. The regressive offender generally has adult heterosexual orientation but has adopted incestuous relations as a response to some acute form of stress.[24] It is in the notion of regression under stress that the significance of the 'incestuous personality' is fully realised; socially introverted, overinvested in his family, suffering from feelings of 'phallic inadequacy', he is driven to resolve his personality problems in an incestuous act when some form of stress, be it economic, emotional or physical, accentuates his particular inadequacies or so disorients him that his normal impulse control is impaired.[25]

While psychology's concentration on the father rather than the mother and daughter is a welcome reorientation, its analysis of the offender remains one-dimensional; social relations are ignored, and the answer to the origin of incestuous abuse is sought at the level of individual personality. This search eventually becomes tautological; the incest offender commits incest because he has an 'incestuous personality', i.e. a failure of 'impulse control' at the crucial moment. This characterisation assumes that normal, natural male sexuality is directed at little girls, specifically daughters, but that sexual abuse is forestalled by acts of individual self-control. Because psychology regards sexuality as merely a personality trait, it takes for granted the power relationship that enables the adult male to enact such an impulse. The offender is studied as though he exists in a social vacuum; as an isolated individual rather than a being in relation to others, specifically a father in relation to his family. So, on the one hand, psychological tests depict the 'incestuous personality' as rather passive, inadequate, introverted, etc. whilst, on the other, these men were found to be very domineering towards their families. As Judith Herman observes:

. . . the solution to this apparent contradiction lies in the fathers' ability to assess their relative power in any situation and to vary their behaviour accordingly. In the presence of men much more powerful than themselves, such as police prosecutors, therapists and [psychologists], the fathers . . . [appear] as pathetic, helpless and confused. Only in the privacy of their homes, where they know they will encounter no effective opposition, do they indulge their appetites for domination. Face to face with men of equal or superior authority they become engaging and submissive.[26]

The feminist literature

The feminist objection to the three perspectives discussed above relates to the systematic misrecognition and displacement of the power relationships involved in incestuous abuse; as evidenced by the psychiatric and family dysfunction literature in apportioning responsibility and agency to mother and daughter, and by the psychological literature in divorcing the father's actions from any social context. The first two virtually represent the experience of incest from the father's position, while the third cannot provide an adequate strategy to address the ubiquities of incestuous abuse; however, all three perspectives maintain the status quo of patriarchy.

Patriarchy is the world view that seeks to create and maintain male control over females – it is a system of male supremacy. In contemporary society men as a class dominate women as a class. This dominance is maintained by men's organisation of and control over the structural systems that constitute the society we exist in, for example, the health, legal, welfare, educational, economic, judicial, religious and familial systems. In addition, the way these systems function is primarily determined by patriarchal beliefs and values. Male hegemony is based on the assumption that men's perception of reality is the only one. Woman is viewed as adjunct, secondary, an object for male manipulation. The mechanics of male supremacy are buffeted by the cross-currents of social class, racial oppression and cultural difference, which also inform our power relationships.

Feminist analysis of incest has been concerned to present the experience from the position of the mother and daughter, to understand the family dynamics of incest as the playing out of a power relationship and to look at the connection between this power relationship and the broader operation of patriarchy.

The starting point for feminist writing on incest has necessarily been the experience of the incest survivor herself. This experience has been presented and utilised in a variety of ways; (i) first person accounts;[27] (ii) theoretical propositions;[28] and (iii) survey-style questionnaires.[29]

Elizabeth Ward draws strong connections between the common female experience and fear of rape and that of incest. She rejects other terms including that of 'incest' because it

. . . focus[es] attention upon who is involved, rather than upon what is happening. What is happening is that a child is being victimised and that she and the offender usually belong to and live in the same family. The particulars of the rape dynamic mean that the offender has almost unlimited access to the [survivor] . . . as well as access of a parent/adult/male over a girl-child . . . I use the term 'rape' because I believe that the sexual use of a child's body/being is the same as the phenomenon of adult rape . . . To be raped, as a woman or girl-child, is to experience . . . an act of aggression in which the [survivor] is denied her self-determination.[30]

Judith Herman places emphasis on the relationship between the 'normal' and the 'incestuous' family, attributing the high incidence of incest to the power that all fathers exercise in the family, but particularly where the father is domineering.

If . . . the taboo on father-daughter incest is relatively weak in a patriarchal family system, we might expect violations of the taboo to occur most frequently in families characterised by extreme paternal dominance. This is in fact the case. Incest offenders are frequently described as family tyrants. These fathers . . . tend towards abuses of authority of every conceivable kind, and they not infrequently endeavour to secure their dominant position by socially isolating the members of the family from the world outside.[31]

By comparing women who had experienced overt incest with women whose fathers had been covertly 'seductive', Herman concludes, 'The similarities between [the two groups] once again confirm the contention that incest represents a common pattern of traditional female socialisation carried to a pathological extreme'.[32]

Ward and Herman also emphasise the powerlessness of the mother within this particular family configuration (the powerlessness which may eventually lead her to deny her daughter's disclosure or to blame her daughter for the incest):

Mothers have many reasons for not being able to 'see' or 'hear' incest . . . All the cultural baggage about marriage, motherhood and Happy Families contains absolutely no information about the possible need to protect children from men within the family . . . For many women there is also a very real economic imperative.

At the moment of disclosure she must choose whom to believe. Most women are dependent on their husbands' incomes . . . Another reason why so many mothers repress stories of sexual harassment from their daughters: such stories touch all women in terms of their own suppressed childhood memories and in terms of our lifelong existence as potential [targets for] rape.[33]

Despite all these factors militating against them, many mothers do act to protect their daughters in any way they can. However, the existence of 'collusive' mothers is undeniable; Herman accounts for this by describing the extreme oppression of many mothers in the family where incest is ongoing:

More than the average wife and mother she is extremely dependent upon and subservient to her husband. She may have a physical or emotional disability which makes the prospect of independent survival quite impractical. Rather than provoke her husband's anger or risk his desertion, she will capitulate. If the price of maintaining the marriage includes the sexual sacrifice of her daughter, she will raise no effective objections . . . Maternal collusion in incest, when it occurs, is a measure of maternal powerlessness.[34]

The 'collusive' mother maintains the incest secret and fails to act for the same reasons that the daughter does; both mother and daughter are powerless *vis-à-vis* the father. Women who collude with the value systems of patriarchal society do so as a personal survival strategy. Such women attach themselves to the trappings of male privilege, protection and security however conditional, unstable and vicarious it may be. This collusion is not from a position of real power or real choice but an effect of Rape Ideology. Elizabeth Ward describes Rape Ideology as

that set of beliefs and practices which causes females to actually live in fear of males or maleness. It assumes that male sexuality is innately active, aggressive, and insatiable; that female sexuality is innately passive, receptive and inhibited . . . War and sexuality are seen as the same battleground.

Rape, actual and threatened, is an effective tool of control that subjugates females – of all ages – and nowhere is this terrorism more insidious than in its application to children; particularly in their own homes.[35]

The individual masculine desire for sexual domination over females is compounded by the propertarian nature of heterosexual relationships. Ward say of incestuous fathers that

. . . they are not aberrant males. They are acting within the mainstream of masculine sexual behaviour which sees women as sexual commodities and believes men have a right to use and abuse these commodities how and whenever they can. The fact that many fathers do not behave in these ways towards their daughters . . . does not alter the fact that they could.[36]

The power theory

Through its analysis of incest as a sexual power relationship, the feminist literature has provided the tools to re-examine the family dynamics described in the family dysfunction and psychiatric literature, in a way that is much more realistic about the mother's and daughter's positions. By linking the phenomenon of incest with the nature of the family and male-female relationships in patriarchal society, it can suggest intervention strategies that are social as well as individual: for example, the very act of reconceptualising the notion of power is part of the empowerment process; an initial step towards recovery and survival.

The Power Theory is a theoretical framework used by feminist workers at Dympna House, a community-based incest centre in Sydney. This theory has its roots in the feminist analysis of incest and has been evolving over recent years with input from researchers, trainers and workers in the field. It differs from many other theories and perspectives as it provides a conceptual framework which serves as a basis for not only casework, but also for socio-political change and prevention as well. The incest models presented to date all have certain limitations. They are limited in their analysis of the problem, for example in emphasising offender pathology, blaming mother or child, or not looking past the family to its socio-political context. They are also therefore limited in their application, as they tend to lend themselves to specific treatment modalities and miss entirely the potential for socio-political change as the basis for prevention programmes.

The Power Theory, as developed to date, provides a broad-based framework that encompasses socio-political factors, familial factors and individual characteristics, and thus provides a springboard for a comprehensive approach to both stopping incest and child sexual abuse in the long term and treating it in the short term. The theory utilises two concepts of power, (1) structural power – power over others; and (2) personal power – power within self. It is vital to the analysis to consider whether this power is being used creatively, or whether it is being misused.

Structural power

This is the power granted to individuals or classes of individuals by society. It is power accorded to one class of person over another, on the basis of certain factors such as gender, age, race, religion, intelligence, education, family status, political affiliation, income, etc. Some examples of this in our society are: the power of the rich over the poor; the politicians over the unemployed; white over Black; men over women; English-speaking over non-English-speaking; adults over children; able-bodied over disabled.

Structural power, or institutionalised power, gives the powerful the opportunity to exercise control over the lives of the powerless, and/or to take up opportunities not available (or less available) to the powerless. It is legitimised by society as a whole. Although certain individuals or groups (e.g. feminists, Aboriginal land rights groups, anti-nuclear groups, children's rights lobbyists) may strongly disagree with where this society legitimises its power, their attempts at change are thwarted by the very institutions which have power over them.

This form of power is hierarchical, static, public, socially legitimised (it has 'authority'); it is a form of control: the 'power over' model, with all its connotations of competition, dominance, and force. This construct is a cornerstone of patriarchal hegemony and, without it, aggression against and exploitation of people who have little or no institutionalised power (e.g. children, females, Black people, working-class people, the disabled, etc.) could not be maintained.

How is structural power misused? Where there is structural power, there is the power of one group over another. Where there is power over others, there exists the *potential* to misuse or abuse that power. When the misuse of power is also legitimised by society, there exists a very real *option* for individuals to act on that potential and thereby abuse the power granted to them.

How does the misuse of structural power relate to child sexual abuse? Child abuse represents a misuse of the power that society 'legitimately' accords to males and to adults. As this structural power of males and adults exists, there also exists the *potential* for every man to misuse his power over women (e.g. rape) and for every adult to misuse his/her power over children (e.g. sexual assault). As well as this potential, there exists the *option* for abuse, as society actually legitimises the misuse of power. The legitimising of the abuse of power is 'ild sexual abuse. It occurs on several fronts. For example, the child who discloses to adults, who she hopes will protect her from abuse, is often not believed. Society reinforces this situation by perpetuating some of the myths about child sexual abuse. Secondly, the legal system allows for relative ease of removal of the child survivor from the family, yet poses difficulty in removing the offender, thus reinforcing the blame on the child and granting the right to continue offending on the male/adult. Thirdly, society provides limited punishments for sex offenders: imprisonment for those very few offenders who are found guilty by the criminal justice system; and the public shaming for those even fewer offenders who become newsworthy for a day. On the whole, most offenders are not punished by society.

By failing to provide effective deterrents, society says 'yes' to misuse of male and adult power.

The potential for misuse of structural power by offenders in families becomes more of a reality when considered in the light of misuse of personal power. Not all males in families do abuse children – the second dimension, misuse of personal power, is quite likely to be the factor which tips the balance.

Personal power

This is the power within the self. It is the inner strength that arises from a strong motivation to survive. Well-channelled personal power enables us to exercise control over our own lives, achieve our own goals and fulfil our own needs while respecting the value and goals and needs of other people. In some individuals, personal power is positive, strong and healthy; in others it is underdeveloped, distorted or neglected. As such, it may be harmful to themselves and to others.

Some individuals who have strong personal power operate from a base rooted in fears and anger, rather than self-worth and the worth of others. Operating from this damaged but powerful stance, they are in a position to hurt themselves and others. The distorted development of personal power may place one at risk of being a persecutor, especially in the social environment which bestows structural power on that individual, e.g. the male adults in a family. Other individuals have been socialised to victimisation of one kind or another. A case in point is an incest survivor who internalises her powerlessness and enforced passivity to an extent that prevents her from developing other parts of herself. The personal power she has goes mainly to survival, with little or no power to protect herself from further victimisation.

Personal power exists in everyone. The challenge then is to ensure its development so that no individuals are at risk of victimisation or persecution; that all individuals develop the capacity for self-love, self-worth and a recognition of the intrinsic worth of others, and thus to empower themselves to act creatively and assertively in controlling their own lives.

The concept of structural power, as applied to child sexual abuse, highlights the need for both structural change to the current distribution of power and massive change to socialisation of our children. In terms of casework, both intervention and treatment would need to address the individual offender's choice to take up his option to misuse the power inherently given to him/her. It would also need to focus on empowering women and children in a familial and structural sense – economic, legal, housing, education, career, etc. In terms of prevention, radical changes need to happen to the structure of our society.

The concept of personal power, as applied to child sexual abuse, highlights the need for the full development of the individual, particularly in terms of self-love, self-worth and the worth of others. In terms of casework, the challenge is to shift our focus from dysfunctional families and pathological individuals to one of empowerment of families and individuals to develop and nurture their own, each other's, and their children's personal power. Such an emphasis on positive empowerment is not just a trite statement; it fully recognises the need for individuals and families to work on old or painful feelings and behaviour. However, in such work, interventionists and therapists, coming from a position of their own personal power, would enhance the development of that in others. In terms of prevention, this concept of personal power is an enormous challenge to our society. A society that, as a whole, nurtures a child's development of self-love and respect for others is considerably removed from our current world as regards child-rearing, education, sexual development, sexist roles, legal position and recognition of children's rights.

The great advantage of the Power Theory is that it can encompass the other perspectives, rather than excluding them. Some examples of this would be that an individual who offends can still be considered 'deviant', both as a function of his misuse of personal power and in the context of the power society has bestowed upon him. A non-offending mother who does not protect her child can be seen as 'dysfunctional' in respect of her lack of personal power and structural power, especially in the context of her dependence on the male for her economic and social survival. The child survivor can be seen as lacking the power to say 'no' or lacking the persistence to keep disclosing until some adults believe her. The family can be seen as 'dysfunctional' in that the power distribution is so unequal that one person persecutes, one is victimised, and a third remains a helpless bystander.

However, if the family as a whole, or its individual members, is seen as dysfunctional, or deviant, or sick, without recourse to the Power Theory, this perspective of incest itself only serves to perpetuate the power imbalance of our society.

Notes and references

1. This article was first published in *Breaking the Silence: A Report Based upon the Findings of the Women Against Incest Phone-in Survey* (Haberfield, New South Wales, 1985). The Power Theory was first printed in New South Wales Department of Youth and Community Services Child Sexual Abuse Trainers' Package, Sydney, May 1986.
2. Sigmund Freud, *Introductory Lectures on Psychoanalysis*, 1933.
3. Sigmund Freud. 'Some Psychical Consequences of the Anatomical Distinction Between the Sexes', in S. Freud, *On Sexuality*, The Pelican Freud Library vol. 7 (Harmondsworth: Penguin, 1977), p. 335.
4. L. Bender and A. Blau, 'The Reaction of Children to Sexual Relations with Adults', *American Journal of Orthopsychiatry*, vol. 7, 1937, pp. 514–5.
5. P. Sloane and E. Karpinski, 'Effects of Incest on the Participants', *American Journal of Orthopsychiatry*, vol. 12, 1942, pp. 672–3.
6. J Rinehart, 'Genesis of Overt Incest', *Comprehensive Psychiatry*, vol. 2, December 1962, pp. 347–8.
7. A. Kaufman, Peck and L. Tagiuri, 'The Family Constellation and Overt Incestuous Relations Between Father and Daughter', *American Journal of Orthopsychiatry*, vol. 24, 1954, pp. 270–1.
8. Ibid., p. 276.
9. Nancy Chodorow, *The Reproduction of Mothering: Psychoanalysis and the Sociology of Gender* (Berkeley: University of California, 1978).
10. Judith Herman, *Father–Daughter Incest* (Cambridge, Mass.: Harvard University Press, 1981).

11. P. Machotka, F. Pittman and K. Flomenhaft, in *Family Process*, vol. 6, 1967, pp. 98–116.
12. T. Gutheil and N. Avery, in *Family Process*, 1977, pp. 105–16.
13. N. Lustig *et al.*, in *Archives of General Psychiatry*, vol. 14, 1966, pp. 31–40.
14. Ibid., p. 39.
15. Machotka *et al.*, p. 113.
16. Ibid., p. 114.
17. L. Webb-Woodard, 'The Larger System in the Treatment of Incest', training paper, *Counselling and Student Services*, North Texas University.
18. N. Groth and J. Birnbaum, 'Adult Sexual Orientation and Attraction to Underaged Persons', *Archives of Sexual Behaviour*, vol. 7, 1978, pp. 175–81.
19. Karin Meiselman, *Incest: A Psychological Study of Causes and Effects with Treatment Recommendations* (London: Jossey-Bass, 1981), p. 50.
20. P. Gebhard, J. Gagnon, W. Pomeroy and C. Christenson, *Sex Offenders: An Analysis of Types* (New York: Harper & Row, 1965).
21. Meiselman, *Incest*, p. 92.
22. Weiner, 'Father–Daughter Incest: A Clinical Report', *Psychiatric Quarterly*, vol. 36, 1962, pp. 623–4.
23. Gebhard *et al.*, *Sex Offenders*, p. 225.
24. Groth and Birnbaum, *Adult Sexual Orientation*, pp. 176–7.
25. Meiselman, *Incest*, p. 106.
26. Herman, *Father–Daughter Incest*, pp. 75–6.
27. Louise Armstrong, *Kiss Daddy Goodnight: A Speakout on Incest*, (London: Pocket Books, 1979).
28. Herman, *Father–Daughter Incest*; Elizabeth Ward, *Father–Daughter Rape* (London: Women's Press, 1984).
29. As is the case with the original report forming the basis for this chapter.
30. Ward, *Father–Daughter Rape*, pp. 78–82.
31. J. Herman and L. Hirschman, 'Father–Daughter Incest', *Signs: Journal of Women in Culture and Society*, vol. 2, summer 1977, p. 741.
32. Herman, *Father–Daughter Incest*, p. 125.
33. Ward, *Father–Daughter Rape*, p. 116.
34. Herman, *Father–Daughter Incest*, p. 49.
35. Ward, *Father–Daughter Rape*.
36. Ward, *Father–Daughter Rape*, pp. 194–5.

3

Through the looking glass: children and the professionals who treat them

EMILY DRIVER

This chapter focuses on the need for childcare professionals to reconsider their attitudes to child sexual abuse and to learn to handle their own personal problems with the subject. It is based in part on experience gained working with abused children in a locally funded project which was founded and run by incest survivors themselves.[1] The project arose from concern amongst community groups that the general response of psychiatrists, social workers, health care workers, etc. was not adequate to abused children's needs, largely because of the ignorance and fear with which professionals were approaching children and their families. Even during the 1980s it was frequently denied in professional circles both that workers themselves had been abused as children and that a proportion of professionals were exploiting their access to children to perpetrate such abuse.[2] Consequently, clients or patients often found their own needs unanswered or their troubles intensified by professional prejudices and projections.

One solution to the power imbalance and sense of alienation thus fostered by professionals was to attempt to bridge the gap between the professional and lay communities by founding a preventive and therapeutic childcare project in which the workers were all incest survivors. Some of these had professional qualifications (as psychologists, social workers, nurses, etc.) and others had gained work experience from the women's movement. All had the advantage of first-hand knowledge of sexual abuse, so that work between them could progress unhindered by ignorance or by the poor professional training then available in London. Whilst many incest survivors might find it unusually painful to work in such an atmosphere, where all one's colleagues are aware of the connection between one's personal and one's professional life, others found the experience creative and rewarding.

The main group who benefited from this project's work was, of course, the children for whom it had been developed, since the knowledge that adults shared their experience of abuse allowed them to feel safe in disclosing it. They would be understood without having to be subjected to the more invasive professional techniques, such as the insensitive overuse of anatomically correct dolls (as discussed below). Children are hindered from reporting sexual abuse where they fear that adults will have a hostile, fearful, prurient or patronising attitude to their experiences. With the best will in the world, this can frequently develop whenever the adult questioning a child has not herself or himself experienced, or is not prepared to admit to having experienced, such abuse at first hand. Children were also able to take advantage of strong role models from their own particular culture or community, where these were represented by workers from the project or consultants to it. The involvement of adults who had successfully survived sexual abuse encouraged children to recognise and develop their own strengths free from the negative 'victim' stereotypes so often imposed by traditional treatment models.

The project provided consultation and training for other professionals, and it was through this work that I first understood the difficulties faced by workers battling against the massive institutional power of their agencies, a reactionary power which in some ways reflects that of an abuser within his family, forcing some into silence and others into collusion. The main problems for professionals were inadequate training and large case-loads which, far from encouraging them to bring their own insights and understandings to their work, actually militated against self-expression and therefore against useful communication with both clients and colleagues. The priority for anyone working with abused children should be to listen inwardly to her or his own experiences of child sexual abuse, before slavishly accepting what are, after all, comparatively untried and abuser-centred ideologies and methods. Until one has heard the child within oneself on this subject, one cannot possibly work from a child-centred position.

What, then, are some of the feelings that professionals may

recognise from their own childhood? I will deal in turn with several emotional consequences of sexual abuse, which influence child and professional alike: the initial confusion, the distancing response, the quest for safety, and the identification with the aggressor which sometimes resolves this quest. When some of the implications of these consequences have been examined, there will follow some suggested solutions, again applicable to both child and professional worker.

The initial confusion

Children have many responses to sexual assault, but these usually fluctuate over time and in differing circumstances. A constant and lasting response is that of bewilderment. It starts in the child's physical sensations and perceptions, continues through her[3] emotional assessment of her predicament, and surfaces as an intellectual, political and philosophical question in later life. However much we try to understand and explain the assaults that we have been subjected to, we are left with that monumental *Why?* to which there is no answer.

Confusion causes insecurity. Perhaps the deepest damage that sexual abuse can do to a child is to shake her trust in her own instincts, so that s/he becomes a stranger and an outcast to her own body. Children's emotions, insights and understandings are denied so often by others that the child-molester has a ready-made foundation on which to build. At a very early age, an assaulted child will usually instinctively know, if not from her own sense of being abused, then from the signals of selfishness and secrecy exuding from the molester, that how he is behaving is a wrong to her; and yet the trust and authority with which the rest of society has invested this person tell her that it is for him a right.

There seems to be no exit from this double-bind. A child's logic may solve the position something like this: 'What is happening is wrong, yet who is doing it to me is right. Therefore I must be wrong. It is 'dirty', therefore I must be dirty. Good children are rewarded and bad children are punished. I am being punished. Therefore I must be a bad child. What did I do wrong? I must have done something wrong without even knowing. Therefore I am not a good judge of whether I am right or wrong.'

Childish logic, of course. Yet these woolly reasonings have a sinister parallel in that psychiatric literature which sets out to project the causes of child sexual assault upon any aspect of the *child's* behaviour or mental make-up. More importantly, this topsy-turvy, looking-glass logic is deliberately engineered by the offender, who seeks to transfer all sense of responsibility onto the child in order to secure her silence and ensure his continued exploitation of her confusion. It is depressing to see professionals being sucked into this game, especially when they are, rightly, so critical of the presumed collusion of abused children's mothers.

Sexual abuse causes children moral confusion; it leads them to confuse their own needs with the desires of the abuser; and it deprives them of the safety in which to explore their own identity so that they can develop as a balanced, integrated whole. I am suggesting that some forms of professional treatment of children are founded in a similar sense of confusion, and that this confusion allows us to fluctuate in our responsibility for the welfare of the child, sometimes subordinating it to the desires of the abuser and sometimes abandoning it entirely.

Confusion may be detected in both the attitudes of individual workers and in the practices of their agencies. So many times one hears from people in the caring professions that they would kill any man who laid a finger on their own child, whilst the other side of their mouth is already formulating excuses on behalf of their offending clients, such as 'family dysfunction', 'intergenerational boundary breakdown', 'complex interacting pattern', and other such diversionary jargon.

For example, when professionals advocate that abuser and abused be treated therapeutically together (under the family dysfunction model, see Chapter 2) or remain living under the same roof, one only has to ask them if they would have a tea party for 'cured' sex offenders whom their agency has treated and leave their own children unattended with these men, and one immediately exposes the deep double-think that underpins the approach to the family as a unit in sexual abuse cases. No professional conducting this type of therapy seriously considers undergoing it herself or himself. It is an inherently patronising form of treatment of the client group as a whole, and insults the child and innocent family members by positing that incest offenders and incest survivors 'belong together' as an indiscriminate class whose interests are similar, so that the child feels tarred with the abnormality of the offender. Family therapy sacrifices the child's need for a sense of safety and self-worth to an ideological fantasy of the perfect nuclear family which in fact does not exist. It fails to recognise the fact that just as a child cannot say No to the abuse from the offender, nor can s/he say No to the treatment with the offender. S/he is not in a position to make any meaningful consent to contact with him and therefore her sense of powerlessness is reinforced. The child is made to relive her incest in a way that does not heal but simply silences, whereas the offender again monopolises attention and finds great excitement in the experience of self-abasement. His power within the family is confirmed rather than challenged by the professional voyeurs who conduct such sessions. Family therapists might claim that the girls involved in the sessions are given permission to show anger and to receive an apology. They have not grasped the fact that an apology from a sex offender is at best a hollow victory, at worst an insult. Any emotion displayed by the girl in such a situation will be a pretence put on for the purposes of stress survival, whilst her inner spirit has long since vacated the room. Many young girls approach voluntary projects and speak of the humiliation, the coercion, and the enforced appeasement of the offender inherent is such therapy models.

The distancing response

Returning to the child's position, how does s/he attempt to resolve the confusion that s/he feels? In many children we may observe variations of the distancing response, whose external forms will be dealt with in chapter 6. In some ways we have to help the child to distance herself from her body, her relationships and her environment in order to secure a healthy separation of identity from those around her. Otherwise s/he will overidentify with either abuser or abuse: in the words of one young survivor, 'He is the liar, I am the lie.'[4] Clearly we must equally support her subsequent attempts to reintegrate the experience, since we are all aware of some of the more cruel effects of the distancing response on the relationship between the child's mind and her body, as are manifested in extreme form in fits, drug abuse, suicide attempts, eating and sleep disorders, etc. In considering her needs we have to avoid categorising her via her external 'symptoms', and try to understand in what ways s/he is striving to establish a distance from her experience, what methods s/he is using, and just what these methods mean to her. We must respect the rate at which s/he is moving, even if this seems to us intolerably slow.

I found in aftercare work with children and adults of all ages that the mental acrobatics that the child has to perform at the point of assault will often determine the specific problems that s/he will face later in life as a survivor. The process that occurs psychologically for the child is technically called 'cognitive dissonance'. In human terms it is Catch 22, and Catch 22 at such a primal level that it may have a profound influence on the child's system of morality, and her whole ethical approach to later life. For many children, the specific helplessness and hopelessness experienced during sexual assault will be dynamic, leading to a general concern for change and for justice, a resolve that others should not experience what they have been through, and that those who commit such harm must be prevented. The child thus distances herself from the abuse, yet retains her empathy with others (there may be problems for these children in over-empathising with others to the extent that they may neglect their own interests, but their concern with justice and compassion provides a healthy basis for later self-healing). For some, however, the reaction might be negative and effect a moral stasis. The helplessness and hopelessness are things that they feel they can escape only by visiting them upon others. This type of distancing – at the expense of others – is found more often amongst sexually abused boys than it is amongst girls. It will be discussed more fully in the section on identification with the aggressor.

When one turns to consider the ways in which some professionals are handling their sense of emotional confusion in the face of child sexual abuse, it can be disheartening to observe to what extent their own distancing response has served to alienate them from the child. As outlined above, family work distances us from children in that it prevents us from facing their true feelings and their betrayal. But even when children are treated on a one-to-one model, there is a desperate flight by professionals from any real communication with the child, perhaps because s/he represents such terror and abandonment. It is as if we cannot accept that in some ways, there is no answer to the child's question, *Why?* Therefore, we refuse to hear it. We cannot bear to tell the child that we do not have any magic solution, that we cannot make people love her, that however sophisticated and caring our treatment of her, s/he must still carry the burden of her experience quite alone. In refusing to admit this to ourselves or to children, we are yet again requiring them to shoulder adult pain. A good example of our adult dishonesty is afforded in this context by the phenomenon of the 'anatomically correct doll'. Those who feel uneasy or titillated[5] when confronted with sexual abuse are all too eager to employ anatomically correct dolls in their work with children. These dolls may arguably have some forensic use, but the suggestion that they are therapeutically useful in that they help children to externalise sexual assaults is often wishful. What is important to the child is communication of feelings, not of events. Adults are sometimes too keen to learn all the exciting and horrifying details of sexual abuse before the child is ready to discuss these. The dolls are said to help children to overcome embarrassment. In fact, some professionals use the dolls to disguise their own embarrassment, and their own inability to get down and communicate at the child's level. It is early as yet to assess the long-term effects of the use of these dolls, but some basic points may be made.

First, the dolls are often not as anatomically correct as is claimed, since the females usually lack a clitoris. The female child is therefore confronted with a doll with three gaping holes in her body, open and ready to accept a penis, with no reflection of her own active sexual potential. Furthermore, the holes are usually lined with pink silk, to facilitate the insertion of the male doll's penis. The message to the child is therefore that penetration is something easy and automatic. This has implications for the socialisation of a submissive female sexuality, but it is also unacceptable because it misrepresents the girl's experience of rape itself. As one adult survivor put it, 'it would be more realistic to make the vagina out of sandpaper.'

Secondly, children's play with such dolls is often misinterpreted by professionals. For example, a child psychiatrist on one televison interview[6] stated that if the child concentrated on playing with the anal area of the doll, this was evidence of anal molestation. Whilst the generalisation is worrying enough in itself, in that the speaker had leapt too readily to his conclusion, it also implies that if a child avoids the anal area then there is no need to suspect anal abuse. Common sense would, of course, suggest that the opposite is equally possible. If a child has had a traumatic assault to one part of its body, it may be that that part of the doll will become too taboo to approach.

Thirdly, the dolls may well have an impact on the child's perception of the human body and sexuality which, far from dispelling the trauma of abuse, simply compounds it. On the one hand, small boys have been known to attempt to have intercourse with these dolls, which in a sense is reminiscent of the use of rubber dolls by highly disturbed adult men. It may thus become easier for young boys to transfer such depersonalisation onto other children. On the other hand, some agencies have reported that children have been frightened by the almost voodoo quality of the dolls and in one case a child later stopped playing with any doll at all.

The one advantage of the technique is that it introduces a 'third object'[7] between patient and therapist, thereby displacing any anxiety about direct communication. I would argue from experience with very small children that other displacement techniques, such as artwork, music or roleplay with ordinary dolls can be equally effective in helping the child to express itself and to heal.

The quest for safety

It has been seen that the distancing response of the child may be an almost automatic consequence of the physical invasion effected by sexual abuse. Emotionally it also protects her by providing a sense of safety. Professionals too are engaged in the quest for safety, only their motives may be less admirable. One of the strategies that we may use to protect ourselves from the panic that can pervade our work on sexual abuse is to fall prey to the assumption that 'it' happens to 'them' out 'there', and never to us 'nice' people. All kinds of abusive, racist and classist theories have fuelled, and have been fuelled by, this assumption.[8] Many of us make vigorous attempts to unlearn such an approach, but as we stifle each myth we often discover that it simply returns to our work in a new form, like the Old Man of the Sea. For example, professionals are surely informed enough to reject the ridiculous 'class' and 'subculture' theories that still permeate a lot of the incest literature. Yet many are influenced by a more recent spin-off of this prejudice – the notion that sexual abuse is on the increase because of growing unemployment. The implication here is that it is only 'the poor' who commit sexual abuse.

In fact, child sexual assault has been widespread for generations. Without it the West would not have the society it does – the family organisation, the male-dominated religion, the economic sub-ordination of females, the abuse of women in pornography, even some of the Hollywood film stars. As one disgruntled survivor commented on unemployment: 'Child-molesting gets you an orgasm, not a job. Unemployment may increase the occurrence of child sexual assault – not because of any sociological dynamic – but because of increased time and increased access to children.' It is not child sexual assault that has escalated over past years but its reportage, as can be observed also with the phenomena of rape of adult women, wife-battering, and physical child abuse.

Another strategy in the quest for professional safety is to concentrate on the superficial aspects of sexual abuse, regarding it as a pathological aberration or set of behaviours which can somehow be contained by definitions of external 'symptoms', and thereby avoiding the recognition of how basic a pattern it is within our society. Justice and welfare systems alike approach the issues of sexual crime from the externals – what actual acts have occurred? What relationship existed between the offender and the target? Was it an attack on a stranger or was it 'domestic'? Of course these factors are important in how hard the experience of sexual assault is for the child and in how that child is going to overcome it – and yet, in my experience, professional concentration on such factors can be irrelevant as well as often leading to dangerous diagnoses and treatments for abused children.

First, an example of dangerous diagnosis: one child abuse prevention worker recounted a situation where a friend of hers had seen her son poking a pencil into her daughter's bottom while they were playing in the garden. She rushed out in a panic, ready to protect the daughter. On getting closer to the children, she heard: 'And now we're taking your temperature . . . ' She heaved a sigh of relief. After all, they were only 'playing doctor'. But why should 'playing doctor' suddenly in itself justify an act which might be independently violent? What's in a name? We are well aware that some real doctors molest children. Why should a play doctor be any less likely to do so? This worker did not question how the friend's little girl might be perceiving the insertion of a pencil into her bottom. To the worker the pencil was a thermometer, the act was a game and the participants of an innocent age. Thus, it was concluded from externals that all was well. Perhaps, indeed, it was — but without verifying that with the child herself, one is not in a position to know.

Examples of dangerous treatment caused by this professional obsession with the superficial have been outlined above. But preventive strategies may also be beset by the same problem. For example, there is a method of warning children against abuse in certain relationships by contrasting them with situations which are automatically assumed to be trustworthy. A school class may sometimes be warned that for a person to demand secrecy about a certain relationship with the child is a sign that the person is probably being abusive. To illustrate the worker may say, 'After all, when mummy and daddy put you to bed and kiss you Good Night, they don't ask you to keep *that* a secret, do they?' This distinction between relationships depends on external roles and is not helpful to the child. It may in obvious ways serve further to silence children. If there is any basic lesson that all preventive trainers must learn well and thoroughly, it is the lesson learnt by every abused child – that trust is what is abusable.[9] Trust must never be taken in advance as automatic: in every relationship it has to be earned afresh.

Identification with the aggressor

Identification with the aggressor is one of the ways in which children can distance themselves from the trauma of abuse and achieve a sense of safety, although it may be argued that this sense of safety is highly precarious in that it requires constant reinforcement by means of further acts of abuse. To trace the development of this response among both children and professionals, we may begin by looking at the visual imagery projected by abused children. Children's artwork produced in sessions that I ran with under fives demonstrated the four basic ways of resolving the moral double-bind of sexual assault which have been identified by Ann Burgess.[10] One is the 'blocking' response outlined above: 'I must have done something wrong without even knowing it. Therefore I am not a good judge of right or wrong.' A blocking response is one in which the child has repressed the memory or believes that her experience is totally unique. S/he makes no statement of right or wrong. Her drawings will be totally disorganised – if s/he can begin to draw at all. This can be her genuine response to the assault, but is more often the result of poor communication on the part of the therapist. A second type is the 'non-integration' response, where the child has a strong sense of right and wrong but blames herself and not the offender: 'I am being punished. Therefore I must be a bad child.' This type of response usually results from a situation where the authorities were not supportive enough towards the child on disclosure. A third type is the 'integration' response, where the child has a strong sense of right and wrong and believes the offender was guilty. This usually results from a situation where the authorities were child-oriented. Last, there is the 'identification with the aggressor' response, where the child develops a sense of 'entitlement' to exploit others, including sexually.

By following the development of children's artwork, we can gain unique insights into their type or combination of types of response and help them to progress, for example, from blocking or from non-integration to an integrated position. A typical progression in such a child's drawings will be from frightening, disorganised pictures or depictions of the assaults where the offender is monstrous ond overwhelming with a tiny helpless child, to a depiction of the child as a strong, independent image and the offender as either absent from the picture or present but controlled in some way – perhaps with a strongly buckled belt or a pair of handcuffs. (Children accept what many professionals will not – that the only sure-fire way to prevent sexual abuse by adults is to use external curbs to control their behaviour).

For the child who identifies with the aggressor, however, the progression is more worrying. The first pictures will, as usual, depict a huge and terrifying monster. But as the pictures progress, we find that s/he is protecting herself not with inner resources such as the emotional certainty of the integrated response, but with external weapons such as guns, knives, swords and laser beams. The child is now a veritable armadillo, and communication with such a child will be a severe long-term problem for any worker. I once interviewed a little survivor of 6 for the purpose of making a legal report, and he informed me that he never needed to tell anybody anything – after all, 'he had his sword to protect him'. A toy sword may be harmless in the hands of a 6-year-old boy, but unless someone works with that boy, his love of the sword may well have developed into something quite other by the time he is an adolescent.

The parallel of violence between such children's imagery, and the imagery marketed in all the militaristic boys' comics available today, is not accidental. British incest self-help groups have suggested that military men make up a high proportion of sex offenders. Indeed, the Police Policy Advisor to the Association of London Authorities has stated that police officers are one of the major categories of wife-batterers.[11] Whether the armed forces are a breeding ground for such men or whether military careers appeal to already-formed child-molesters, may never be known. But the brotherhood, the emphasis on male identity, and the rituals of dominance and submission observed by all fighting men must be taken into account seriously when we examine child sexual assault as a societal phenomenon. Many researchers have gathered statistics on the numbers of female prostitutes who are incest survivors. Of greater interest perhaps are the figures these statistics ignore – for example, the proportion of the male population that causes prostitution to exist. Who charts the disturbance, let alone the absurdity, of the punter's pathology? And who takes large populations or men, such as soldiers, similar to prostitutes in that they follow a highly depersonalising and gender-oriented profession, and analyses what proportion of them are incest survivors or incest offenders? What is the relationship between the professional fighter and the victimised or victimising male? One can only be struck by the similarity between macho advertising images as on film posters and the images projected by some abused boys. For example, one flyer featured a photograph of the huge and hunky wrestler 'Big Daddy'. The caption below read 'Big Daddy Fears No Man'. Although intended to sound tough and impressive, to anyone who has worked with abused boys this reads as a cry from the heart.

The sexual violence of little boys is something that all who have worked with them have observed. It is hard to believe that it is biological, although given that most child-molesters are boys and men, the process of identification with the male aggressor will obviously be easier for boys than it will for girls. It is more likely that the root of the identification is psychosocial. In some ways, our society ensures that women can never escape childhood. We are expected to keep young, soft and childlike as long as possible into our adult lives; our clothes, our make-up and our children are packaged for us like toys, sweets, and dolls; our legal rights as wives reflect our dependency as daughters; and apart from a male-defined 'age of consent', there is no real transition in our social roles as plaything, nurturer and nurse. Ironically, although women are infantilised politically and sexually throughout our lives, psychologically and emotionally we are forced very early into a mothering role. We often take on nest-building, family-making, and relationship-supporting responsibilities in a constellation where men remain the irresponsible consumers. The most extreme example of this pattern is, of course, the kind of incest in which an adult man rejects his very adulthood and responsibility by projecting them, along with all his other problems, onto a little girl, who is thereby thrust headlong, like Alice in Wonderland, into a looking-glass world where every role is reversed. The offender sees himself as a child and her as an adult – and so, unfortunately, do others, including often the caring professions, the community, and even the child herself.

For boys, however, the socialisation is different. Through adolescence they are seen to graduate, to achieve not only a change of voice but also a change of power in the world, an initiation into the public brotherhood of man away from the privatisation of woman and child back home. For them the overriding aim will be accession to that power and alienation as soon as possible. Abused boys hate as much as girls do the powerlessness imposed by men over women and children, but abuse may teach them that the easiest escape for them is by identification with the powerful. Their adult power will be gained at the expense of others, amongst them yet more boys: and thus sexual abuse may be viewed as essentially a battle between males for dominance over each other, with the sexual abuse of women and girls almost as a side-issue to this battle. A large-scale 'cycle of violence' so continues from generation to generation: it is a cycle not of 'family violence', but of male violence, with females as the unfortunate witnesses and sacrifices to a power struggle in which they have no stake.

What of professional identification with the aggressor? The cognitive dissonance of Big Daddy and Little Boy may shed light upon the moral imbalance within ourselves as a society, and especially within those who work professionally with sexually abused children. Just as the morality of an abused boy who has become an abuser may be distorted by the experience of sexual abuse because he turns his face outwards and denies his inner hurt, so professionals who divide the public technique from the private experience of assault are subjecting children in their care to the same hobbled morality.

Some male professionals quite plainly identify with the aggressor in a sexual abuse situation and express this identification through, for instance, sex therapy techniques.[12] But the identification may not be conscious and is more usually displayed in collusive behaviour by professionals. The collusion may be innocent, but with increasing information available on the behaviour patterns of sex offenders, it is becoming less and less excusable. As an example, recent research has documented the fact that sex offenders are by and large 'repeaters'.[13] Many of them make what one might call a career out of sexual abuse, repeating many assaults against the same or different children. Unless controlled externally, they will not stop their behaviour – they find it too rewarding. Yet even today professionals are prepared to sacrifice children's safety to their idealistic trust in such offenders. Until we can convince the health and welfare services that there is a general pattern to the child-molester's behaviour, we shall keep seeing the kind of justice that voluntary groups monitor in the courts today – cases where the offender stands alone and crestfallen in the dock, the ultimate victim, whilst every 'mitigating' circumstance is pleaded by his defence and every slur is heaped upon his wife and children. It is often suggested in mitigation that the offender regrets his acts. He does not. He regrets his arrest. I have actually witnessed an able-bodied offender pretend to be disabled in court. He hardly needed to do so. Reports from social workers who had never even interviewed his children stated that he was a good father to them and that his imprisonment would therefore do them irreparable harm. The man was released, and when his ex-wife attempted to fight his divorce-court application for custody of the children, the local authority took them into care, denied her access and proceeded to arrange sole access for the father. With friends like these, what abused child needs enemies?

Ann Burgess, a criminologist who works with sexually abused children in Virginia, USA, has drawn up a pattern of reactions which every child-molester follows on being exposed. She explains that sex offenders have had to become very manipulative people in order to get their way. She warns that their manipulation affects not only the child and its family, but also professionals dealing with the case. Each strategy that the offender takes is geared to throw the professionals off the scent and bring them into a position of supporting the offender, at the expense of the child.

1. The first strategy is denial. The offender will feign indignation or shock, or claim that he has lost his memory, or been 'misunderstood'. These excuses can be utterly convincing and the offender is often knowingly or unknowingly aided in the cover-up by friends and associates.[14]

2. If the offender is forced to admit the offence, he then shifts his tactics to the second strategy – minimisation of the evidence. He will minimise the quantity and quality of the assault, trading on our alienated concern with externals – the fact that we will consider certain crimes against a child's body to be less serious than others, basing our judgement purely on anatomy.

3. Given that the child's witness of the assaults has been believed and that his own minimisation has failed, the offender now turns to justification. He claims he loves the child or that he was acting under stress. He suggests that his wife would not sleep with him or that he was drunk. Ignorance of the girl's age is also put forward as a justification for abuse. All such excuses amount to victim-blame.

The reader may well have recognised these three strategies, if not as strategies then as typical behaviours of offenders. In most cases the accusations against the offender will already have failed or foundered before he has to resort to the fourth.

4. This is the 'sick' game. He will claim that he cannot control himself or that he is mentally ill. These are arguments that he is not morally responsible for his action. Paedophile manuals actually advocate them as a last-resort tactic, when all else has failed. At this point the professional may well be duped by the offender's obvious personal disorders, and let him off the hook for his offence. But one must ask oneself, if he is *compos mentis* enough to be so acutely aware of all his psychological problems, then why ever did he not go for help before? Why does his mental health become an important issue for him only when he is afraid of being imprisoned and thus denied access to children

whom he was happy to assault before, regardless of his overwhelming mental suffering?

5. The 'sick' game combines effectively with the 'sympathy' game as an escape tactic. The offender's supporters emphasise what a respectable, stable pillar of the community he was, how he fought for his country,[15] etc. The image of a model citizen suddenly having a tragic mental lapse is convincing to many. But for that very reason we must inform ourselves as to why some offenders ensure that they are well liked by their communities, and why they curry favour with the powerful in the first place. It helps them to prepare the ground for their offences. Too many offenders have a Nice Guy face for us to ignore the phenomenon as accidental.

6. If he is still not believed or supported, the true nature of the offender finally emerges. He has nothing to gain by hiding it. Therefore, he is finally prepared to take the offensive against the professional. Attacks, harassment, threats and bribes are now used not only against the child and family, but also against the authorities. It is only at this point that the violence and selfishness at the heart of his crime are visible to all. And, sadly, few offenders are ever exposed at this level. For the vast majority, it would be true to say that only the people who really understand their brutality, their self-centredness, and their powers of manipulation are the children whom they have assaulted.

An example of how difficult it is not to identify with the aggressor may be provided by the following case. A young woman, molested by her father, discovered that he had been assaulting several younger sisters also. She had by now left home but decided that, in order to protect the sisters, she would try to resolve the situation. She rejected the idea of involving the police and courts, as she did not want to cause trouble to her family. Instead, she had faith in the therapeutic approach. The family consequently signed up for treatment at a children's hospital in London. Social workers came to an agreement with the father that he would leave the marital home and have access to the family only during therapy. In spite of this the man began regularly to harass his wife and children, turning up on the family doorstep, and once breaking into the eldest daughter's flat. She lived in constant fear of his violence and was disgusted by the lies he had told the social workers. At a public seminar in another city I saw a video show involving one of this family's therapy sessions. To all intents and purposes the offender appeared a harmless, submissive person. No one watching could have guessed that this man was violating the terms of his agreement with social workers and the hospital, still less that he was terrorising his family. Most of the video extract was devoted to a long discussion between the offender and the therapist of the notion that the offender was truly a caring person underneath. This illusion is a perfect example of the way in which all of us can be duped by the appearance of an individual case when we do not have access either to the truth of the matter, or to a generalised analysis of the nature of sexual crime.

Nor does the problem of misinformation stop at professional naivety and collusion. Without a children's rights model of working, it soon develops into one of further exploitation of the child. For example, the videotape in this case was shown in the other city without the permission of the young woman, although she had expressly been given a verbal commitment that the video would be used only for training purposes *within* the London hospital. At no time had she been given any contract or information on the possibility of refusing her consent – not even when she made a complaint about the showing outside London. All she received at this point was an apology to the family as a whole, which failed to include any indication as to the fate of the tape. The Royal College of Psychiatrists' Audio-Visual Subcommittee were contacted on behalf of the young woman, and refused to comment on the problem of clients' rights being disrespected in the matter of videos and transcriptions of therapy sessions.

In terms of what might charitably be called his cognitive dissonance as a professional, the psychiatrist involved in this case is not exceptional. He has simply been influenced by his wishes as a professional to serve the furtherance of science without any concern for the rights or interests of the human being in treatment. But once he has sacrificed the means to the end, he too becomes subject to the looking-glass logic of the incest offender. In some cases where girls under 16 have wished to refuse consent to the making or disseminating of therapeutic videos, professionals have chosen to ignore them and have accepted the consent of the abusing parent on their behalf. This demonstrates a refusal either to respect the feelings or to uphold the rights of the sexually abused child, and betrays a shocking degree of identification with the aggressor.

Some suggested solutions

Many of the feelings of helplessness and hopelessness that professionals have when confronting sexual abuse in others are actually projections of their own experience which they have had neither the time nor the opportunity to resolve. We must therefore search our own memories as far back as we can, in order to activate our own understanding of sexual assault for maximum efficiency. In urging workers to deal with these experiences, I am suggesting a cycle of healing which in turn will influence their clients. The insights that we gain from our own abuse are invaluable assets when it comes to relating to abused children. Likewise, if we examine the stress responses of the children themselves, these will show the way for us in finding our own answers to our past.

Consider some of the feelings a child will have while s/he is being sexually assaulted, and at the solutions each child finds for the fix s/he is in. First, unless a child is actually killed by the offender, then we may be sure that s/he has found a way of resisting the attack. The resistance may not prevent the attack, but it does provide her with her own way of bearing and surviving it.

By now we can recognise the fallacies of blaming a child for not resisting assault. Those old prejudices are laughable to us all. But have we considered just how strenuously, with what inner power, each child actually *does* resist? A child is assaulted. Throughout the assault s/he perhaps remains completely soundless. Not a limb moves. S/he apparently makes no attempt to fight off her attacker – not surprising, since he is twice her height and four times her weight. But you may remember that this child has her eyes closed. A tiny gesture. Yet in that gesture is a complete and utter refusal to accept her violation. A pair of eyelids for this child are actually her will. We must not underestimate the massive emotional energy behind the tiny physical frame. With every child there is at least a grain of resistance that keeps her inwardly undamaged, and that resistance is the key we must find in working with her to resolve the trauma later.

Just as at present we have not adequately fathomed the fact of resistance in every child, so we have denied the power of that resistance by mislabelling the child's subsequent behaviour. Take a response like running away from home or attempting suicide. This behaviour is considered disturbed or delinquent. Yet when it is seen in its proper context – survival from a life-threatening situation, escape from Catch 22 – we can recognise the child's strength for what it really is.

Instead of underestimating children, there are ways we can learn from them. There are ideas that each child has devised on her or his own which could help us to combat child sexual assault as adults. If readers feel that they cannot get in touch with their own memories of childhood abuse, it might be helpful to try a simple exercise, in which you put yourself in the position of someone who is being sexually abused as an adult.

In this exercise you must imagine that you are at a crowded party. The host introduces you to a friend of his, a very small, weedy and rather off-putting man. He is wearing platform shoes, yet even so you would be taller than he is in your stockinged feet. This man looks your body up and down in an irritating way but you are not at all intimidated, as he is so evidently a weakling. You decide that he is becoming boring and move away. As you pass him, however, he suddenly molests you.

What would the reader consider to be the average person's reaction to this event? Fear? Confusion? Self-blame? Surely not. A first reaction would be quite straightforward – a righteous anger at having one's body space invaded. And whether you feel mild annoyance or extreme indignation, this natural aggressive instinct of yours has one physical purpose – to propel you away from the problem; and one emotional purpose – to preserve your sense of integrity. It is not only the most obvious reaction, but also the most healthy for you.

Now take an example of a somewhat less healthy situation. Perhaps it is the host at the party who molests you, and not a simple stranger. You have added complications here, since you know him, you do not want to offend him or his partner, or to upset the other guests or the atmosphere; you do not want to appear a spoilsport or a prude. This time your anger may not have such an easy outlet because it is compromised by such conflicting requirements as the need to protect others, your loyalty to his partner, the gratitude for some favour he has done you or the expectation of a favour, such as a lift that you desperately need to get home. The possibilities are endless but his motives are always the same. He is trading on your needs and he knows it, so that the feelings you have will be made even more complicated by any understanding you have of his cunning.

Finally, take a third situation. You are molested this time by the same little weakling whom you would normally brush aside like a fly. All his personal characteristics and his actions are the same. But this time he is a police officer who has arrested you for an unnamed offence, and he is alone with you in a cell. You have no knowledge of the law, no access to outside help, and no idea of your rights. When will you be released? You do not know. Do you push him away? Or will he then become even more violent? Who will protect you from him? Who will even believe you when you get out of the situation? The chances are, however, at this point, that this last worry will not yet have occurred to you. Your overwhelming survival reaction will undoubtedly be fear. And until you are released from police custody you will never have complete access to the normal emotions of a free person, the freedom to express the anger that was yours by right, the indignation of an ordinary human being and the aggression of an ordinary animal avoiding a problem. Your healthiest reaction – anger – has been confused and complicated by abuse of power and of access.

For any agency working therapeutically with sexually abused children, exposing and releasing the child's anger must be central. Many teenage problems which have been linked with sexual victimisation, such as depression, promiscuity and self-mutilation, can be considered partially from the point of view of misdirected anger. The power thus forced underground is phenomenal – imagine the sheer force of will and the dynamic intensity that would lead you to cut into your own body. But such examples are obvious; one must also consider the concentrated energy that it takes to disguise anger, perhaps by a child who becomes a model pupil, an immaculately dressed and groomed example of normality. The 'normal' children that we know do not underestimate their anger – and that is why they are doing all that they can to hide it.

Anger is a tool that can be channelled for the healing of a child. Too often we deny the possibility of anger to clients, thereby wasting a valuable resource which could save us a lot of time and effort. Before I began to work with sexually abused children, I had spoken with more than a thousand adult women who called themselves incest survivors. Anger is one of the major reactions of adult women towards their childhood experience, yet, interestingly, this is not often recognised by researchers or welcomed by professionals. It was suggested by child psychiatrists in the early 1980s[16] that this anger was purely adult reaction, created by our selective memory processes with all their accompanying distortions. Only adult women, it was argued, perceived incest as a betrayal. Children, it was suggested, do not have comparable feelings towards their abusers. With this in mind I began to meet the project's child clients. The individual work with children was conducted on the play therapy or 'creative listening' model.[17] The therapist's role is to reflect back any feeling that the child may have, without imposing adult value judgements. By this method it is hoped that children will receive the permission to find and explore their own most basic reactions to assault. Children are not told what to do or ordered not to be destructive. Within the limits of their own safety and respect for others' bodies, they may make any noise, use any words, or wreak any havoc that they wish. And one of the major emotions that is discovered through such work is anger. In the safe knowledge that project workers will never confer with or listen to their abusers, the children are free to express every feeling towards the offender – including any wishes for revenge. With adolescents, too, permission and the total exclusion of the offender release feelings that otherwise would not be allowed expression. Girls whose fathers and stepfathers are awaiting trial have, in such an environment, felt safe to say that they want the man sent down for life.

The urge for vengeance is not a 'nice' emotion. Nor is it a basis for running a country's penal system. I am in no way advocating that the desire for revenge be the basis from which we deal with either children or offenders. But neither should professionals dismiss such feelings as excessive or irrelevant. If you think that some children's wish for an offender to be put away for life is inappropriate, then you have not understood the enormity of sexual assault as a crime and the terror and humiliation that the targets of it can undergo.

Therapeutic work with children must be conducted in the absence of the offender. This is essential if we wish them to understand that they deserve respect in their own right, and do not need to gain our approval by engaging in 'naked ape' interactions with people who have denied their very right to a separate existence. To pretend that an offender is less offensive to the child simply because another adult is busily observing everything they say and do, simply serves to exacerbate the child's sense of being 'alone in a crowd', acting a part in someone else's drama, unprotected even in the presence of others.

Art therapy is an excellent tool in working with abused children since it allows the therapist access to the child's inner world without any sense of violation on the child's part. The child can gain strength and self-confidence through her creative interaction with the work, thus counteracting any feeling of helplessness or passivity consequent on the abuse. If the pictures or models made by the child are collected and preserved for her use in adulthood, they will have the same therapeutic effect as the life-story book has for fostered and adopted children.[18] It must be stressed here that if professionals really respect the children whom they work with, they will not seek to retain the original artwork, however tempting for research purposes, but will either hand it to the child or keep it aside until court proceedings and therapeutic sessions are over so that the child remains in control of her own material. The same goes for videos, photographs and taped material involving the child. They are part of her history, and should not be destroyed, publicly exhibited, or otherwise exploited.

Whatever the method used in treating the sexually abused child, a great deal of thought must go into the environment in which the therapy is conducted. It must not be forgotten that to someone who has been sexually abused at home, indoors is not a safe place to be. The child must always feel that s/he has access to the door and that no adult is blocking her exit from it. Neither must s/he feel that people are watching and recording her every move, since this behaviour will be reminiscent of the visual control that many offenders exercise over members of their household. It is also important for treatment to take place outside a hospital, since children will invariably associate these with medical problems and assume that they are suffering from a sickness rather than going for help. I have worked with children in many environments, and the best I have found was, interestingly enough, a law centre. This is because children felt they were approaching an agency as independent individuals capable of defining their own requests, and that this agency was committed to representing them alone. Child sexual abuse was treated by the law centre as just one aspect of a general package of children's rights, along with those affected by education, immigration, welfare benefits and relations with the police. Young people could enter the agency with a sense of pride and in the knowledge that no one witnessing their entry would make any prejudiced assumptions about their sexual abuse or mental health. Finally, the involvement of workers representative of all cultures and lifestyles in many British law centres means that the child is allowed to feel that, despite any sexual abuse s/he may have experienced, s/he will be helped to heal within her community rather than in isolation from it; that there are people from within that same community who will accept her and will not cast her out.

These are some of the ways of working that may be helpful for children. As far as professionals are concerned, the way forward is to work on a purely personal level at first, and ensure that there is enough support to discuss one's own experience of sexual abuse. It is a constant surprise to hear that professionals expect children to disclose all their feelings to adults when adults have not yet even dared to break their own silence in the workplace. Of course it is frightening for those working with sexually abused children to expose their own experiences to colleagues and superiors. The myth that incest survivors are somehow so damaged and perverted by abuse that they cannot be entrusted with the care of children operates to block many a promising career. Such workers are easy targets for accusations of paranoia which conveniently deflect public attention from the widespread reality of child sexual abuse, and act as an electricity conductor for all the public and professional terror which this reality engenders.

Support groups should be formed so that those workers who are incest survivors can get some solidarity and discover that their collective understanding is a source of great insight and healing power for the agency as a whole. This would in turn encourage greater professional accountability to clients, since identification with the aggressor would thereby become less of a viable option for professionals who were being challenged by survivors within their ranks. The professional who has not experienced sexual abuse must be prepared constantly to question her or his assumptions both in situations where incest is assumed to be involved and where it is not. What happens to our clients may well yet happen to our own children or friends' children. Only when we accept this shall we discard the urge to try to differentiate ourselves from clients.

I have criticised the professional tendency to be deflected from a child-centred approach into collusion with the abuser. Another type of collusion must be mentioned here, and this is the agency-centred cover-up. Often workers within an agency will choose not to challenge or question what they see as unjust or abusive practice.

This is understandable when one's job depends on one's silence, as workers in one children's home found to their cost when they tried to expose the head of the home who was molesting many of the boy residents.[19] However, it is to be hoped that as more child abuse survivors gain an active voice within the childcare professions, so it will be harder for those above them to achieve such concealment. It cannot escape us how similar this enforced protection of institutional power is to the incest dynamic within a family.

It is certainly time that all of us examined the interplay of childish helplessness and thoughtless abuse of power that can combine so destructively in our approach to sexual abuse cases. Until we deal with our own pain and our own alienation, we shall be allowing children to continue to carry on their shoulders the mighty moral confusion that masquerades as treatment of their assaults.

Notes and references

1. The Child Sexual Abuse Preventive Education Project, founded in 1984 and funded by the Greater London Council to service the London area.
2. See Introduction, note 96.
3. The pronoun 's/he' in this chapter is an abbreviation for 'she or he'. I have used 'her' meaning 'her or him' or 'her or his' for the sake of brevity.
4. See also *Our Girls' Group*, leaflet published by Liverpool Children's Admissions Unit, 1984.
5. Titillation is unfortunately a very common reaction to reports of child sexual abuse, amongst both lay public and professionals. For a mention of the effects of this on working with the child see Jacquie Roberts, 'Fostering the Sexually Abused Child', *Adoption and Fostering*, vol. 10, no. 1, 1986. For the effects on the specialist's morale of professional prurience see T. Crolley and J. Paley, 'Sexual Problems and the Probation Service', *Probation Journal*, vol. 29, no. 4, December 1982: 'one officer . . . was made to feel [by colleagues] that he himself was sexually obsessive'.
6. 20/20 Vision, *Child Sex Abuse: Some Solutions*, Channel 4, December 1984.
7. The 'third object' technique encourages the child to play without having to confront the professional in any head-on interaction. See Clare Winnicott, *Child Care and Social Work*, Codicote Press; 'Communicating with Children', *Social Work Today*, vol. 8, no. 26, 5 April 1977.
8. See Myths nos 6 and 7 in the Introduction.
9. Irwin Dreiblatt, 'Issues in the Evaluation of the Sex Offender', a

presentation at the Washington State Psychological Association Meeting, May 1982: 'The [offender] is on an adversarial footing with the authorities and, to some degree, with the examiner. Lying and deception on the part of the client are typical . . . Effective assessment and treatment of the offender require a degree of skepticism and cynicism on the part of the professional. I tell my clients that I do not operate on a trust basis. Trust is what is abusable. I communicate to them that I have no intention of feeling confident in them. Feeling confident about them can be dangerous.'

10. Dr Ann Wolbert Burgess, 'The Sexual Exploitation of Children: Sex Rings, Pornography and Prostitution', paper presented at a symposium on child sexual abuse at Teesside Polytechnic, Middlesbrough, 20 May 1984.

11. The suggestion has been made by Incest Survivors' Campaign and Incest Crisis Line, amongst other pressure groups. For the police statistics on wife-battering, see M. M. Hall, 'Why the Police don't give a Damn about Domestic Violence', *Cosmopolitan*, January 1988.

12. For male therapists identifying with the aggressor, see for example, J. Herman and L. Hirschman, 'Father-Daughter Incest', *Signs*, Journal of Women in Culture and Society, summer 1977. For therapists sexually assaulting incest survivors, see Elizabeth Brown, 'A Child *Is Being Molested*', *Maenad: Women's Literary Journal*, 1980.

13. See Introduction notes 109 and 110. As Dreiblatt states in the article above, 'Most offenders go through a cycle of being sexually attracted to offend: offending – feeling regret – promising themselves they will not reoffend – feeling confident that they are under control – feeling attracted to a deviant sexual choice – reoffending . . . the problem typically becomes chronic . . . One must . . . fully understand the importance of past behaviour in risk prediction. There can be little question that the strongest predictor of future sexual offenses is past sexual offenses.'

14. See Introduction note 96.

15. This plea was made on behalf of Watson-Sweeney in the case illustrated in Chapter 6, note 4.

16. For example, Danya Glaser, 'The Treatment of Sexually Abused Children', paper presented at a symposium on child sexual abuse at Teesside Polytechnic, Middlesbrough, 20 May 1984.

17. The 'Creative Listening' model of play therapy is based on the work of Virginia Axline (*Dibs in Search of Self*, Pelican Books, 1971) and taught in Britain by the Children's Hours Trust.

18. See Anne Marie Jones, *The Foster Child, Identity and the Life Story Book*, Social Theory and Institutions Publications, University College, Bangor, 1985.

19. Ronald Cooper, Leeways Residential Home, Lewisham: *The Guardian*, 4 June 1983.

4

Child sexual abuse and the law

SIMMY VIINIKKA

This chapter examines the law and criminal procedure dealing with child sexual abuse, and analyses the limitations of the criminal legal process in protecting the child. It has not been possible to undertake a study of the complex civil framework of care and wardship proceedings which take as their starting point the 'best interests of the child', and to which the comments contained in this chapter do not necessarily extend.

Criminal statistics

Whilst the popular press readily endorses the view that the child-molester is society's most hated criminal who deserves and receives the full rigour of the law, the reality is far less straightforward. The closer to home the abuse, the more ambivalent the legal and indeed the popular response, and the more the inadequacies of the criminal process become apparent.

Most sexual abuse of children goes unreported.[1] A random survey of 930 adult women conducted in San Francisco, in 1978, found 647 instances of child sexual abuse. Yet only thirty cases or 5 per cent of the total were reported to the police.[2] Seven of these resulted in a criminal conviction and in a further two cases the outcome is unknown. Overall, 0.5 per cent of incestuous abuse and 1.3 per cent of abuse outside the family led to the eventual conviction of the offender. The Child Advocate Association of Chicago has estimated a reporting rate of only 3 per cent out of a

132

total estimated 22 000 cases of incest per annum in the State of Illinois.[3]

Statistics such as these led one writer to conclude that 'incestuous fathers have little to fear from the law. Even if a complaint is made, which is unlikely, the chances are slight that the case will ever go to trial, still slighter that the father will be found guilty and even slighter that, if convicted, he will be sent to prison.'[4]

Any discussion of the criminal process must be severely undermined by the knowledge that the number of cases in which it is invoked at all is a tiny proportion of the whole. The case which reaches a police file, let alone a court, is by virtue of that very fact in a substantial minority from which it would be dangerous to draw general conclusions. Diana Russell,[5] who conducted the San Francisco survey, points out that the sex offender who gets caught or ends up in treatment is likely to have behaved abnormally, even for sex offenders, and she gives examples such as unusually repetitive or flagrantly bizarre behaviour.

Legal definitions

In terms of the British criminal law, there is no one offence called 'child sexual abuse'. Rather, it is composed of a number of sexual offences, some of which, for example unlawful sexual intercourse, are age-specific, and others, for example rape, are not, but apply to both adults and children. Whilst very few cases of child sexual abuse reach the courts, it is as well to remember that sexual offences against children constitute a high proportion of reported sexual offences overall. In Britain in 1985, for example, 20.8 per cent of all recorded rapes and 40.3 per cent of all recorded charges of indecent assault involved girls of 15 or under, and 24.9 per cent of recorded cases of buggery and indecent assault on a male in fact involved boys aged 9 or under.[6] Similarly, 72 per cent of incest cases in 1983 involved children under the age of 16.

These figures expose the level of violence which is masked by the term 'child sexual abuse'. I therefore make no apology for including the offences of rape and buggery in this discussion along with offences such as incest which are more readily associated with child sexual abuse. Many people have examined child sexual abuse in the context of works on child abuse and neglect. It is right that child sexual abuse should be centrally located in that discussion. It is time it was also located within the context of crimes of sexual violence.

Legal intervention

Sexual offences against children share certain characteristics with a number of forms of criminal conduct, in particular, domestic violence, all forms of rape and sexual assault, and physical child abuse. All are under-reported, and in all legal intervention is less than satisfactory. Unsatisfactory not because, as some would say, the law should not intervene in 'domestic matters' but because it should, and generally does so badly or not at all.

On paper, legislation offers what Florence Rush describes as 'an academic basis of justice'.[8] In practice, enforcement is problematic. The legislation seeks to operate against deeply entrenched social assumptions of male dominance over women and children. Society reinforces the view of many men that they have the 'right' to chastise a wife or child, or to have sexual access to her. The criminal justice system itself, whilst offering theoretical justice, in practice does little to interfere with such views. The criminal process is most effective in dealing with extremes, for example cases of great violence. It is progressively less confident in its role as it is invoked in situations where the conduct complained of more closely resembles that of so-called normal adult male behaviour. It is precisely because, as one judge remarked, 'this is the sort of thing that could happen to any man'[9] that the law, which understands so well the predicament of the offender, is unable fully to address the demands for protection of the assaulted child.

Legal intervention is therefore paradoxical. Theoretically legislation against all forms of child sexual abuse is harsh and maximum penalties severe. However, legal practice in the form of the rules of evidence, the process of investigation, and sentencing policy, tends towards a reversal of the position, putting the child 'on trial' in place of the accused.

The offender

There is a double vision within the criminal process which reflects the double vision of the world outside. On the one hand, the child-molester is universally condemned and despised to the extent that his safety in prison cannot be guaranteed. On the other hand, society in fact sanctions a high level of sexual exploitation, and the child-molester, particularly if he confines his activities to family and friends, receives a great deal of sympathy. He could be any man, misunderstood, perhaps sick, perhaps driven to it, perhaps the victim of a lying child, a vindictive wife or a seductive daughter. He is described by Susan Forward as 'an otherwise law-abiding, hardworking guy next door who somewhere along the line lost the ability to control his impulses'.[10] Sarah Nelson points out the irony of the situation, in that those who view the child-molester as the worst kind of criminal, and call for strong and unequivocal measures, do not believe that child sexual abuse happens much, while those who know that it does, and that many men abuse their children, are calling for a reduction in penalties.[11]

Types of offence

The offences involved divide into two main categories, the offences of sexual penetration (incest, rape, unlawful sexual intercourse and buggery), and sexual assaults (called indecent assault and gross indecency in the United Kingdom). They reflect society's preoccupation with the act of penile penetration – for which the worst punishments are reserved. Many children, particularly if they are very young, are systematically violated over long periods of time, but unless sexual intercourse or attempted sexual intercourse has taken place, the abuse falls into the secondary category of sexual or indecent assault. In the case of a girl, her virginity is assumed to be her prize and some men do not think their activities 'count' if a girl remains technically a virgin.

Rape

The crime of rape originated in the desire to protect female chastity as a commodity. Rape was an offence which could be prosecuted by the husband or father of the woman concerned and he could apply for damages against the rapist, effectively for taking or damaging his property. Whilst these legal actions are long gone, their legacy remains in the view of a wife or child as a man's sexual property.[12]

Incest

Although a statutory offence in Scotland since 1567, incest did not become a specific offence in England and Wales until 1908, following widespread public campaigning.[13] The definition of incest is very narrow. A man can only be convicted of incest if he has, or attempts to have, sexual intercourse with his daughter, granddaughter, sister or mother. There are parallel provisions for female offenders. The incest legislation does nothing to protect children against any form of abuse other than sexual intercourse, nor against abuse by other relatives such as uncles, and other members of the household such as stepfathers. It has been suggested that stepfathers are the single category most prone to perpetrate sexual abuse,[14] yet a recent review of the law in England and Wales recommended only that adoptive fathers and not stepfathers should be subject to incest legislation.[15]

Incest laws are concerned with the absence or presence of a biological relationship. They do not thereby necessarily address the needs of the child, so much as society's concern to regulate public morality. Incest is popularly seen as a terrible crime, not so much because of the abuse of power involved, but because, first, it is seen to violate a taboo, and secondly, it carries a vague fear of 'inbreeding'. For these reasons incest is an offence regardless of the age of the parties and the degree of consent involved.

A child-centred approach would look at incest legislation from the point of view of how best to protect the child, and the effect on a child of an assault involving a breach of trust by a person close to him or her.

A number of states in the USA reformed incest legislation in the 1970s by abolishing or amending the traditional offence.[16] It has been replaced in some states with provisions against any form of sexual penetration or assault, aggravated by the youth of the child and by the breach of a relationship between the adult and child. In other states, the traditional offence still applies but has been widened to include possible offences by stepfathers and other family members. Maximum sentences for such offences vary widely from a fine to life imprisonment. Similar legislation has been passed in France and the Netherlands. In New South Wales, Australia, sexual offences against children have been redefined into categories based upon the age of the child. Harsher penalties apply where the child is under the care or supervision of the offender at the time of the offence.[17]

Unlawful sexual intercourse

The offence of unlawful sexual intercourse means sexual intercourse with a girl who is under the 'age of consent'. It is sometimes defined more descriptively as 'statutory rape'. The age of consent was raised from 13 to 16 in 1885 in the United Kingdom. In the United States it varies from 12 to 18. It is not in law possible to consent to sexual intercourse under the 'age of consent'. However, we shall see that in practice consent will very often become an issue, and the courts are reluctant to intervene in many cases. Between 1972 and 1982, for example, for every adult man prosecuted for the offence in England and Wales, two were cautioned instead.[18]

Like incest, the offence carries a maximum life sentence where the girl is under 13, and a maximum two-year sentence (seven years for incest) if she is over 13. The girl (only if under 17 in the case of incest) cannot herself be prosecuted for either offence. Both incest and unlawful sexual intercourse charges can (and often will) be brought in circumstances amounting to rape, because they are easier to prove, and because the offender may be willing to plead guilty to the lesser charge. As a result, however, the extent of violence and coercion involved may be disguised, and maximum penalties are significantly reduced, at least if the girl is over 13. The reality of incest in the case of a child will almost invariably, in view of the difference in age and authority between the offender and the child, resemble rape.

Buggery

Buggery is penetration, forced or not, of the anus by the penis. It is not possible in law to consent to heterosexual buggery. The maximum sentence in the UK is presently life imprisonment, ten years for an attempt. In the USA many statutes refer to 'sexual penetration' and therefore specific offences of buggery may no longer exist.

Indecent assault

Until 1985 indecent assault (any sexual act other than intercouse or buggery) was punishable in England and Wales with a maximum sentence of five years if the girl was under 13, two years if over, and ten years in the case of any man or boy who was assaulted. Whilst such an anomaly may come as no surprise, it speaks volumes as to the bias of the law, and the readiness of male legislators to protect their own. Indecent assault covers an enormous range of abuse, including penetration by fingers and objects and oral and manual sex. Unlike the law in many countries, there are no degrees of seriousness, and until recently very little scope for relative gravity to be reflected in sentencing practice. The maximum sentence is now ten years in all cases.[19]

It was said in defence of the former maximum sentences that sexual abuse was more traumatic for boys than for girls.[10] It is certainly less widespread, and since abusers of both boys and girls are overwhelmingly male, it was more likely to be of a homosexual description. The abuse of boys is therefore seen as 'unnatural' and presumably the abuse of a girl, which follows more closely the accepted norms of sexual behaviour in which she will be expected to participate in later life, is more 'natural'. Many men delude themselves into not seeing the abuse of a girl as a serious matter because they consider that she is being 'initiated'. This viewpoint is endorsed in the administration of justice which continues to treat the abuse of girls less seriously than that of boys.

Legislative change

It has been pointed out[21] that legislation against the abuse of children, unlike sexual offences legislation, has a very short legal history, mostly dating back only a few decades. This late development has been explained by the traditional abdication of the state from responsibility in family matters, and the state's willingness to delegate to parents, or more particularly, fathers, virtually total authority over children. In such an analysis, the state will avoid, so far as it possibly can, interfering with the family unit. A gradual shift in perception is signalled by the passing of mandatory reporting legislation in most states of the USA during the 1970s. Such legislation requires a large number of people who come into professional contact with children to report suspected sexual abuse to the authorities. There are both civil and criminal sanctions against a failure to do so. There is no similar obligation to report crime in the UK, and agencies to whom child sexual abuse is revealed may for various reasons decide not to do so. The only equivalent is in the various published guidelines for dealing with non-accidental injury, and the internal procedures of voluntary agencies such as the National Society for the Prevention of Cruelty to Children which requires its staff to report. UK registrations of sexual abuse on the 'non-accidental injury register' increased by 126.5 per cent in 1985.[22]

A decision to report suspected abuse sends a child along a confusing legal obstacle course which makes few concessions to the needs of young children. The focus in criminal proceedings is on the offender and not on the child, whose role is purely as witness for the state. In this context, the child's needs will invariably come second to those of the accused.

Investigation

Cases are investigated by the police with varying degrees of involvement by social service agencies, from almost none to a close formal liaison over the interviewing of children and the decision to prosecute. In Sweden and Denmark, statements are taken jointly by a woman police officer and a social worker and video recordings of the interview can be used in court proceedings.[23] It was proposed in Great Britain as long ago as 1925[24] that specially trained women police officers and women police surgeons should be employed to deal with child sexual abuse. Although individual areas may have introduced practice which improves the overall picture, in general police training continues to be patchy, and there is no specific requirement that women staff should be used. A Women Police Surgeon Scheme has been set up in Northumbria in conjunction with the local hospital and Rape Crisis Centre to deal with all cases of sexual assault. In Dublin, a sexual assault unit is run by fifteen women doctors based at a maternity hospital, providing 24-hour cover and forensic reports as well as counselling and support. Proposals put forward by a Scottish Office research study[25] on investigating sexual assault asked the police to prioritise the well-being of the child over other goals, and made practical suggestions such as interviews taking place in pleasant environments, away from police stations, and the importance of not keeping children waiting. They also point to the need for specialist police training in interviewing young children.

In many parts of Australia and the United States, procedures have become more sophisticated, and, for example, sexual assault centres have been set up in hospitals in some areas dealing with all initial reports of child sexual abuse, in co-operation with the police and statutory agencies.

Evidence

Evidence, or rather the lack of it, is a legal problem in many cases, particularly where so-called 'non-violent' abuse has been going on for a considerable time. The decision to prosecute is based in part on the availability of evidence, and problems invariably arise, not so much in establishing the identity of the attacker who may be well known to the child, as in proving the offence 'beyond reasonable doubt'. On a practical level, the police may well, if they wish to proceed, try to elicit a confession from the man instead. In Bexley, South London, experiments are under way whereby the man is confronted by a video recording of the child's statement.[26] Ultimately, the police will be interested in a good disposal rate, and will therefore sift out at this stage those cases they do not think strong enough in evidential terms, or where they feel the child will be unable to withstand a court appearance.

Practical difficulties in obtaining evidence are compounded by a widespread unwillingness to accept the extent of child sexual abuse, and a consequent readiness to believe that children are not telling the truth when they allege that it has taken place. This belief is enshrined in the legal system in the corroboration rules. The evidence of a child 'of tender years' must be corroborated if she is considered too young to take a formal oath, but intelligent enough to justify her evidence being received by the court. The relevant age is not defined. The evidence of an older child, taken on oath, can be accepted without corroboration but, as in all sexual offences, the court must be warned as to the dangers of convicting on the basis of uncorroborated evidence. Corroborative evidence is defined as 'independent testimony which confirms in some material particular not only that the crime has been committed but that the defendant committed it'.[27] Examples are medical evidence, or the evidence given by a third party of the child's distress. Children cannot corroborate each other when both give unsworn evidence. For example, even where a man is accused of abusing a number of children at the same time, all of whom give evidence, the man may still be acquitted. It will be obvious that corroborative evidence is often very hard to come by, and that many prosecutions fail as a result.

Available research contradicts the view that children lie more than adults. It has been found[28] that children are at least as accurate as adult witnesses and that they do not lie in court. Studies[29] have shown that children as young as 3 can give coherent and truthful accounts.

On the strength of such findings, the corroboration rule has been abolished in New South Wales, Australia. The child has to make a declaration 'to tell the truth at all times' and thereafter need not be corroborated, and a corroboration warning is not required. Until recently there appeared to be no sign of a similar move in the United Kingdom, and the most recent UK government report on sexual offences failed to recommend any reforms, although the problems of the corroboration rules have been pointed out to the Home Office since the beginning of this century. It seems that at last, following its own recent research study, the Home Office is considering a relaxation of the rule.[30]

Court proceedings

Many cases which are investigated by the police are subsequently dropped. A study[31] of 250 police reports of cases of child sexual abuse in New York City found that in 31 per cent of cases no arrest was made, and in 44 per cent of cases the proceedings were withdrawn. The most common reasons for not going ahead are lack of evidence, or else a wish to spare the child a court appearance.

More writers have remarked on the detrimental effect of court proceedings than almost any other aspect of child sexual abuse: for example, Susan Forward says, 'The experience of pressing charges and testifying in an incest case can be almost as traumatic to the [survivor] as the incest act itself.'[32] The answer, however, is not to suggest a virtual decriminalisation of child sexual abuse but to improve court proceedings and to challenge those responsible for law enforcement to take account of the child's feelings. The decision to prosecute will seldom, if ever, be the child's, and it is all too easy for an adult to conclude that the anxiety of a court case will outweigh or equal sexual abuse. It is a heavy responsibility to maintain in the face of allegations of abuse that they should not be criminally investigated. To do so is to come close to colluding with child sexual abuse.

Months can elapse before a trial takes place, particularly in the more serious cases and those where the man is pleading not guilty. It should surely be possible for cases involving children to be dealt with more quickly. Court delays often amount to little more than administrative inefficiency or backlog, and should be reduced to an absolute minimum. In Scotland, there is a '110 day rule' in all criminal cases, meaning that the trial must take place by the end of that period.

Whilst waiting for the case to be heard, the child may find herself in continued contact with the alleged abuser who might take the opportunity of persuading or coercing her to retract her complaint. If he has been charged he can be remanded in custody or required to reside elsewhere. He may also be ordered not to approach the child, but if he lives in the same neighbourhood, the child may well have to see him. The courts have no power to remove a man from the household if the case is not going ahead, and the child may well find herself removed instead under childcare legislation. Such a procedure is of dubious benefit to a child who may feel she is being punished instead of the abuser. Every effort should be made to get the alleged offender to leave the home. A child should only be removed where there really is no alternative, for example, if neither her mother nor any other female relative is able and willing to care for her in safe surroundings, or if there are additional concerns, for example, of physical neglect, to be addressed.

In many cases, whether or not a prosecution is likely, the mother will take matters into her own hands either by leaving home with the children or by seeking a divorce and/or court orders in family proceedings to exclude the man from the home and from contact with the children. 'Protective' mothers, unlike 'collusive' mothers, do not receive much attention. There is no comprehensive published research on the actions and reactions of mothers to child sexual abuse. This has not, however, inhibited a great volume of writing,[33] mostly based on clinical opinion, to the effect that the mother is at least as much to blame as the abuser, either by not policing him more effectively, for example, leaving the children in his care while at work or in hospital, or by having an alleged psychological investment in the abuse. Clearly a representative study, to include those cases where the mother acts decisively and independently, is long overdue.

Ultimately, the case which has survived the legal maze will come to court. If the man is pleading not guilty the child will be expected to provide a detailed account of what happened to a room full of strangers.

Courtroom architecture and procedures show scant regard for the interests of children, who are singularly out of place in what can seem to be an all-male club. The child will have difficulty in understanding the language and terminology used, the judge and lawyers are dressed in unfamiliar and archaic garb and the child herself may have to sit in a witness box all on its own and in direct line of vision to the alleged offender. Until the early twentieth century it was quite usual for courts to be cleared of women present while evidence of sexual offences were given,[34] accentuating the child's alienation. Whilst this no longer goes on, women are still usually outnumbered by men in court. There are no provisions to ensure that the child can have a trusted friend or relative sitting with her while she gives evidence. It is easy for lawyers and those familiar with the courts to underestimate the difficulty for a child for whom the only familiar face in court may be that of the accused.

Concessions to the needs of children are presently few. They include the clearing of the public gallery while the child is giving evidence in abuse cases and press restrictions on reporting the identity of complainants.

Most courts do not have proper facilities for children who have to wait outside in smoky, noisy rooms, sometimes with the defendant's family. Separate waiting rooms with toys, supervision and toilet areas should be available for use by child witnesses, and should lead directly into the court area. Courtrooms themselves could easily be made less intimidating and designed in such a way that the defendant was out of sight, and the judge or magistrates less remote. Most serious offences are dealt with by jury trial which limits the extent to which a court can be made smaller, but there is no reason why the main parties should not be placed in close proximity to each other in one small part of the room, perhaps a sunken area, so that the child will at least not have to shout her evidence to be heard. In all cases the court should be designed in such a way that the defendant is out of sight of the child, perhaps behind a screen, two-way glass[35] or on a video link while the child is giving her evidence.

Videotape recordings

It has been suggested that the child's evidence should be videotape-recorded. Use is already being made of such evidence in some courts in the USA and in civil proceedings in the UK.[36] Legislation authorising the use of a live video link is at the time of writing before the British Parliament.[37] The benefit to a child of careful questioning at an early stage in the investigation by someone with special training, in congenial surroundings, is apparent if a recording of that interview is subsequently made available to the court. In some areas initial police interviews are videotaped to save the child from having to repeat her story. It is more difficult to see that the giving of live evidence on video will really constitute much of an improvement. Questions will be put by the lawyers in the same way and presumably the same manner as at present, but with the additional confusion of talking through a television screen instead of in person. In a pre-recorded interview the child's questioner is in the same room as her, but the live video proposal appears to be that everyone apart from the child, and presumably a technician, is in court. This seems suspiciously like solving the problem by getting rid of it. The child is put out of sight, and court procedure and attitudes avoid the challenge of taking on board a child-centred approach. Above all, if the process of cross-examination continues to reflect the belief that the child is a liar or deluded, or that she encouraged or enjoyed the defendant's advances, the use of videotapes is little more than cosmetic. It is a technological way out which fails to address the central issue, the power imbalance between accused and accuser which is reflected so crudely in the nature of cross-examination.

Cross-examination

Cross-examination involves an attempt by the man's lawyers to discredit the child's story as far as possible, by suggesting that it is a fantasy or a fabrication, or that the child's motives are malicious, or that she has a propensity to make such allegations.[38] Although 'consent' to sexual activity is immaterial, since a child under the age of consent is unable to do so in law, cross-examination on sexual history and motives is not infrequent, more so as the child is approaching the age of consent. Such questioning rests on the premise that a girl whose sexual purity may be open to question is less worthy of legal protection. The accused is therefore less to be blamed. It is the morality of 'soiled goods' and originates in a socially constructed definition of female sexuality with reference to which a child, despite her youth, will be judged unless she is either extremely young or has been physically injured during the sexual abuse. As in rape cases, such questioning undercuts the child's own experience of the assault and measures her against a scale of sexual virtue.

In an effort to reduce such questioning, and to make it easier for cases to be brought, in Israel[39] all cases are dealt with by youth examiners who are trained in both criminal investigation and child psychology. The youth examiner takes the child's statement and decides whether or not she should give evidence in court. The youth examiner may give evidence on behalf of a child under 14. In Israeli law evidence given by the youth examiner has to be corroborated as a safeguard to the defendant. Such a system has a good deal to recommend it from the point of view of the child, not least because it implies that only one person will be responsible for her case. It is very confusing for a child when she is greeted by different detectives on each interview, and a new set of faces again in court.

Hearsay

The drawback to the above from the point of view of the English legal system is that it offends against the rule against hearsay. This rule prevents the admission of any evidence which is not first-hand, with few exceptions. It is strictly followed in criminal proceedings, much less so in civil proceedings dealing with the welfare of the child such as wardship proceedings in England and Wales where the hearsay evidence of social workers is commonly admitted. It is tempting to propose that the hearsay rule be generally relaxed to admit some such evidence, with adequate safeguards in criminal proceedings.

With the political will and sufficient funds, it should be quite feasible to make dramatic improvements in the police investigation and court procedure without hindering the defendant's right to a fair trial. There is a lot to be said for the child being present, with suitable adult support, in a sympathetically constructed courtroom with the defendant out of sight, her oral evidence being supplemented by the use of pre-recorded videos where appropriate, and again, in appropriate cases, the admission of the hearsay evidence of social workers and police officers. Lawyers as much as police officers should be trained in questioning child witnesses.

The balance of power

Such innovations can only be of limited benefit as long as entrenched attitudes to child sexual abuse remain untouched. Those professionally involved in dealing with sexual abuse of children are frequently reluctant to examine its wider social implications, or to acknowledge the manifest inequality of power between adult and child on any other than an individual level.

This is sometimes masked by a concern to protect the rights of the defendant in a criminal trial. For example, the use of the pre-recorded video interview, with provision for pre-recorded cross-examination, has been rejected in the UK because it is said to offend against the 'oral hearing' tradition. The implication is that nothing can be changed because it might undercut the defendant's position. Yet the rules can be bent to suit the needs of the state if it chooses. Does not the 'no jury' Diplock Court in use in Northern Ireland offend the tradition of trial by jury? Does not the proposal contained in the same Bill as that for live video links seek to abolish the defendant's 'right' to challenge a juror without cause?[40]

I have no wish to become an ally of repressive measures, far less to interfere with the right of an accused in a child sexual abuse or any other case, to a fair trial. But in fact the defendant in a child sexual abuse case gets much more than a fair trial. He is at an immense advantage, both psychologically and legally, compared to the 'average' defendant because of the nature of the case. Children are habitually used to deferring to adult authority, frequently that of the defendant; they may easily be intimidated into withdrawing their allegations, and they are used to being disbelieved.

Instead of addressing the power imbalance in this unique situation by giving the child some protection or status, the legal system intensifies the odds, already stacked high against the child, by institutionalising prejudice against sexually abused children.

To spell it out, compare a case of, for example, theft with one of rape or incest. In the theft case it will not usually prove fruitful to the defence to argue that the complainant brought the crime upon himself or herself or made it up for reasons of her or his own. Yet this is just the argument that is frequently employed in any sexual offence case. It is intensified where a child is concerned because children are treated as even less credible than adult survivors of sexual assault. The court, when faced with a man accused of theft, has no particular resistance towards finding him guilty, if justified on the evidence. Society takes crimes against property in its stride; it cannot accept the widespread sexual abuse of children. To acknowledge its true extent would be to recognise a fundamental defect in the family system which permits it to go on. So the child, already at a substantial disadvantage in the 'adults only' legal process, has to battle uphill against public and judicial reluctance to accept that sexual abuse may have taken place. Any proposal that the child's position in court proceedings is strengthened, even marginally, so as to put the case of child sexual abuse on a par with other offences, will be strongly resisted, simply because it will be recognised as a challenge to those fundamental assumptions which legitimate the sexual abuse of children in the first place.

One way of strengthening the child's hand is in the use of Child Advocacy programmes. Such programmes arose in the USA out of feminist initiatives and aimed to make the legal system less frightening for children. The child advocate sees a child right through a case, offering her support, counselling and an interpretation of the legal process. The advocate can go with the child on interviews and sit with her at court. She is a bridge between the child's needs and the demands of the legal process. She takes the child's part and aims to redress the power imbalance between the child and the accused. Even the presence of a child advocate has been found to lead to increased numbers of guilty pleas from abusers who recognise that someone is on the child's side, perhaps for the first time. One such programme dealing with incest cases found that in 75 per cent of cases the father pleaded guilty.[41]

Sentencing policy

The accused may, during the period leading up to the trial, have been at liberty. He is reasonably likely to remain at liberty even if found guilty of an offence. In the New York City study,[42] of the thirty-eight men who pleaded guilty to lesser charges, and the fifteen who were found guilty, thirty men or 21 per cent received fines or suspended sentences. The remaining twenty-three men were imprisoned, the majority for less than one year. In Great Britain, in 1982,[43] of 6 600 persons convicted of an indictable sexual offence (one triable in the Crown Court, i.e. a more serious offence), half were dealt with by way of fine, or conditional or absolute discharge. Out of 129 convictions for incest in England and Wales in 1973, nine out of ten offenders were imprisoned where the girl was under 13 and three out of four where the girl was under 16. Only 24 per cent of men convicted of indecent assault where the girl was under 13 and 42 per cent of men convicted of unlawful sexual intercourse where the girl was under 13 were imprisoned in 1982.

Sentencing policy in the British courts posits two main categories:[44] the 'tariff' principle, which is intended to be a deterrent and to indicate society's disapproval of the crime; and the individualised sentence which is said to be 'tailor made' to the needs of the individual offender, with a view to influencing his future behaviour. Such sentences will be applied, for example, in the case of the young offender, or of one who is considered to be in need of psychiatric treatment.

Incest and unlawful sexual intercourse are usually dealt with on the tariff basis and a custodial sentence is generally considered appropriate where the girl is under 13. The sentence will in practice be a good deal shorter than the possible maximum.

However much it may be thought likely that the offender has committed other offences, he can only be sentenced on the basis of those specific instances to which he has pleaded or been found guilty. He is at an advantage if the child is unable to recollect specific dates, or to fulfil the corroboration requirement for each occasion. A study[45] of convicted child-molesters in the USA found that they had been convicted and sentenced for less than half of the total number of offences which they admitted to the researcher.

Mitigation

Any sentence is subject to mitigation or reduction on the basis of personal circumstances and the circumstances of the offence. These are factors which, in the court's view, tend to lessen the guilt of the offender and/or increase the culpability of the complainant. Common mitigating factors are an admission of guilt, extreme youth or age, and absence of physical violence. Other factors are constructed around perceived notions of the causative elements of child sexual abuse. For instance, in incest cases, marital problems will sometimes be a mitigating factor. In one case, a sentence of five years for several acts of sexual intercourse with a 13-year-old daughter was reduced to eighteen months because the man had been 'punished enough' by the resulting breakdown in his marriage.[46] In another case of unlawful sexual intercourse with a teenage girl who became pregnant as a result, the sentence of a man of 32 was reduced from twelve to six months 'because his background speaks so well for him'.[47]

As with sexual offences against adults, the behaviour of even a young child is considered relevant and a sentence may be reduced because her manner was found to be 'seductive'. In one such case the sentence of a man of 62 who had sexual intercourse with two girls aged 13 and 15 was suspended in view of 'the girls' depravity'.[48]

As long as male sexual dominance over women and children is a feature of society, the courts will hardly be in a position to treat the child-molester with dispassion. His offence comes too close to the bone to be criticised too harshly by those other men whose job it is to police, prosecute and sit in judgement upon him. While a minority of offenders, in particular the stranger who abducts and assaults someone else's child, are popularly condemned, the legal response to the majority who are so representative of the so-called normal male population is at best bizarre. Returning to our theft example, a man who robs and steals cannot *per se* be a 'model citizen', yet the courts will often describe the man who abuses his own or his neighbour's children in these terms. The typical child sexual abuser has been described as 'of normal intelligence, a good worker, not involved in other criminal activity'.[49] Faced with such a man, particularly if he is white and his family has a comfortable lifestyle, the courts are unlikely to be severe.[50]

Punishment or treatment?

Although the incest offender may be imprisoned, this is on moral grounds – because he has transgressed 'God's law',[51] rather than because he is dangerous to people. The legal system finds it difficult to accept that someone whose offences take place at home is nevertheless a dangerous criminal. Sarah Nelson explains why: 'The property offender threatens wider sections of the community. Incest aggressors within their own four walls do not.'[52]

Many writers on child sexual abuse agree with the assessment that the abuser is not dangerous and therefore should not be imprisoned. They advocate therapeutic schemes to keep the family together, based upon the premise that it is in the child's interests to maintain her relationship with the abuser, even to the extent of continuing to live with him. Such an idea would be fantastic if it were not so widely held. Whilst it may be the case, all things being equal, that children do better with a father-figure who is present rather than absent, the reality is that all things seldom are equal, and certainly not, one would have thought, where sexual abuse has been taking place. Large numbers of children are brought up in single-parent households without comment. Many men are removed from their families and imprisoned for relatively minor property offences without regard for the possible distress of the wife or child who is left behind. Women who are being battered are encouraged, for the sake of their children if not themselves, to take legal action or to leave home. A parent, mother or father, suspected of physically neglecting or abusing a child runs a risk of having that child taken away.

Yet an apparent exception is being made of child sexual abuse. As Sarah Nelson explains:

> No-one would suggest that muggers and mugged, burglars and burgled, rapists and raped should live in the same house for the next five or ten years . . . Still fewer people suggest that parents proved or suspected of battering their children should be left to continue behaving in this way.[53]

One is driven to the conclusion that the primary goal of such a policy is not protective but ideological, to rebuild the family unit. Such programmes seem not to accept that some things are worse than the collapse of a family structure. They also do not accept that the breach of trust may be so absolute that, as far as the child is concerned, the family may never be safe again. Of course, those who advocate such programmes base them upon a belief that once you have a properly reconstructed family, child sexual abuse will no longer be a problem. In fact one could as well say that the problems are only just beginning.

Treatment programmes are formulated upon a given perception of the offender, in particular his ability and willingness not to reoffend. Although research data is available, unfortunately its conclusions are sometimes contradictory and confusing. Further, if we are to believe that only a minority of abusers are ever caught, the research findings, based inevitably upon that minority, may or may not be representative of child abusers as a whole.

Research does not bear out the conclusion that all sex offenders are mentally ill.[54] It would seem that they represent a cross-section of society as a whole, some of whom will betray symptoms of mental disorder and many of whom will not. However, the effect of labelling them as sick tends in practice to shift the emphasis away from criminal proceedings to psychiatric treatment. The danger in this arises if the needs of the offender (for treatment) are set against the needs of the child (for protection), i.e. that they are both 'victims'.

There is conflicting evidence suggesting both that sex offenders are, and that they are not, prone to reoffend. Gebhard, in 1965, found that 40 per cent of convicted child-molesters studied had at least one prior sexual offence conviction, 20 per cent more than one.[55] Dreiblatt says, 'There is little question that the strongest predicator of future sexual offences is past sexual offences.'[56] However, the nature of child sexual abuse, and the unlikelihood of its ever being reported in the first place, let alone a second time, make accurate research very difficult.

A number of treatment programmes have been set up in the USA specifically to deal with child-molesters and to provide an alternative, and in some cases an adjunct, to imprisonment. For example, the Incest Diversion Programme at El Paso, Colorado,[57] will treat first-time 'non-violent' offenders who plead guilty and agree to undergo a two-year treatment programme. Criminal charges will be pursued if the offender fails to complete the programme. He must volunteer freely to undertake the programme and be free of mental illness. This programme, in common with many others, is designed primarily for incest or incest-type offenders, and treats incest as 'a symptom of serious family problems'. One of the earliest programmes is the Child Sexual Abuse Treatment programme at Santa Clara County, San José, California,[58] which co-operates with law enforcement agencies who agree not to pursue charges if the offender undertakes treatment and admits his guilt.

Initial claims that there was virtually no recidivism have been found to be over-optimistic, and a number of recent surveys conducted over periods of five and ten years have found virtually identical rates of re-offending in both treated and untreated groups of offenders.[59] According to Dreiblatt and others, statements by sex offenders about future behaviour (such as reoffending) cannot be viewed as reliable, and it is easy to be misled by their law-abiding and co-operative stance.

The view that the sex offender is to some extent inadequate and driven to sexual abuse by outside forces has less threatening implications for male sexuality and control than the view that the abuser knows what he is doing, and believes that he is entitled to do it. In the latter model, the offender is likely to resent outside interference with his perceived right to treat his own as he wishes. The offender therefore must be prevented from doing what he wants, whether by imprisonment, removal from the home, or directive treatment based, for example, upon a model of addiction therapy. This model is followed at the Harborview Sexual Assault

Centre, Seattle,[60] which works on the premise that while the offender's behaviour can be modified and checked, his basic inclinations cannot, i.e. that there is no cure but 'a relative mastery of a serious behavioural problem'.

Ultimately, one must ask oneself, 'How do these initiatives protect the child?' In most cases, they do not eliminate the need for a distressing investigation of the alleged offence, as all treatment programmes make it clear that they are only effective when backed up by the sanction of the courts. Clearly, the child who has been abused is already in a terrible situation, and there is no perfect way of dealing with abuse which does not risk either revictimising the child, or leaving her vulnerable to further abuse. It is a case of weighing up relative risks. Those who run treatment programmes are not prepared to risk the child's distress if her father goes to prison, but are prepared to risk permitting him to return to the household and to continue the abuse, all in the interests of 'keeping the family together'. Others, including those mothers who do not wish to take the man back, obviously run the risk that the child might feel responsible for his removal.

Those who argue that prison does the child-molester no good may well be right. Prison may not help any offender much, but it at least has the merit of expressing social disapproval, and of putting the man out of children's way, at least for a time. Many, perhaps rightly, question the entire prison system, and wish to work towards alternative rehabilitative methods of dealing with all offenders. There is a danger in singling out child-molesters in a call for a reduction, or the elimination, of custodial sentences. Within present sentencing policy, the length of the potential sentence represents society's condemnation of an offence. To reduce such sentences is to make a social statement, whether intended or not, that the sexual abuse of children has become more tolerated in our society, or is less than criminal behaviour. It is surely risky to do anything which might reduce even further the deterrent value of the criminal sanction.

Some argue, however, that one of the reasons why mothers and children may be reluctant to report is their fear that a lengthy sentence of imprisonment will result. As we have seen, such a fear, if it exists, is usually misplaced. Even if maximum sentences were to be reduced or imprisonment to be less widely used, would this change in policy filter downwards to the abused child? The only information a child is likely to receive about sexual abuse is that supplied by her abuser. He will continue to use the threat of imprisonment to buy the child's silence. On the other hand, the call of the mass media and reactionary elements for increased sentences is largely irrelevant and diverts attention from the real issues involved in protecting the child and detecting the crime.

Conclusion

Child sexual abuse can only be effectively challenged within the context of developing a critical analysis of the socialisation of sexuality and the structure of the family. At the same time, practical efforts must be concentrated on prevention, detection and on working towards a more sympathetic investigative and judicial process which reflects the needs of the child.

Notes and references

1. For incidence studies see, for example, David Finkelhor, *Sexually Victimised Children* (New York: Free Press, 1979) and Diana Russell, *Sexual Exploitation: Rape, Child Sexual Abuse and Workplace Harassment* (Beverly Hills, CA: Sage, 1984). For an overview and tabular analysis of various surveys see Judith Herman, *Father–Daughter Incest* (Cambridge, Mass.: Harvard University Press, 1981).
2. Diana Russell, *Sexual Exploitation*.
3. Quoted by Judith Herman, *Father–Daughter Incest*.
4. Ibid.
5. Diana Russell, *Sexual Exploitation*.
6. HMSO *Criminal Statistics*, 1985.
7. HMSO *Statistical Bulletin*, quoted in *Unlawful Sex*, the Report of the Howard League Working Party, Waterlow Legal and Social Policy Library, 1985.
8. Florence Rush, *The Best Kept Secret: The Sexual Abuse of Children* (Englewood Cliffs, NJ: Prentice Hall, 1980).
9. See Chapter 6, note 4.
10. See Susan Forward and Craig Buck, *Betrayal of Innocence* (Harmondsworth: Penguin, 1978).
11. Sarah Nelson, *Incest: Fact and Myth* (Edinburgh: Stramullion, 1982).
12. For an account of the criminal law in England and Wales see, for example, Glanville Williams, *Textbook of Criminal Law* (London: Stevens, 1983). For a critique and historical analysis, see Anna

Clarke, *Women's Silence, Men's Violence: Sexual Abuse in England, 1770–1845* (London: Pandora Press, 1987); Susan Edwards, *Female Sexuality and the Law* (Edinburgh: Martin Robertson, 1981).

13. For an account of the campaign, see Sheila Jeffreys, *The Spinster and her Enemies* (London: Pandora Press, 1985).
14. Diana Russell, *Sexual Exploitation*.
15. Criminal Law Revision Committee, 15th Report, Cmnd 9213, 1984.
16. For a detailed breakdown of incest legislation in the USA, see 'The Incest Statutes' by Leigh Bienen in Judith Herman, *Father–Daughter Incest*.
17. Nicholas Harrison, 'Child Sexual Assault', *Law Society Journal* (Australia), April 1986. Harrison described the recent legislative reforms in New South Wales in child sexual abuse cases.
18. Howard League, *Unlawful Sex*.
19. Sexual Offences Act 1985 S5(4).
20. See, for example, Kempe and Kempe, *Child Abuse* (London: Fontana, 1978); they argue in relation to incest that 'it can be overcome by many girls, but it is ruinous for boys'.
21. Melvin J. Guyer, 'Child Abuse and Neglect Statutes', *American Journal of Orthopsychiatry*, January 1982.
22. *Family Law*, vol. 17, April 1987.
23. Howard League, *Unlawful Sex*.
24. *Report of the Departmental Committee on Sexual Offences on Young Persons*, Cmnd 2561, 1925. This report, written at the very end of the last 'wave' of concern about child sexual abuse, gives a fascinating historical perspective to a discussion on legal reforms.
25. Gerry Chambers and Ann Millar, *Investigating Sexual Assault: A Scottish Office Research Social Study* (London: HMSO, 1983).
26. Described in Eileen Vizard, 'Interviewing Child Victims of Sexual Abuse', *Family Law*, January 1987.
27. *R v. Baskerville*, 1916.
28. Research of Elaine Goodman in USA referred to in Standing Committee on the Sexual Abuse of Children Newsletter, November 1986.
29. Research of Dr Graham Davies, Aberdeen, quoted in *The Independent*, 5 December 1986.
30. Reported in *The Guardian*, 2 May 1987.
31. Vincent de Francis, *Protecting the Child Victim of Sex Crimes Committed by Adults* (American Humane Association, 1968).
32. Forward and Buck, *Betrayal of Innocence*.
33. For example, Susan Forward, ibid; Blair Justice and Rita Justice, *The Broken Taboo* (New York: Human Sciences Press, 1979). For a critique of this position see Kevin McIntyre, 'The Role of Mothers in Father–Daughter Incest: A Feminist Analysis', *Social Work*, November 1981; Elizabeth Ward, *Father–Daughter Rape* (London: Women's Press, 1984).
34. Cmnd 2561, *Report of the Departmental Committee on Sexual Offences on Young Persons*.

35. Proposed by Libai in 'The Protection of the Child Victim of a Sexual Offence in the Criminal Justice System', *The Sexual Victimology of Youth*, ed. L. G. Schultz.
36. For a recent account of the development of the use of pre-recorded videotapes in wardship proceedings, and the evidential problems which have been encountered, see Gillian Douglas and Christine Wilmore, 'Diagnostic Interviews as Evidence in Cases of Child Sexual Abuse', *Family Law*, May 1987.
37. The Criminal Justice Bill 1987.
38. Trevor Nyman, *Australian Law Society Journal*, April 1986.
39. Libai, 'The Protection of the Child Victim of a Sexual Offence in the Criminal Justice System'.
40. See note 37 above.
41. Harborview Sexual Assault Center, Seattle, described by Judith Herman, *Father–Daughter Incest*.
42. de Francis, *Protecting the Child Victim of Sex Crimes Committed by Adults*.
43. HM Government, quoted by Howard League, *Unlawful Sex*.
44. For a text on sentencing practice, see D. A. Thomas, *Principles of Sentencing*, Cambridge Studies in Criminology (Heinemann, 1979).
45. Nicholas Groth, 1982, quoted in *Unlawful Sex*.
46. *Carter*, 1975, in D. A. Thomas, *Principles of Sentencing*.
47. *Shuck*, 9–2–76, in D. A. Thomas, ibid.
48. *Doman*, 28–2–75, in D. A. Thomas, ibid.
49. Kaljner, quoted in Lena Dominelli, 'Father–Daughter Incest', *Critical Social Policy*, vol. 16, summer 1986.
50. Russell found a 100 per cent conviction rate for Latino and 30 per cent for Black offenders tried, compared to 13 per cent white offenders in those cases which were reported. Although a very small sample, she says, 'It nevertheless seems clear that the perpetrator's race/ethnicity is a major determinant of who is convicted of child sexual abuse. It is also clear how extremely unrepresentative incarcerated sexual offenders are of sexual offenders generally in terms of race/ethnicity.'
51. Susan Forward, *Betrayal of Innocence*.
52. Sarah Nelson, *Incest: Fact and Myth*.
53. Ibid.
54. See David Finkelhor, *Sexually Victimised Children*; Diana Russell, *Sexual Exploitation*; Gebhard (1965), quoted by Howard League, *Unlawful Sex*.
55. Quoted in MacNamara and Sagani, *Sex Crime and the Law* (Free Press, 1977).
56. Irwin S. Dreiblatt, 'Issues in the Evaluation of the Sex Offender', presentation at Washington State Psychological Association Meeting, May 1982.
57. Described by Jean Renvoize, *Incest: A Family Pattern* (Routledge and Kegan Paul, 1982).
58. See Henry Giarretto, 'A Comprehensive Child Sexual Abuse Treatment Program', *Child Abuse and Neglect*, vol. 6, 1982, for more detail.

59. Mayer and Romero, 1982, Hall, 1983, both in David Finkelhor, *A Sourcebook of Child Sexual Abuse* (Beverly Hills, CA: Sage, 1985).
60. Described by Judith Herman, David Finkelhor.

5

Racism and anti-Semitism

AUDREY DROISEN

> For those of us
> who were imprinted with fear
> like a faint line in the center of our foreheads
> learning to be afraid with our mother's milk
> for by this weapon
> this illusion of some safety to be found
> the heavy-footed hoped to silence us
> for all of us
> this instant and this triumph
> we were never meant to survive
>
> Audre Lorde, *Litany for survival*

Spend your time immediately in learning the English language and its correct pronunciation.
Do not talk in a loud voice.
Do not criticise any government regulation or the way things are done over here.
Do not make yourself conspicuous by your manner or dress.
Do not join any political organisation or take part in any political activities.

> German Jewish Aid Committee in conjunction with the Jewish Board of Deputies, *Helpful Information and Guidance for Every Refugee*

Sexual abuse is not worse for Black and/or Jewish children but the

158

pressures and prejudices of racism and anti-Semitism compound the abuse, thereby making it more difficult to ask for assistance or to get appropriate and sympathetic help from the police or the caring professions.

Racism and anti-Semitism are systems of oppression with very different histories and present-day modes of operation. Both can be defined, however, as the prejudiced belief of the majority (or the ruling group in such places as South Africa) in their own superiority and the backing up of this prejudice with power.[1]

The prime condition for the maintenance of a status quo of inequality, formal or informal, is the unequal distribution of power – political, economic or military. Two major psychological correlates of this distribution of resources help to ensure the maintenance of its stability: the perception of the system of inequalities as being *stable* or *legitimate* or both simultaneously.[2]

Historical background

Briefly, racism as an ideology and an institution developed out of imperialism. Westerners needed to see the African and Asian people as inferior and even subhuman, in order to rationalise slavery and colonialism. Black people who live in the western white world today continue to be seen through this myth and continue to be exploited and discriminated against socially, politically and economically.

The development of anti-Semitism as a theory is a consequence of Christianity. Engaged in an early struggle with the Synagogue for converts in the Hellenistic world, the Church took to equating Jewry with a satanic influence trying to take over the world and to stressing a doctrine which indentified Jews as Christ-killers.[3] Today, in this secularised western world, the devil is no longer trying to rule the world through the Jews. But Jews themselves are seen as trying to rule the world through a capitalist-communist conspiracy that controls money and the media.

Stereotyping

So both Black people and Jews are stereotyped by the majority as having certain distinct unpleasant characteristics which are directly attributable to their Blackness and/or Jewishness. By defining ethnic minorities as being inferior, those individuals who belong to the dominant group are collectively able to legitimate their superior position and individually able to project their conflicts, fears and anger on to those in a weaker position.

Racism and anti-Semitism are not a product of human beings' 'natural fear of the unknown'. We have only to look to the many examples from history of white men being originally greeted with hospitality by the indigenous population of the Americas and Asia, to disprove this theory. Rather these prejudices are products of certain conditions in history and continue because they justify the present balance of power and continue to be pumped into each generation.

> There was a denial of the most terrible thing the Germans did to us, namely that many of us identified with the oppressor in the ways that we accepted the picture of the *Untermensch* the Nazis were painting of us. Of course, we wanted to survive, but we weren't at all sure we had the right to survive. We weren't sure that they were wrong about us.[4]

So the messages of racism and anti-Semitism fill our minds, seeping down to unconscious levels until they become a part, more or less, of everyone's vision of themselves and others. Children need to learn in order to survive and to grow. They are taught the ABCs of racism and anti-Semitism. Black and/or Jewish children are taught that they are inferior, guilty of some quality that makes them unworthy and somehow dirty.

Echoes of abuse

These are exactly the messages that children receive when being sexually abused. It's as if society is echoing the voice of the abuser: 'There's something wrong with you, not me', 'You don't deserve anything better', 'This is what life is all about, so you have to accept it', 'You're the cause of your own misfortune', 'You're dirty'. With this doubling of negative messages, the child feels that s/he doesn't have any rights, and is even more unable to demand recognition as a human being. To fight abuse you have to be sure that you're worth defending, that you have certain basic rights. How can you be sure when everyone seems to be saying that there is something wrong about you, that what is happening to you is somehow part of the scheme of things?

In the end it can become impossible to unravel whether your feelings of unworthiness are due to the abuse or the racism or anti-Semitism. They merge and intensify each other. For survival, they need to be unravelled.

Being an outsider

For to be Black and/or Jewish in the West is to always be treated as a guest in your own country, to live on the periphery, to be an outsider. But being an outsider in society at large means that you are, at least, an insider in your own community. There is one place where you belong. You might not have the same ideas as everyone else in your community but every thing is familiar. You know the rules, the language, the humour, the music, the food. You share the bond of the same oppression. The 'they' and 'us' are reversed. You're not in fear of your life (unless you're being physically or sexually abused). What 'they' take for granted is something special but necessary for you or any human being to survive – a safe place.

The continuous and daily interactions with the outside world, and the consequent *psychological* participation of a group in the system of values and the network of stereotypes of the society at large create a degree of acceptance by the minority of its deleterious image; at the same time, *some* measure of protection is offered by the social and cultural links surviving within the group.[5]

Needing a community to feel safe and validated in, it is vital that a child separates her or his feelings about sexual abuse from feelings about being Black and/or Jewish. By absorbing the negative stereotypes from outside, it is understandable that a child may connect the 'wrongness' of the abuse with the 'wrongness' of her/his people.

She had been in England over four years and always she had seen it and now, at the reception centre, she was forced to live with it. 'All them white people trying so hard to hide their hate', she thought sadly. 'Yet they could kill you because you are so different from them.' She always had to remind herself that they had not hurt her yet. Of course, they let her know she was not wanted, did not belong, but at least they were not violent like black people.[6]

Of course, white people are just as violent, but no white child would make that connection between their 'race' and violence or abuse, because being white and christian is the norm. A man and his family are not *seen* to be what they are *because* they are white and christian.

So if a white man abuses his child, the situation is looked at in terms of his individual problem. But if a Black man abuses a child, racist stereotyping will point the finger at Black Culture.

If a white child is removed from his or her family because of sexual abuse, that child can attempt to start life again somewhere else. The culture of that 'somewhere else' will be very similar to what they left behind, but that wouldn't be noticed. The culture itself wouldn't 'trigger' past unpleasant memories of abuse.

But if a child is part of a despised community, that community is like an oasis in the desert. Its sights, sounds and aromas make it unique and therefore identifiable to the child and everyone else. If that culture is associated through memory or through internalised oppression with abuse, and cannot be separated out, then every time the child touches that safe place, pain will be felt. There will be no safe places.

It is through the family that ethnic minority children are part of their communities. If a child is removed from the family, that access is denied. So even when children do not associate their abuse with their communities, they still lose the support of those communities.

They may also be alienated from their mothers. There is a great deal of confusion about why children who are being sexually abused do not tell their mothers. Fear, guilt and need to protect the family and mother are all part of the picture. But in addition, Black and/or Jewish children may be further distanced from their mothers by specific racist and anti-Semitic stereotypes such as the 'black mama', 'Jewish mother' and 'docile Asian women'. The love, strength and courage these women have shown should be applauded. But instead they are defined as animal-like, vulgar and dumb.

It is very likely that children will pick up these negative attitudes that the legal authorities and people from the helping professions may have towards their mother, and feel even more alone and confused. The mother is probably the most important person who can help the child, but if she is not believed, not supported or is viewed as an unhelpful influence, then that help may be lost.

Even if the child has not been directly discriminated against by a teacher, social worker or police concerned, children have learned that prejudice exists. How can they be sure, therefore, in what light their abuse will be seen.

'Are you sure that is all there is to it?' The teacher's kindness reached out to her, begged to be confided in. Miss Maxwell was one of the few teachers who had always been nice to her, and she felt the words burning on her tongue. She had to bite down hard, fingers clenched, to prevent the truth being trapped with someone; but suddenly her father's words came to her – 'You think you get bad treatment here?' he often asked, 'Well let me tell you, if you run go tell the white teacher them going to take you away'. She had felt her heart leap with hope for the first time she heard this until he explained, 'They don't like neaga in this country. All them white people smiling up them face with them plastic smile, and then when you trust them, them kill you'. She looked at the woman warily, fancying that she was looking at her with hatred, plotting her death. She felt sick with fear, trapped, sandwiched between the hate and spite of the white world and the dark dingy evil that was the house of her father.[7]

Protecting the community

Many children do not tell anyone about their abuse because they feel responsible for holding their families together. They think that if their mother or anyone else knew, their families would be torn apart and so everyone else would be hurt. If they keep quiet, only they are being hurt. So they take on the burden of keeping the family together by sacrificing themselves. Because they are not sure if they have any rights, to assert them might be selfish. Abuse is better than guilt.

So too children protect their communities. They don't want to add fuel to the fire or prejudice. They don't want to be disloyal.

Children are taught not to tell family secrets in public. How much more do they feel this pressure when they know their communities are despised and they are telling someone who belongs to the group which is doing that despising. The doubled division of loyalties becomes too confusing; too traumatic for a child to bear.

In a very real sense a woman of colour abused and raped by a black male inherits the complex contradictions of loyalties, and social pressure to repress her anger, such as an incest survivor inherits. The conjunction of white racism and black male violence to women has helped ensure that horrid legacy for women of colour. And she owes neither of them, either white oppressor or black male violator, a jot of thanks for it.[8]

Children from ethnic minorities also can assume that their sexual abuse will not be taken as seriously. If they are treated as if they don't matter, then why should their abuse matter? As Edgar Hoover, former and long-term head of the FBI said, 'Some niggah bitch gets herself raped.' If they could be sold and murdered, why not raped.

The words 'pure' and 'innocent' are rarely associated with Blacks and/or Jews. Closer to nature, insatiable, rapists, more sensual – these are the words associated with ethnic minorities who have been labelled by the majority. Just as the abuser projects his sexuality on to the child and blames her/him for his desires, so too do whites and christians project their sexuality on to Blacks and Jews and accuse them of being over sexed. Since children can feel that their report of incest will confirm this racial stereotyping can they be so disloyal to their own people and play into the hands of racists and anti-Semites?

Protecting the child

So how do we help these children to tell, feel supported, survive and become strong again? Given that most people in authority are white and christian, is there any hope for them?

Some years ago I went to a meeting of radical health visitors who were discussing child sexual abuse. One of the health visitors said that she was working with a Nigerian family whose 2 year-old daughter had gonnorrhoea. She described how the girl's parents had told her that the child had been assaulted by a man in Nigeria, but was now safe with them in London. The health visitor said that as a white English woman she felt very uneasy about intruding into these people's home, and basically she had just accepted their explanation and was letting them alone. She didn't feel as a white woman that she could do anything more. Not one other health visitor in that room (they were all white) questioned her response or actions. I assume that not one of them would have treated a white family in the same way.

Who was protecting that child? This was a group of women, most of whom would have been at least sympathetic to feminism and aware of the problem of male sexual violence. But from a misguided idea of what not being a racist is all about, they were not willing to confront a Black man's possible sexual violence on his 2 year old child.

A white woman's challenging of racism must surely be based on her own sense of honour and awareness that racism must be fought because it is an odious evil in itself. And not an evil either she, or women of colour, can combat by being prepared to overlook or collude with the evil of rape *by, or of, any*.

Racism and rape do not unfortunately cancel each other out. (Both are so prevalent did they do so, we would have long been rid of both.) But the two evils cannot be traded off against each other. Although patriarchy has done this.

As women we must try to cut through that knot. For it strangles . . . Neither Black, nor white males, should have their male violence, inclusive of rape and violence against women, protected by white women, or women of colour.

It is an unholy protection of unholy acts and women should *quit* doing it.[9]

Allowing Black and/or Jewish men to violate their children is not showing awareness of racism or anti-Semitism. Rather, it is an example of inverted prejudice. It shows an inability to confront and work through uncomfortable feelings, but those uncomfortable feelings are part of the problem, part of the fear, part of seeing minority groups as the 'other'.

That doesn't mean that people in authority shouldn't be aware of the power and privilege they have in society over the people they are dealing with and that there aren't different ethnic experiences and expectations. Being aware of privileges means not abusing them and understanding the confidence and position that they have given you as compared to other people. (It doesn't mean thinking that a man has been so oppressed as compared to you that he couldn't help abusing a child.) It means being empathetic and open enough to see reality from another point of view and to see this as an opening up of one's horizons rather than threatening or condemning of one's own point of view.

It is also being aware of what are genuine different cultural norms and what are individual injustices that happen in all cultures. So people expressing themselves loudly are only loud as compared to a more repressed culture. But men abusing their families are not merely part of a so-called more patriarchal society, rather they are abusive personalities and need to be stopped. We must assume certain basic needs and rights for all children and all women.

Training

The other side of all this, of course, is acknowledging the pervasiveness of racism and anti-Semitism and trying to minimise its effects. This means that educational institutions must train their students, who will later become social workers, lawyers, police, probation officers and so on, to be aware of their prejudices and the need to eradicate them.

There are many different types of training and all students should go through all of them as a matter of their course requirements. First, there is a training for self-awareness in which students learn about socialisation and the cultural basis of their behaviour. They become aware that how they think and feel is not any more natural than people of another cultural upbringing. They become aware in fact that they belong to an ethnic group as much as anyone else. Also, within this perspective, prejudices can be sen to have been learned just as are table manners.

Then students need to learn about other cultures: their customs, foods, music, and so on. It means enriching a limited way of understanding the world.

Cognitive training in which students learn facts about other cultures is also necessary. Historical and socio-economic factors are vital in understanding other people's position, expectations, philosophies. For example, it is important for white British people to know that Asians from East Africa came to Britain with British passports and therefore didn't expect to be treated as aliens.

The oppressed have learned to identify with the oppressor through the positive and powerful representations of him everywhere. But this process does not work the other way round.

The more she saw other girls dressed up, the more she envied them and wished she had been anything but black. They could never understand what it was like, how much she hated her brittle hair, the thickness of her lips. How could they understand what it was to be born like her? she often thought in bitterness.[10]

I hated my parents for being Jews and thereby making me Jewish.[11]

What is white and christian in this society has been constructed, by those who had the power to enforce their own image, as being the measure of beauty and value. It is obvious who benefits from this.

Blacks and Jews have had painstakingly to develop a sense of their own beauty, and whites and christians must learn from this. To see other peoples' beauty, to feel like them or to want to be like them at times, to feel their side is one's own, is the moment of breakthrough. Identification is an essential bridge.

No professional who has not seriously and actively worked on his or her racism and anti-Semitism in this way should attempt to work with Black and Jewish children. The assumption that it is not necessary demonstrates the problem.

So far anti-racist training has been discussed in terms of set courses. But real change can't happen by putting a week or two extra into an existing syllabus. An anti-racist perspective must be consciously integrated into every course because it should affect every aspect of a person's work as long as that person is dealing with other people. It must never be seen as an afterthought. It needs to be an assumed mode of operation.

Conclusion

But training students will never be enough. No matter how well the course is structured and the students are eager and become aware professionals, prejudice will continue to exist for a long time. The divide will continue and empathy does have its limits.

So it is vital that minority groups from the local community are involved in the working of social services, schools, the police force, and so on. They should be advising, monitoring and, when feasible, involved in case studies.

Given the fact that most authorities are mainly white and christian, these things need to be done as a matter of course. Only in this way can these bodies be truly representative of the interests of all people. Why should it be resisted if service is the priority? Wouldn't this 'open door' policy facilitate the trust of ethnic minority groups in the community?

In working with sexually abused children from the ethnic minorities, trust is crucial. It would, therefore, be preferable for these children to be able to talk to adults from their own background, as this would greatly alleviate their fears of individual prejudice on the part of the professional and fears of betraying their own community. When this is not possible then ethnic minority paraprofessionals should be sought to facilitate communication and understanding.

With the expectation that this will often not happen, I make a plea that the special position of Black and/or Jewish children should be recognised. This means understanding the particular obstacles these children have faced and are still dealing with.

It means helping the child to unravel racial abuse from sexual abuse, even though the messages echo each other. It includes making sure the child understands that sexual abuse happens in all cultures. If children are removed from home, they should have regular positive contact with their own community. If they are put into a foster home, every attempt should be made for their foster parents to be from the same background as they are. If they aren't, then again, contact with their own community is essential.

But it would be impossible and foolish to go on and try to outline a complete set of guidelines. Each case is individual and there are no easy formulas. What this chapter has tried to do is to give some insight and some direction. It grew out of a number of discussions with Black and Jewish incest survivors and reflects a number of perspectives.

These discussions also highlighted the need for a 'safe place' for adult Black and/or Jewish survivors.

There had to be a way of easing this pain, or at least starting to deal with it, but how? Sure I knew about the 'Incest Survivors' Group', and groups like 'Rape Crisis' and 'Lesbian Line', but there was the whole thing about how white these groups were, and the risk of exposing myself, making myself vulnerable to the racist assumptions about Black families.[12]

Autonomous Black groups have developed in many Western countries and there is now a Black Incest Survivors' network in Britain. This coming together has not just been important in terms of self-help but as a campaigning strategy to raise the consciousness of agencies working with Black children who have been abused. This is the kind of group that needs to be supported. After all, they are the experts.

Notes and references

1. T. Hall, 'Teaching About the Awareness of Prejudice', *Minority Rights Group*, Report no. 59, 1985, pp. 12–13.
2. H. Taifel, 'The Social Psychology of Minorities', *Minority Rights Group*, no. 38, 1978, pp. 3–20.
3. S. Cohen, *That's Funny, You Don't Look Anti-Semitic,* (Leeds: Pale Collective, 1984) p. 11.
4. The Jewish Women's History Group, *You'd Prefer Me Not to Mention It . . .* ,(London: The Jewish Women's History Group, 1982) p. 29.
5. Taifel, op. cit., p. 13.
6. J. Riley, *The Unbelonging,* (London: The Women's Press, 1985) p. 69.
7. Ibid., p. 51.
8. A. Hearne, 'Racism Rape & Riots', *Trouble and Strife,* no. 9, 1986, pp. 9–14
9. Ibid., p. 12.
10. Riley, op. cit., p. 78.
11. The Jewish Women's History, op. cit., p. 47.
12. Kris, 'Another Kind of Coming Out', *Gossip*, No. 2 (1986) pp. 80–89.

6

Positive action

EMILY DRIVER

Given all the obstacles to acknowledging, detecting, stopping and preventing child sexual abuse, how can we develop our awareness and skills in order to work positively and effectively against it? This book has attempted to suggest some strategies. So far we have considered child sexual abuse as a social problem, caused by individuals who exploit positions of power and access to those weaker than themselves; we have also examined how the power of individual child-molesters is underpinned by the general imbalance of power between the sexes, and how the institutionalisation of power in general may condone or even encourage child sexual abuse. The problem is clearly vast and leaves many of us with a feeling of hopelessness. This chapter therefore seeks to encourage some recognition of our own powers in combating the sexual abuse of children.

Political power

This first power lies in the historic impetus afforded by the women's liberation movement. Child sexual assault is not a new issue for women. It has long been associated by them with other forms of sexual violence. From the 1870s, female activists petitioned the British Parliament against sexual abuse of girls. Child prositution was rife and the public was quick to respond to feminist information campaigns, as a result of which the age of heterosexual female consent was raised from 13 to 16 in 1885. But public understanding of the extent of child sexual assault, then as now, fell far below women's ideals. People were happy to be outraged at assaults committed by strangers – for these were no challenge to their sense of social structure and family coherence. To this day, outrage at assault by 'outsiders' can mask class hate, race hate and homophobia. An example is the reaction to the rape of a boy in Brighton in 1983, described ironically by Katharine Whitehorne:

> We all tend to shy away [from incestuous assault] and think about something more cheerful – like getting angry with those rotten Huns who came over here and attacked one of our boys . . . There's an unpleasant element of queer-bashing in the howls of outrage – with little girls, it's only when they actually get killed that there is normally this sort of fuss.[1]

Nineteenth-century women campaigned, in the face of reactionary state strategy and without the benefit of a vote of their own, to have sexual abuse within the family declared a criminal offence. In 1908, the incest laws of England and Wales were duly passed. These, as the Lord Chief Justice of the time declared, were long overdue considering 'the frequency of assaults by fathers on their daughters'.[2] One could not have had a clearer statement from a more prominent public figure to the effect that incest in Britain, then as now, was *known* to be widespread. And yet such witness has been lost to us.

The Women's Freedom League was a suffragette organisation active in the movement for Votes for Women. This league was also involved in the campaign against rape. A column in their weekly paper included regular bulletins from women who monitored court cases, and compared the very low sentences pass on child-molesters with the much higher sentences dealt out to people who committed property crimes. For example, one offender at that time got three months' hard labour for sexually asaulting two girls aged eight and nine, whereas someone who stole four coats received a sentence of twelve months' hard labour. On monitoring court cases in London, women's groups have found that similar comparisons can be made today. In November 1985 at one London magistrate's court, a white man who had molested and raped his three Black step-children was kept on unconditional bail until trial, where he was pronounced guilty of indecent assault against the eldest and released on a year's probation. The next defendant, a young Black man who had stolen a £10 bottle of brandy from an off-licence, received six months' imprisonment. Finally, another defendant was imprisoned for car theft. The magistrate stated of this last sentence, 'My concern is further offences. I am not going to put the public at risk.'

One magistrate, reported by the Women's Freedom League, had said in mitigation of a man who had sexually assaulted a 3-year-old: '[such crimes] are committed by the very best-conducted men, just one of those things that the very best in all walks of life are apt to commit in some unguarded moment.'[3] Compare Judge Brian Gibbens in December 1983, on the man who had committed rape (in legal jargon, 'unlawful sexual intercourse') against a 7-year-old girl: 'No force was used . . . It is one of the accidents that can happen in life, although of a different kind, and could almost happen to anyone . . . I felt compassion . . . This was a momentary lapse.'[4] The rapist got a sentence of two year's imprisonment. As one suffragette put it early this century: 'Men say, in reference to lenient sentences, that magistrates are only human. It's our complaint, not that magistrates are only human, but that magistrates are only men'.[5] And, as the women's movement might put it today: What's new?

Discredit of women and children in the courts may be slow to change, but ordinary women have moved fast. In the 1970s Rape Crisis Centres were established in many countries, and began to receive calls from or about sexually assaulted children. In the 1980s we have witnessed the burgeoning throughout the world of networks of self-help groups for adult women who are survivors of child sexual assault and aim to use the insights and skills gained from the assault in order to help others. These groups perform a variety of functions, from running girls' refuges to founding drop-in centres or holding preventive workshops for children and developing professional training and policy.

The incest secret is a magic circle imposed by the abuser on each child, preventing any deep or honest contact between herself and her peers, friends, family members, and society at large. In refusing to tell another person's lies, each incest survivor who shares her experience with others finds that she has stepped outside the circle, and is free to question not merely the abuse of herself as an individual, but also the societal institutions which cause child sexual abuse, allow it to flourish, and reinforce its oppression on the survivor. When incest survivors break that circle, we begin to wield a great political power which has for centuries lain dormant.

Emotional power

Our second power is our forgotten ability to empathise with the child, to study the options that children have and to try to learn from the ways in which they themselves deploy those options. In taking the child's eye view on sexual abuse, we have to unlearn many of our adult assumptions about the phenomenon. We are prone to interpreting positive strengths as negative weaknesses. We communicate this interpretation to the child and thereby undermine her[6] confidence even further. Her deterioration then confirms our interpretation, and so we help to set up a self-fulfilling prophecy of destruction and despair. Let us look at two popular adult misconceptions of the dynamics of sexual abuse as illustrations to this proposition. They are that children rarely resist it and that they rarely tell people about it.

Children's resistance to sexual abuse

Resistance, admittedly, is hardly ever effective given the determination of sex offenders, but still many children do resist sexual abuse – either because it is painful or frightening; or because they perceive that it is not an activity of sharing but one performed solely for the benefit of the offender; or because they are enjoined to secrecy in a way which causes them to mistrust the offender. Resistance may take the form of physical struggle or verbal challenge, or it may be expressed in the form of physiological changes, such as when a child stops breathing, stiffens her body, closes her eyes, turns her head, grits her teeth, etc. In every single case the offender is perfectly aware that these gestures or changes mean 'no'.

Why do children resist? Sexual assault upon a child is an inherently threatening act. Young children who have no sex education or understanding of the physiological changes that occur in a man's body when he is aroused, may fear that the abuser is metamorphosing into a monster which will eat them or kill them.

One small boy was heard to describe the male orgasm as a 'bomb exploding'. Children do not know what will happen next and have no way of telling either that the act will come to an end, or that the behaviour will not get worse with time. Indeed, their fear is well-founded: offenders may follow set patterns of abuse, but in general these patterns grow progressively more extreme as the offender gains more and more success in his exploits. The offender also takes care to manipulate and threaten the child explicitly. He need hardly do so, since the child is usually well primed to take full blame for his actions. The offender attempts to build on her guilt by saying that if s/he tells anyone about what has happened, various pets or loved family members will leave her, punish her, die, etc. Or he may resort to overt threat of punishment or death. This exploits the child's very real fear of disfigurement or death from sexual assault. There are cases where fear and the threat of death may play little part in the physical assault itself, and yet it is often implicit in sexual violence: most adult women remember a sense of the murderousness of the offender and a response to incest in which they felt that a part of them 'died' or was 'killed' by the assault. Because children can be made at the point of assault to feel so utterly alone and abandoned by others, they may well project this feeling onto a sense that their mother has 'died' in spirit or a fear that she really will in fact die and abandon them to the offender. This fantasy is extremely powerful in undermining the child's psychic strength and is readily exploited by sex offenders.

Children's reporting of sexual abuse

The second tribute to children's courage and resilience is that, initially, despite the intimidation described above, many of them are not deterred from reporting the abuse to another child or a trusted adult. Unfortunately, the child's report may go unnoticed because it is misunderstood or presented in a cryptic manner – for example, s/he may be too young to speak or to express herself clearly; or s/he may deliberately mask what s/he is saying, half hoping and half terrified that the adult is going to understand. What busy relative or nursery teacher will stop to analyse the statements 'my tummy hurts', 'I don't want to go to the toilet', or 'I don't like the doctor'? Yet these are typical ways in which toddlers and young children expose sexual abuse.

Power over our emotions

Our power to understand sexual abuse from the child's point of view will teach us to overcome our own reluctance to cope with the subject as adults. At present, not only abused children but all children are made vulnerable by adults' ignorance and apathy. A far more dangerous obstacle, however, is adult fear.

Overcoming adult fear

When we are confronted with the suspicion or certainty that a child has been sexually abused, whoever we are our first reaction is usually one of fright. Such fright is complex and not necessarily conscious. Much of it is a reflection of the interests of the community at large, since one case of child assault may pose questions that threaten the very foundations of our social hierarchies and family structures. On the individual level, though, fear can be influenced by: concern for the child's safety, feelings, or future; panic at having to face experiences from our own childhood; worry that we are wrong or that our accusations will be made to look foolish; implications for our relationship to the offender (be he husband, brother, father, son, friend, employer or public official), our sexual relationships, our role within the family, and our status at work or in the community; a sense of being besieged by state agencies who may place more emphasis on containment and social control than on helping and supporting the child. We may feel frightened at our ignorance of our options or confusion over possible consequences of any action that we may take, such as shame or ostracising imposed on us by outsiders; we may fear violence to our own selves from the offender; and finally, for some, there is the threat that their own personal or professional abuse of children may be exposed in the wake of someone else's disclosure.

In the past, individuals and agencies have rarely overcome these obstacles in dealing with child sexual abuse. Naturally: a common survival strategy in reaction to a situation that causes fear is not acceptance or confrontation, but denial and flight. We may well feel so helpless and immobilised that we prefer to deny that a child has been abused rather than face up to the massive shifts of loyalty, the change of lifestyle, the years of sheer emotional hard work and responsibility that must follow if we choose to believe the child. And in this adult reaction, we are often no different from children themselves, who well perceive the implications of reporting. After initial attempts to tell have failed, a child may often learn to deny abuse, perhaps through fear of retribution or of causing others pain. By pretending that nothing has happened s/he may attempt to block out each assault psychologically as it occurs; to lead a normal life amongst her peers; to hold her family together; s/he even hopes, perhaps, that the abuser may desist of his own accord if s/he does not complain. Children who use these strategies, though misguided and ill-informed, at least have well-founded motives for their behaviour. As adults, our motives are less honourable. Whilst the fear we experience may well feel as intense as that of a child, unlike her we have other options. The child appeases fear by sacrificing herself. The adult appeases fear by sacrificing a child.

Overcoming institutionalised fear

Adult denial may be expressed in the form of disbelief. Concerned adults frequently disbelieve children's testimony both within families and in institutions such as schools, the caring professions, the religious establishment and the courts of law. We may add to this betrayal by projecting fear onto the child. It is a truism that the nature of bad news infects the teller, but with incest it is the teller alone who becomes in other people's eyes both the bad news and the infection. In many cultures the incest taboo holds far greater stigma for the person who reports the act than for the one who commits it. Our media and justice systems stereotype sexually abused women as dirty, lying, and unchaste. For younger women these stereotypes crop up on case notes and socal services files in a more sophisticated and apparently objective form: labels such as 'delinquent' or 'promiscuous' are still in widespread use.

If we have the strength of character to avoid aiming at safe targets and thereby scapegoating the child, we overcome our personal fear only to discover the terror of society at large. Massive obstacles are placed in the way of any adult attempting to defend a child's right to safety and justice. For no one is this more so than a child's mother. Most reports of child sexual abuse are made by the mothers of the children concerned,[7] and refuges for battered wives are familiar with the situation where a woman leaves home for the sake of her children's safety rather than for her own. Yet few of these women's reports are taken seriously by the police; even where a case is taken to court with the mother as witness on behalf of the child, her character is routinely assassinated by the defence counsel in a similar manner to the treatment of rape survivors in court;[8] and no state welfare provision is made for such women to lead a life independent of economic support from the offender. Family, friends, neighbours and colleagues may stigmatise mothers who have attempted to help their children; as has been outlined in previous chapters, professional intervention may well work against their rights, and professional influence may even be used unfairly to their detriment. In the face of all these pressures and threats of isolation, it is astounding that any mother is prepared to report sexual abuse at all.

Overcoming professional fear

For the professional who attempts to take child sexual abuse seriously and to protect the children who come under her agency's supervision, there may also be obstacles, especially when s/he has to use institutional authority and interfere with adults' privacy in order to uphold children's rights. At this point s/he will usually encounter a political backlash whereby the privileges of parents are strenuously upheld, whilst workers are painted by the media as ogres thirsting to devastate family life[9]. Usually inter-agency strife ensues and professionals accuse each other of empire-building or of using techniques which themselves amount to child sexual abuse.[10] Meanwhile, the rights of children remain unheeded.

Perhaps the most urgent problem is lack of public information. Until the public can accept how widespread the problem of sexual abuse is, the professional will be frightened to use her power to combat it. Whilst any individual diagnosis may well be mistaken and therefore unjust to parents, it does not help to criticise it on the subjective ground that one just cannot conceive that a high proportion of children in our society are molested.[11] This is no way to approach a subject about which so many of us are so appallingly ignorant.

Then there is the manner in which the child's interests are bypassed or ignored, as so often happens when the parent is seen as the powerless, innocent party: this is a common societal pattern of collusion with the offender. More subtly, the child's interests are presented as subsumed under the notion of 'family' rights which are seen as being besieged by the invading state – hence the championing of alleged abusers' causes by many a left-wing politician,[12] when one might usually expect radicals to associate themselves with the interests of the most powerless. Because the issue is felt to be one between the paternalistic, bureaucratic state and 'the people' or 'the little man', a socialist sees no dilemma in unquestioningly supporting parents, who within their homes may well be conducting their own tyrannical regime.

Another way in which such controversy serves to shift the focus of care away from children and their needs is demonstrated by the agency conflict that predictably arises in these cases. A power struggle is exposed in which professionals battle for the deployment of their clients. There is no denying that work with sexually abused children gives many people a sense of power and excitement for which they will fight other workers or agencies tooth and nail. Not only are individual psychiatrists keen to present themselves as gurus on the subject, but refusal of different agencies to share information, skills and access to clients means not only that children are once more exploited for the gratification of the adult ego, but also that they are subjected to constant repetition of the diagnostic examination which in reality need only be performed once.

Lastly, the woman professional working in this area is particularly vulnerable to public criticism. As a female, she provides a scapegoat for all the fears of a society just awakening to a recognition of the horrors of child sexual abuse. She is a safe target for accusations of 'paranoia' from both public and colleagues alike. In Britain, for example, the psychiatric and medical community which specialises in child sexual abuse is currently disproportionately dominated by men. Any woman who dares to place the interests of children or women within the family before those of male offenders may easily be discredited for 'bias' and is therefore under great pressure to suppress such opinions for the sake of her career. The situation is even worse for those professionals who are also incest survivors themselves. I have met several female psychologists and psychiatrists who are in this position, but they have stated that they would never inform their male superiors of the fact since this would bring them too under the suspicion of paranoia and jeopardise their future within the agency.

A child-centred approach

All of us, whether we are relatives of children or whether we work with them in a professional capacity, share the fear of making mistakes as a result of uncertainty. On discovering that a child has been through an upsetting or potentially life-threatening assault, no one wants to cause her further pain or anxiety. Yet despite all the obstacles outlined above, it is true to say that responsible adults who do not interfere in a situation where a child is being abused actually add to the ill-treatment and injustice that the child is going through.

Whilst as a society we can make some progress in preventing and stopping child sexual abuse, our attempts to deal with its effects on children are as yet quite rudimentary. Projects which place the interests of the child before any other consideration, such as parental 'rights', are rarely state-funded and consequently lack many of the resources granted to statutory bodies. But most statutory organisations are obliged in practice to attend to the interests of 'the family' before those of the child.

In families where sexual abuse occurs, the family dynamics usually centre power and influence in the offender and consequently sacrifice the needs of other members to his interests. Concern for 'the family' from those attempting to intervene usually means continued support for the offender at the expense of innocent family members, with the child being considered as an appendage to the parental relationship rather than an individual with needs and rights of her own. Many workers, not to mention ordinary friends and neighbours, have expressed frustration with the dilemma that they experience when visiting a family where abuse is, or is suspected to be, occurring, since they are in effect policing the parents, and yet their relationship is such that either they are in sympathy with the parents' problems or they have to curry favour with these parents in order to gain access to the children. In both cases, they find that their relationship with all members of the family is compromised and leads to professional dishonesty and collusion with abuse. It is therefore important in our work with abused children to ensure that each member of the family has separate representation, so that the issue of divided loyalty does not block our effectiveness from the outset.

What then is the most practical way in which we can represent children alone, in order to take positive action against child sexual abuse? There are many useful books on crisis intervention and therapeutic work with incest survivors and their families, designed for both professionals and for the ordinary public. Since the main problem for the public, especially parents, is still in accepting that sexual abuse can happen or has happened to a child, this chapter will deal solely with recognition, and readers are referred to the booklist for guidelines on communication with abused children and therapeutic or preventive strategies.

Detection and recognition of child sexual abuse

A common assumption which prevents parents or childcare professionals from recognising the fact that a child has been abused is that sexual abuse is rare. For example, teachers regularly approach child counsellors or community education projects with requests for interviews or consultation with individual abused children. Whilst the children in question certainly need support, the whole emphasis of attention on them alone perpetuates the myth that abuse is a rare phenomenon which only happens in exceptional circumstances. To single out specific children for counselling will cause those children to feel even more isolated, and can turn them into scapegoats amongst their peers. The scapegoating process also protects teachers from facing the possibility that more children in the class have been abused. In such cases it is advisable to educate the class as a whole and to acknowledge that most children in it will have experienced some form of sexual abuse; many children will find public discussion of the subject strengthening, and those who have been through abuse can thus find a positive role in teaching and informing their classmates.

For those who have endured sexual abuse as children and carried its burdens into their adulthood, incest is neither shocking nor a hidden mystery. Media and professionals have made great play of the recent Western 'discovery' of incest, hailing it as the exposure of a 'veiled secret' that goes on 'behind closed doors'. For children, on the other hand, it is not so much a skeleton in the family cupboard as part of the furniture of their everyday lives. Many, although they are aware that they are suffering, are unaware that they are being wronged in the eyes of society; few, although they are aware that they have been betrayed, have any understanding of their legal or moral right to protection. They live the lies imposed on them, not because they accept those lies, but because they have no conception of any other life.

The following hints may be helpful in detecting or confirming suspicions of child sexual abuse, in both girls and boys. Many of the emotional responses are signs of pain, fear, anxiety and grief (which may, of course, have other causes than sexual abuse). It is important to examine the emotional dynamics underlying the acting out of distress rather than simply envisaging the child as a bundle of pathological 'symptoms'.[13] This list is not comprehensive – indeed, no list could be, since reactions to sexual abuse are as unique and various as the people abused. Those who rely too heavily on checklists would do well to remember the commonest 'symptom' of all: this occurs when the child 'seems perfectly all right'. An abused child may have the impression that s/he has been made somehow abnormal by the abuse, and this idea is often consciously imposed by the offender in order to obtain her continued silence. Therefore s/he may well react to abuse by keeping her suffering hidden behind a mask of 'normal' or socially acceptable behaviour, to the extent that concerned adults would find it very hard to believe that s/he has suffered anything at all. Those attempting to detect and combat child sexual abuse are often deterred by the fear that concern for children may lead them to be over-zealous and diagnose abuse where there has been none. Failure to diagnose existing abuse is in fact the greatest problem in this area, but even where one's suspicions turn out to be ill-founded, as Roy Meadows has pointed out, we must not be too afraid of false positives, for the only way to avoid making any false positive diagnosis is never to make *any* diagnosis.[14]

It is often assumed that incest starts in early childhood and continues into adolescence. This is only one of many patterns. Sexual attacks may be made against very small babies (these may even have been planned whilst the baby was still in the womb[15]), or toddlers who are then left untouched by the offender for the rest of their childhood. Or he may only start on them towards adolescence. An incest offender may suddenly rape a girl at 18 after no apparent build-up whatsoever. For those who are too economically disadvantaged to leave home, and for disabled children, the experience of incest may well continue right into adulthood, until the abuser himself leaves home or dies.

Physical indications

Babies can be killed by rape. Choking from penetration of the mouth by the penis can cause suffocation, which may result in death. When children are examined for sexual abuse, it is often forgotten that the offender may have assaulted them orally. In very young children there may be physical damage caused directly by the force of the abuse, although the practised incest offender usually aims to leave no marks. Injuries can include laceration, bleeding, bruises, abrasions, grasp or bite marks; the child's lips may be bruised within if the offender has held his hand over her mouth to prevent sound; other physical damage caused indirectly by the abuse could be urinary tract infection, discharge, or venereal disease (infecting either vagina, penis, anus, or throat);[16] the child may suffer from anal dilatation or dropped bowel, or may have paid urinating; her ability to sit down comfortably or walk properly may be affected; s/he may suffer from vomiting, stomach ache or abdominal cramps. Symptoms which could have a psychosomatic as much as a physical origin might be incontinence; eczema; asthma; allergies; paralysis; nausea; fainting; s/he may be subject to fits which resemble epilepsy. These symptoms express a range of responses, from disgust to self-defence, as described below. The fact that such conditions are brought on by incest rather than by disease or organic factors does not make them any the less real, but they may well not respond to traditional medical treatment.

Physical effects on the adolescent will be the same as above, with the addition the of pregnancy, miscarriage or abortion, especially when the identity of the father is kept secret. Girls may also suffer from gynaecological problems such as premenstrual tension or loss of their period due to stress. There may be increased frequency of menstruation, for example when the girl knows that the offender is repelled by menstrual blood so that her cycle is psychosomatically accelerated; or, in rare cases, girls may show the signs of pregnancy when they are not in fact pregnant. The stress of the experience may express itself for adolescents in the form of migraines, digestive problems, cramps, extreme gain or loss of weight, or even general hypochondria. An osteopath or holistic therapist would assert that every physical and psychological trauma is fully recorded by the body and retained within our bone structure and the distribution of our muscle tension, much as the rings within a tree trunk bear witness to its age. Thus as children grow older, some may develop back problems and it is particularly common to see adolescent incest survivors whose heads hang permanently downward, so that their whole posture is an indication not only of their physical experience of violence but also of emotional stances such as fear, distrust, avoidance of contact, depression, shame, etc.

Emotional/behavioural response

Toddlers and school-age children have difficulty verbalising fears and concerns. They are likely, however, to present physical and behavioural signs and symptoms. Emotionally the very young child will respond to sexual abuse in various ways.

At onset of abuse The most obvious sign is an abrupt change in behaviour, whether the child suddenly becomes shy and clinging or whether s/he suddenly behaves in a brash, outgoing manner. The change usually indicates the onset of abuse and the behaviour is used as a way of coping with it; thus if the child hides behind her mother or under furniture, s/he may be showing fear and apprehension; if s/he runs up to strangers and begins to behave in a sexual way with them, s/he may be showing that s/he believes that this behaviour is expected of her. When abuse begins to happen at an older age, the child may respond to the change by redefining her relationship to the offender: s/he may call him by a name, such as his first name, which is considered inappropriate within her culture; s/he may refer to him as simply 'him' rather by name, or as 'it', 'X', etc.

Confidence and energy Abuse saps a child's energies and the energy necessary for survival may be diverted from that usually directed towards growth and development. The emotional neglect inherent in sexual abuse may induce failure to thrive. Sexual abuse invariably produces a sense of powerlessness in children, and this may decrease their confidence in their bodies and mental abilities. Children may thus develop learning disabilities comparable to dyslexia, or problems of expression such as poor eye contact, tics, stammering and blushing. Stress may affect their play or school work, reducing the ability to concentrate and inducing hyperactivity, destructiveness, aggression, etc. In children who have been abused very young, such stress behaviour has sometimes been misinterpreted as mental disability, brain damage or even autism. Co-ordination and concentration powers are also seen to be affected in the child who as a result of abuse becomes noticeably 'accident prone'.

Fear   Fear may affect the child's pattern of sleeping; for example, s/he may suddenly request a night-light in her bedroom or suffer from nightmares, insomnia and bedwetting. Assaults committed at night can result in the child developing patterns of sleep-walking or sleep-talking. They may also lead to drowsiness during the day, if the child has kept herself awake in order to ward off abuse (strangely, we are always concerned by such sleep problems in adults, and yet in small children we have accepted them as entirely normal). Sleep disturbances show that however the child may succeed in repressing the experience of sexual abuse by the use of her conscious and rational strengths, the fear that it induces will be expressed by her subconscious mind. Similarly, the child's fear may be expressed in behaviours which largely draw on the subconscious, such as trance states, 'freak-outs', or spell-like repetition of words or chants. The heightened sexual state of the offender may communicate itself to children as a kind of magical power, and it is common for small children to believe that the offender can somehow read their mind, know where they are hiding, etc. Clearly in cases where the offender is also a religious officiary or medical professional, the process is exacerbated, since he may accompany his acts with suggestions that they are the will of God or medical treatment that will do the child good.[17] In response to the fear engendered by this 'supernatural' aspect of sexual abuse, children can develop obsessively ritualistic behaviour to combat it. All are familiar with childhood games such as stepping away from the cracks in paving stones, chanting magic words, or holding one's breath for as long as possible; these are often used by children who are being sexually abused. The daydreaming adolescent who appears to have a 'faraway look' or is 'wrapped up in a world of her own' may also be using mental distancing techniques either to retreat or to fly away from the fear induced by her experience. Finally, fear may cause a child to do everything in her power to appease adults, and the behaviour of 'model' children who are extremely quiet and polite must be considered in this light.

Disgust Disgust can affect a child's eating habits, for example by refusal to eat or to drink, especially egg or milky liquids (perhaps because they remind her of semen). The child also expresses disgust by washing or wiping herself repeatedly. Obsessive cleanliness is usually associated with adolescence, but in fact may be seen in toddlers as a reaction to sexual abuse. Conversely, a child may appear to regress and begin to soil herself with food, play materials, earth, body waste, etc, in order to demonstrate the way that s/he feels the abuse has made her dirty. Displaced disgust will often take the form of phobias such as irrational fears of insects, birds, reptiles, etc; the reason being that these are socially acceptable objects of a revulsion which it is impermissible to direct openly towards the offender. The sense of 'dirtiness' is also expressed by the adolescent who conforms to punk-style fashions, wearing ragged or patched clothes, the modern equivalent sometimes of sackcloth and ashes.

The disgust felt in response to sexual abuse finds an easy outlet in self-hatred. This begins at the point when one perceives that physically one is vulnerable to abuse, as an anger that one's own body has let one down. Some children rationalise this experience by the feeling, 'my body is not my own'. Hence they begin to hate their bodies, distancing themselves either by self-neglect or by excessive cleansing or purifying rituals, such as constantly picking or scraping at their skin, the very organ of touch which represents contact with the outside world, that magic boundary which both separates us from and connects us with the feelings of others. The vast array of skin products available on the modern market bears witness to the fact that many adult women are still suffering from the child's sense of disgust at the violation of her organ of touch. As for the body as a whole, some survivors continue to feel that it is betraying them and has almost taken over from the abuser in this respect. As one survivor bitterly replied when asked what legal punishment she thought was appropriate for child molestation, 'I can't sue my father for loss of peaceful enjoyment of my own body, can I?' But our body also represents the mother within us, since it emerged from within her. That our body is felt to have betrayed us is one reason why so much of the survivor's sense of disgust may be projected as anger towards her own mother for failing to protect her, and why so much self-disgust is acted out by the abuse of nurturing media such as food, drink, air and medicines, as when the young person becomes anorexic or bulimic, alchoholic, addicted to smoking/sniffing solvents, or uses harmful drugs.

Self-hatred in females is so fostered and encouraged in our culture that it is not necessarily an accurate indicator that a girl is being overtly sexually abused. But when it is strongly expressed by an adolescent girl, especially in the form of clinical depression, self-mutilation, or suicide attempts, it should be borne in mind that incest is highly likely to have caused it.

Trust   Trust is an important issue for the sexually abused child, especially if s/he has been betrayed by a close relative. The child may develop various behaviours which express mistrust of all adults, such as jumpiness, watchfulness, repeated flinching, or covering the mouth with the hand as s/he speaks. The notion of 'covering' can extend to a heightened sense of personal modesty, but it can equally well be externalised by the development of the Mask, a concept familiar to all of us who have been forced to endure abuse in private. We put on a 'brave face', 'grin and bear it', become the 'life and soul of the party', but suffer from a feeling of acute isolation within. A favourite image chosen by abused children to represent their Mask is that of the Clown (or Fool), often present in their drawings, posters, toys and other personal bric-à-brac. The Clown is one who laughs to hide his tears, or smiles when in pain; the Fool is inner wisdom presented as an incomprehensible joke. The best way to detect a Mask is first to recognise your own.

Children may display introversion or secretiveness in other areas of life than the sexual abuse, and some will act their mistrust out by dishonest forms of behaviour such as stealing. Because adults so manifestly do not want to know about child sexual abuse, children become expert about hiding not just that but all their other feelings too. An extreme example of children's mistrust is elective mutism, where the child stops speaking altogether. This can be a shock reaction, or it may be a conscious choice, as described by Maya Angelou:[18]

> Then there was the pain. A breaking and entering when even the senses are torn apart. The act of rape on an eight-year-old body is a matter of the needle giving because the camel can't. The child gives, because the body can, and the mind of the violator cannot.

I thought I had died . . .

In those moments I decided that although [my little brother] loved me he couldn't help. I had sold myself to the Devil and there could be no escape. The only thing I could do was to stop talking to people other than [my brother]. Instinctively . . . I knew that . . . if I talked to anyone else that person might die too. Just my breath, carrying my words out, might poison people and they'd curl up and die . . .

I had to stop talking . . . for a while I was punished for being so uppity that I wouldn't speak; and then came the thrashings, given by any relative who felt himself offended.

Pain and grief   Two of children's responses to sexual abuse which are often glossed over in the orthodox literature are their pain and grief. These can be experienced simultaneously as both physical and mental sensations. They are to be found in young people whose chests are hunched or whose arms are constantly protectively folded, or in those who seem much older than their years. We see grief in the teenage girl who appears to be in 'mourning' – she is permanently wearing dark, drab clothing. We see children attempting to deny or take control of their pain by wearing thin summer clothes in the middle of winter, acquiring tattoos, slashing their arms, and so forth. These feats of endurance are often a source of pride to the child, much as an old war veteran or prisoner shows his scars or as many cultures throughout the world use tattooing or scarification as signs of initiation into adulthood.

Anger   Anger, another frequently unmentioned reaction, is commonly expressed by abused children, and even very young children may have a grasp of the injustice of their experience which they will challenge through temper tantrums, rebelliousness, apparently unrelated outbursts of rage, and so on. For an analysis of the origins of children's anger, see Chapter 3.

Power and control   The child, especially as s/he grows older, attempts to assert some form of power or control over her life. All the behaviours described above may be seen as assertions of personal power from the child's point of view. Besides these, there are the more recognised forms of rebelliousness and disobedience to authority. Examples are disruptiveness in class groups, or truanting/running away from home or institutions. Adolescence is considered a time of hormonal imbalance and general rebellion without a cause. This popular view of teenage disturbance as causeless and unavoidable begs many questions about incest. Young people's distress at their general powerlessness is quite understandable. By adolescence the majority of girls will have been sexually abused or exploited in one way or another. Most adolescent girls' emotional distress, depression and delinquency are a direct and logical reaction to this abuse, and are some of the few ways in which they can assert the force of will to resist it.

Direct communication

Symbolic behaviour   So far we have considered ways that sexual abuse can be detected indirectly from children's behaviour. The above examples may be unconscious manifestations on the child's part, but sometimes they may be interpreted as unspoken appeals for help, as when a child hides an object not intending to prevent the adult from finding it but in the hope that the adult will notice that it is hidden. Unfortunately, because of the ignorance of the audience, many of these hidden appeals are doomed to blow up in the child's face. This happens to the teenage girl who is seen as a hysterical female indulging in repeated 'self-dramatising' scenes. When she finally dares to name the real reason for her upsets, she is seen as inventing yet another story for effect.

Verbal reports   But many children will tell us directly about the sexual abuse they are experiencing. Such reports must always be taken seriously, since small children do not have the mental or emotional equipment to invent sexual stories or to manipulate adults with them; and in the few cases where older children fabricate allegations of abuse against someone, the young person is usually protecting another offender or indicating that something else is desperately wrong. Some children are unaware of the fact that they may shock others with details of the abuse, and the straightforwardness and matter-of-factness of their accounts must not prevent us from recognising that they have suffered. In some cases, children even boast about abuse to other children in the playground or nursery.

Visual representations   Children tell us about sexual abuse by drawing pictures of it. Of course, with visual imagery the interpretation depends very much upon the world picture of the artist and the attitudes of the viewer, but there are four cases in which one should be alerted to the possibility of abuse. First, if a child resists drawing any human figures at all, but sticks to objects, animals, landscapes, etc, it would be worth asking oneself whether s/he is not drawing human figures because s/he finds them frightening. Secondly, one can note the anatomy of any figures drawn. For example, if they have no arms or hands, this may indicate that s/he wishes that someone would stop touching her, or, conversely, that s/he is getting no comfort or protection; if s/he draws human faces without eyes or mouth, there is a chance that s/he has been made to feel watched or to see something that upsets her, or to keep an unpleasant secret. Third, the image of the house for all of us represents the body or the self. If the child draws houses without windows and/or doors, this may be because s/he feels trapped at home or unable to escape from abuse. Fourthly, if a little boy repeatedly draws representations, of himself or a man with emphasised nipples, he may be feeling upset and confused about gender roles as a result of being sexually used by a man.

Acting out Children approach other children and adults sexually in the effort to demonstrate and expose what is happening to them in secret. It is a difficult task for us all to distinguish harmless sex play from abuse or a cry for help amongst small children, but with sensitivity and experience these distinctions can be drawn. Children may also act out their abuse with their dolls or toys. For some children, compulsive public masturbation can be a way of showing that something sexual is disturbing them.

It will be clear from this outline on children's and young people's reactions to sexual abuse that the variations of response are infinite. Much of the behaviour described may not indicate sexual abuse at all; the point is not to fasten onto a 'symptom' as if it were a key or talisman, but to consider the child as a whole person, with human needs and feelings. As Finkelhor suggests, by homing in on the survivor of sexual abuse in order to seek 'signs' and 'symptoms' of the experience, we are further victimising her.[19] Consequently, it is only fair to conclude below by focusing on the offender, who after all, is the source of the problem.

External factors

There are some events or situations which, although they are unrelated to the child's personal behaviour, alert us to the fact that sexual abuse could be going on. For example, if a pupil persistently arrives very early at school and leaves late, with few absences, this might be a way of avoiding abuse at home. If you notice that your child has more sweets or money than usual, check whether these are bribes. Any clubs that children attend where secret games or rituals are enacted should be a matter for concern. If s/he consistently avoids the company of a particular person without apparent justification, then it might be worth investigating the reason. If s/he keeps refusing to sleep in her own bed at night or sleeps there in her daytime clothes, this is a strong indication that s/he is not feeling safe in it. Likewise if s/he wants a lock on her door.

The child-molester

One of the hardest facts for people to face about child sexual abuse is that all of us are acquainted with child-molesters without necessarily knowing it. We may be related to them or employed in the same workplace; they may be our friends, our lovers, our parents or our children. They are usually indistinguishable in their general behaviour from people who do not molest children. However, it is important to note certain patterns of behaviour which are common to child-molesters in order to help us to challenge and prevent sexual abuse at its root, instead of patching up the devastation of individual children as and when they are attacked. This section is intended neither to scare readers into suspecting everyone around them nor to suggest that one can infallibly identify every sex offender as soon as he appears on the scene. However, offenders depend on our trust of them and doubt of our own gut reactions in order to continue with their abuse. For this reason we might need some concrete guidelines to clarify any suspicions we have. The following open-ended checklist is derived from the experience of women and children who have shared their experiences with me over a seven-year period.

Recidivism   The highest indicator of future offences is known to be past offence; if you know a man to have molested children in the past, it is in no circumstances safe to leave children alone with him. This is an important issue for those who have been molested by brothers. As brothers grow up and start their own families, one cannot dismiss the possibility that their own children are at risk, even though one may have rationalised their boyhood behaviour as childish experimentation. It is also important for those molested by fathers to try to ensure that they do not get lone access to their grandchildren. In many women's experience, the offences continue with each new generation. This point is stressed here because many people who were abused as children have been led by the offender to believe that it was some special quality in them that induced abuse. There are numerous accounts by adult women who were under the impression that if they 'permitted' abuse to themselves, their sisters would be left in peace. When these sisters grow up and find the freedom to speak openly with one another, they often find that the man has pulled exactly the same trick on each of them. Some are also given the impression that the offender is molesting them precisely because they are his kin, and therefore that anyone who is not his kin will be safe – or the reverse. The facts that emerge when survivors grow up and make enquiries amongst their friends/stepsisters, etc., do not bear this myth out. Of course, morally speaking, it is hardly the survivor's responsibility to protect further children from assaults by her abuser: the responsibility lies first with the abuser and then with society at large. However, until society chooses to accept that abusers are continuing to molest children, the adult survivor may feel a practical responsibility for exposing her abuser so that further assaults can be prevented.

Sexism   As stated in the Introduction to this book, child-molesters are 97 per cent male, a large proportion of them boys. This marked gender imbalance is in part attributable to the sexist socialisation of the male as described by Rich Snowdon.[20] Consequently, any man who is markedly sexist or misogynist may well be capable of sexual offences against children. Particularly suspect here are men who evidence an infantile and depersonalising sexuality, such a those who read pornography or use prostitutes. Pornography is frequently used as a tool in child sexual abuse, and shown to the child either before or during the assaults.[21] Therefore any child living in a house in which pornography is known to be in use must be considered to be in danger.

Domination   Another feature of sexist male socialisation is the emphasis on paternal or patriarchal power within the family. Thus, a father who appears obsessed with discipline, punishment, 'law and order', etc, or has a rigidly disciplinarian religious streak, may be likely to be molesting or assaulting his children. This is particularly apparent when a father tries to restrict his family's contact with the outside world (for example, by keeping a tight control over family finances), especially when he shows jealousy over his daughter's attempts at going out with her peers and starting sexual relationships of her own. In addition, wherever a man is battering his wife or children, this is almost invariably accompanied by a pattern of sexual abuse.

Hypocrisy/abuse of trust   We can all recognise the bully; harder to detect is the offender with the opposite characteristics, namely the supremely 'gentle' man who appears very caring and affectionate towards children, often gravitating towards careers concerned with childcare, such as youth work, teaching, etc. The existence of this kind of sex offender must be particularly upsetting to and undermining for the male anti-sexist movement, since these types sometimes involve themselves in men's groups, which provide the ideal camouflage for their activities. There are cases where rapists and child-molesters have developed this pretence of fashionable anti-sexism to such a convincing degree that they have managed to infiltrate rape crisis centres[22] or battered women's refuges as workers whom the feminist agencies have hired from a spirit of idealism, in order either to support abused boys and men or to ensure that children benefit from a gentle male role model. By raping and molesting in these circumstances, offenders betray not only those whom they abuse but also other men who are genuinely caring or trying to work for change. The only solution to this problem is for truly anti-sexist men to develop their awareness on rape and child molestation, and to ensure that they challenge and exclude from their collectives anyone known to be guilty of sexual assault.

The 'anti-sexist' offender is a new political animal, but he does have something in common with a more basic type of child molester, who is often known as 'Mr Nice Guy' by survivors or 'the Pillar of the Community' by professionals combating child sexual abuse. Professionals tend to concentrate on the perceived contradiction inherent in the behaviour of a man who is a good citizen, model employee, liked by his family, popular amongst friends, and so on – and yet who can abuse women and children in private. Survivors, however, are not so surprised by the phenomenon, since they would argue that the socially approved behaviour is simply a mask or strategy by which this type of offender consciously attempts to gain the trust of his community, thus ensuring that if ever a child were to allege sexual assualt, s/he would be disbelieved and cast out whilst he retained his status and privileged access to other children. For the survivor to be treated as an outcast is a particularly painful experience when the molester is a religious leader, or if he is prominent within an oppressed cultural, racial or political community, in which case the pressing need for coherence within the community will lend the offender even more authority. Any child accusing him of molestation will be seen as a threat to the solidarity of the minority group whilst he apparently is the champion of its rights.

Manipulativeness The child-molester often has a strong sense of 'entitlement'. This can be expressed in an open manner, as with the patriarchal father described above. But it may also be expressed in a manipulative, self-pitying manner, by the type of man who presents himself as a victim of, for example, a 'nagging wife' who 'doesn't understand him', or 'a terrible childhood', or who seems to feel in general that the world owes him a living. Such a man might flit from relationship to relationship with adult women, vilifying the last partner and suggesting that the present one is the centre of his world and the only person who understands him, etc. This manipulation of the current partner by pitting her against the former, who is seen as a punishing parental figure, is directly analogous to the method of gaining sexual access to children, especially girls, by pitting them against their mothers ('your mother doesn't understand me', 'I love your more than I love her', etc.). It is important for the new wife or partner in these cases to consider just how much objective information is available about the man's previous life. Many of them seem to have a 'mysterious' past, perhaps even travelling from town to town or from job to job in order to escape it.

Behaviour with children Some researchers have suggested that child-molesters frequently have problems with peer-group rela-tionships and see themselves as loners. I have not found this categorisation to be useful except in relation to the type of adolescent offender who keeps company only with adults or with children much younger than himself, With adults, more instructive than an examination of peer group relationships is a consideration of how they relate to the children in their care. Obviously some of the following behaviours are frequently perfectly innocent, but they also accompany sexual abuse and are therefore listed not as a foolproof checklist, but as a guide to clarifying any suspicion one may have. They are: idealising sentimentality over children; treating children as one's personal property; erratic discipline of children, involving harshness to one, and favouritism to another; manipulating children against each other or against adult women, especially the offender's wife; violence, insults, or disrespect for children's integrity (this is demonstrated by squeezing, teasing, tickling, horseplay, etc., which continues even though the child is clearly upset); threatening behaviour towards a child which appears to cow the child inordinately (i.e. the apparent threat to the child is small but the child is aware of other, more serious threats, which the offender does not even need to mention – hence the child appears over-obedient for no reason); comments expressing either sexual interest in or harsh criticism of a child's personal appearance; the deliberate isolation of individual children or secret private meetings/clubs with children; asking children to keep secrets; giving children sex education lessons one-to-one and in private; showing children pornography; insisting on 'tucking children into bed' alone, or hanging about the bathroom/bedroom in a surreptitious manner when a child is undressed; giving children an excessive amount of money or presents; giving children age-inappropriate presents (such as make-up or adult-style clothes given to a small girl); constantly stating or implying that a particular child is untrustworthy or a liar (i.e. preparing a defence against any chance of future allegations by the child).

Responses to current developments   Since child sexual abuse has been so much in the public eye of late, it has been interesting to note how child-molesters are attempting to deal with the subject in the hope of deflecting attention from themselves. As might be expected, many have continued to be extremely skilful. Some have moved to the forefront of the professional anti-abuse lobby; others have taken the same stance at home. Several survivors have reported their own abusers' indignant comments addressed to friends and family members during a discussion or television programme on the subject ('They ought to be shot'; 'String 'em up'; 'How could anybody do such a thing to a child? I can't comprehend it').

Mothers have reported that after such programmes have been screened, and they have made some general comment on the subject, their partners have suddenly become unduly defensive and indignantly accused them of paranoia ('Are you suggesting I would do such a thing? How can you have such a dirty mind?'). Later the mother would discover that the partner was indeed molesting her children.

The *New York Times* has reported the case of a man who headed a child protection organisation in Minnesota:

> When 13-year-old Sarah Ann Rairdon disappeared in May, the people of Underwood rallied together to search for her and comfort her family. Afterward, with her father, John Albert Rairdon, they organised to help missing children. Mr Rairdon was chosen to lead their new group, Search and Find Missing Persons Inc. No one can forget the many appeals for Sarah's return that Mr Rairdon made on television after her disappearance May 20. Nor the fact that just a week before his arrest he had appeared on a panel with the Minnesota Attorney General . . . to discuss missing children and sexual abuse.[23]

John Rairdon was arrested in August that year for the murder of his daughter, who had been stabbed in the stomach with an awl.

The molester may also take advantage of current professional misapprehensions about child sexual abuse: when generalising about the subject, he blames children or their mothers; he suggests that many women molest their sons; he will insist that child sexual abuse is a family dynamic and not solely the problem of the offender.

Conclusion

It is hoped that these guidelines will offer readers some support in the task of understanding the dynamics of child sexual abuse and the ways in which we can identify it within our own communities. What is so remarkable about the above behaviour patterns is that they are reproduced over and over again in our society, and yet for each individual child the imprisonment imposed by the offender can result in feelings of total isolation from the rest of the world – the sense that one is not, and never can be, fully understood. But as the survivor self-help network is extended and increasing numbers of children, teenagers and adults break one another's silence, so more and more people are experiencing the intense relief and excitement that can accompany any recognition of ourselves in others. Survivors have frequently commented on the healing power of such a meeting of minds. At last we can relax at the thought that in each other's company we can be understood without the need for excuses, lengthy explanations, or even any words at all.

Communication on a personal level further empowers us collectively to influence our environment, to educate those who have no personal experience of sexual abuse and to expose those who are abusing. Only people who have been through sexual abuse face to face with the child-molester are in a position to describe his behaviour first-hand to those attempting to define or control it. Survivors are the ideal advisors on methods of interviewing children in such a way that they build up the confidence to disclose their experiences of assault; survivors have devised preventive education projects confident in their approach because they are clear about how they themselves would have liked to have been advised as children. Besides, they can provide invaluable insights into therapeutic techniques with children and adolescents, whether conducted on a one-to-one basis or in groups. Hence throughout the modern exposure of sexual abuse as a social problem, and the vast proliferation of agencies set up all over the world to study, prevent, combat and treat the sexual abuse of children, the contribution of adults who have themselves experienced child sexual abuse has been paramount.

This book has in part attempted to show how a feminist analysis exposes the flaws in the traditional approach to child sexual abuse. Feminist frameworks may help us to clarify our ideas and to improve our practice. However, it is no practical solution to the problem merely to substitute one theory for another and to refuse to evolve further. Any part of an ideology which fails to serve the needs of children must be rejected or reshaped. Hence feminism itself is useful only in so far as it is synthesised with other approaches to reflect the interests of the people whom it claims to represent.

It is important for those, including feminists, who have not been through sexual abuse first-hand to acknowledge the experience and expertise of female and male incest survivors. And for those of us who do have inside experience of the subject, it is time to recognise our strength for what it is and to reclaim our right to share it with others.

Notes and References

1. Katherine Whitehorn, 'Fear in the Home', *The Observer,* 4 September 1983.
2. From an interview with the historian Lucy Bland, filmed for *Crime of Violence* (Channel 4 Television, 1986). For full details of the suffragette campaigns and aims, see Sheila Jeffreys, *The Spinster and her Enemies: Feminism and Sexuality 1880–1930*, Pandora Press, 1985.
3. Ibid.
4. From the trial of Watson-Sweeney, Old Bailey, London 19 December 1982. Reported in *The Times,* 20 December 1983.
5. See note 2.
6. The pronoun 's/he' in this chapter is an abbreviation for 'she or he'. I have used 'her' meaning 'her or him' or 'her or his' for the sake of brevity.
7. See Introduction note 145.
8. Part of the cross-examination of one mother in a London court in 1983 may illustrate the problem.
    Barrister: 'You have [previously] threatened to divorce [your husband] because of [his] drunkenness and [the] rows? . . . And of course you would have appreciated, would you not, when you were contemplating divorce, who would look after [your child]? . . . You've been married once before haven't you? . . . You had 2 children by that man? . . . Of course that marriage ended in divorce? [Your first husband got custody of the two children.] Looking back, is it a matter that you very much regret that you didn't have the care and control of them? . . . After you had been going out with [the defendant, didn't you have] another child by a man other than [him]? . . . When you were contemplating threatening the defendant with divorce, because of as you say the drunkenness and squabbles, is it not right to say that you were desperate to get the custody of [your child]? . . . In the past, at times of stress, it's right isn't it that you have been susceptible to mental breakdown? . . . Would you not agree that since what you have referred to as some slight breakdown, you've never been quite normal?
    Mother: 'No.'
    Barrister: 'So you're abnormal . . . Are you close to your parents? . . . Is it right that last year they separated? . . . In October last year, was your home burgled? . . . You'll appreciate that you never fully

recovered [from post-natal depression] . . . In January 1980 you were convicted . . . of shoplifting . . .'

9. A case in point is the judicial inquiry of 1987–8, before Mrs/Lord Justice Butler-Sloss, into a controversial diagnostic system of detecting sexual abuse developed by paediatricians working for the Cleveland Health Authority in Britain. A tabloid reported: 'In a quiet and forgotten corner of England a misguided woman's crusading zeal tore a county apart [and] wrecked family life . . . within nine months . . . a chasm [opened] in Cleveland which came close to swallowing the social fabric of the community' (*The Evening Standard*, 5 July 1988). Not even respectable, 'quality' newspapers managed to avoid the cheap. personal insinuations. For example: 'One of the paediatricians . . . unblinkingly defended her . . . professional view of what the town is today – a place where an unthinkable proportion of its men sexually molest . . . their own children. Sometimes she confessed herself puzzled by the legal form of the questions from . . . counsel to the inquiry . . . But doubts about the scientific merits of her tests? – never . . . Still to be heard in the days ahead are the legal voices of . . . the disapproving police and the irate nurses who worked at her side in a year which has seen 120 children away from their parents with unchallenged authority, as though they were no more than the litter of an over-fertile cat. [She] is seen as an Australian Joan of Arc among the keenest of the social workers she has clearly persuaded that up to one in ten children are abused by the adults who have them in charge . . . and it was the collective crusading duty of them all to reveal all. The odd nods and smiles at her more confident answers show that here . . . are those already sniffing the air for the whiff of burning martyr' (*The Times*, 18 November 1987).

10. A Manchester police surgeon and consultant to the NSPCC accused the Cleveland paediatricians of 'outrageous sexual assault' on children they examined in hospital (*The Times*, 24 November 1987). It was suggested to her in court that she herself had been guilty of the same in examining a boy aged 4 to reinforce her findings before giving evidence to the inquiry (*The Times*, 15 November 1987). Lord Justice Butler-Sloss ultimately found this surgeon an unreliable witness, who was 'unable to provide us with a cool, detached and considered testimony' (*The Independent*, 5 September 1988).

11. In the Cleveland case, a steep increase in care orders being placed upon children considered to have been sexually assaulted within their homes led to public shock. Altogether, 121 cases of sexual abuse had been diagnosed over the first six months of 1987. One of the groups involved in the dispute was Parents Against Injustice, a national organisation of people who consider themselves wrongly accused of child abuse. The director of this group said that she 'could not believe' that all the cases could be genuine, simply because there were too many (*The Guardian*, 24 June 1987; *The Independent*, 15 September 1987). But for one hospital, let alone one urban health authority, to diagnose 121 cases over a period of six months is, far from an overreaction, a severe underestimation of the sheer numbers involved.

12. Stuart Bell, Labour Member of Parliament for Middlesbrough, who was the final witness in the Cleveland inquiry, alleged that doctors and social services had conspired against his constituents. He claimed that there had been 'many miscarriages of justice' and that the diagnoses of abuse made by two paediatricians at the centre of the controversy had been a 'fundamental attack on family life' in the county (*The Times*, 17 December 1987). He was reproved in the final report of the inquiry for his 'intemperate and inflammatory remarks' in the course of his media campaign, and was shown to have defended as innocent several parents who were in fact guilty of abuse (*The Independent*, 7 July 1988).

13. 'Child abuse cases can make workers feel de-skilled and there is a passionate search for rules to follow. Hence the flood of guidelines that have characterised the last decade. We almost believe that these rules will act as a talisman if followed to the letter . . . Yet we know each case is unique. No rules can be a substitute for sensitivity, skill and experience. (Jean Moore, 'Like a Rabbit Caught in Headlights', *Community Care*, 4 November 1982).

14. In 'Staying Cool on Child Abuse', *British Medical Journal*, 1987, vol. 295. See also the *Women in Medicine* Policy Paper on child sexual abuse, independent publication, London 1988.

15. As evidenced by research conducted by Dr Brendan McCarthy, of the Tavistock Clinic, London (paper addressed to the British Association of Social Workers, Obstetrics and Gynaecology Subgroup, St. Thomas' Hospital, London, 7 June 1985).

16. For the importance of these infections as virtually certain indicators of sexual interference, see Suzanne M. Sgroi, 'Child Sexual Assault: Some Guidelines for Intervention and Assessment' in Ann Wolbert Burgess, A. Nicholas Groth, Lynda Lytle Holmstrom and Suzanne M. Sgroi (eds), *Sexual Assault of Children and Adolescents* (Lexington, Mass.: Lexington Books, 1978).

17. For an account of one doctor who claimed spanking was religious therapy, see *The Independent*, 13 March 1987.

18. Maya Angelou, *I know Why the Caged Bird Sings* (London: Virago, 1983).

19. David Finkelhor, 'Risk Factors in the Sexual Victimization of Children', *Child Abuse and Neglect*, vol. 4, 1980.

20. See Introduction note 38.

21. A man with an eleven-year history of court appearances for sexual offences against children was found to be in possession of a stash of pornographic videos and magazines, photographs of boys whom he had abused, and babies'/children's outfits. One 12-year-old boy whom he had assaulted was repeatedly shown pornographic videos involving children (*Streatham and Lambeth Comet*, 20 November 1987).

22. See Dr Ann Wolbert Burgess, 'The Sexual Exploitation of Children: Sex Rings, Pornography and Prostitution', paper presented at a symposium on child sexual abuse at Teesside Polytechnic, Middlesbrough, 20 May 1984.

23. 'Father's Arrest Deepens a Small Town Mystery', *New York Times*, 19 August 1985.

Further reading

This book highlights specific areas which may be of further interest or of practical use to readers. The books and articles are recommended for their sympathetic approach to incest survivors. For more conventional academic and research works, please refer to the notes on individual chapters.

First-person accounts

Angelou, Maya, *I Know Why the Caged Bird Sings* (London: Virago, 1984).
Bass, Ellen and Thornton, Linda, *I Never Told Anyone* (New York: Harper & Row, 1983).
McNaron, Toni and Morgan, Yarrow, *Voices in the Night* (London: Cleiss Press, 1982).
Rider, Rose, 'Pater Familias', in U. Owen (ed.), *Fathers, Reflections by Daughters* (London: Virago, 1983; New York: Pantheon, 1985).
Sunna, 'Transformations', in P. McNeill, M. McShea and P. Parmar (eds), *Through the Break* (London: Sheba, 1986).

Fictional accounts

El Saadawi, Nawal, *Woman at Point Zero* (London: Zed Press, 1985).
Walker, Alice, *The Color Purple* (London: Women's Press, 1983).

Analysis

Brownmiller, Susan, *Against Our Will* (New York: Simon & Shuster, 1975).
Campbell, Beatrix, *Unofficial Secrets: Child Sexual Abuse – the Cleveland Case* (London: Virago, 1988).
El Saadawi, Nawal, *The Hidden Face of Eve: Women in the Arab World* (London: Zed Press, 1980).

Herman, Judith, *Father-Daughter Incest* (Cambridge, Mass.: Harvard University Press, 1981).

London Rape Crisis Centre, *Sexual Violence: The Reality for Women* (London: Women's Press, 1984).

Masson, Jeffrey, *The Assault on Truth (Freud's Suppression of the Seduction Theory)* (London: Faber, 1984).

McIntyre, Kevin, 'Role of Mothers in Father-Daughter Incest: A Feminist Analysis', *Social Work*, National Association of Social Workers Inc, USA, November 1981.

Miller, Alice, *For Your Own Good: The Roots of Violence in Child-Rearing* (London: Virago, 1983); *The Drama of Being a Child* (London: Virago, 1986).

Nelson, Sarah, *Incest: Fact and Myth* (Edinburgh: Stramullion, 1982; new edn. 1987).

Rhodes, Dusty and McNeill, Sandra, *Women Against Violence Against Women* (London: Onlywomen Press, 1985).

Rush, Florence, *The Best Kept Secret* (Maidenhead: McGraw Hill, 1980; Englewood Cliffs, NJ: Prentice-Hall, 1980).

Ward, Elizabeth, *Father-Daughter Rape,* (London: Women's Press, 1984).

Preventive work with children

Adams, Caren and Fay, Jennifer, *No More Secrets* (London: Impact, 1981).

Colao, Flora and Hosansky, Tamar, *Your Children Should Know* (New York: Berkley, 1985).

Kraizer, Sherryll, *The Safe Child Book* (New York: Dell, 1985).

Lowe, Judith, *et al.*, *Street Wise* (BBC, London: Ariel Books, 1984).

You're in Charge (Independent Publication, Salt Lake City, Utah, 1983).

Therapeutic work with children

Burgess, A.W., Groth, A.N., Holmstrom, L.L. and Sgroi, S.M., *Sexual Assault of Children and Adolescents* (Lexington, Mass.: Lexington Books, 1978).

Meiselman, Karin, *Incest: A Psychological Study of Causes and Effects with Treatment Recommendations* (London: Jossey-Bass, 1981).

Stevens, Doris and Berliner, Lucy, 'Special Techniques for Child Witnesses', in L. Schultz and C. Thomas (eds), *The Sexual Victimology of Youth* (Springfield, Ill: 1980).

Work with offenders

Dreiblatt, Irwin, *Issues in the Evaluation of the Sex Offender* (Washington State Psychological Association, May 1982).

Snowdon, Rich, 'Working with Incest Offenders; Excuses, Excuses, Excuses', in *Aegis*, no. 29, autumn 1980.

Literature for children

Bass, Ellen, *I Like You to Make Jokes With Me, But I Don't Want You to Touch Me* (Chapel Hill, NC: Lollipop Power, 1981).
Chetin, Helen, *Frances Ann Speaks Out – My Father Raped Me* (New Seed Press, 1977).
Freeman, Lory, *It's My Body* (Seattle Parenting Press, 1982).
Wachter, Oralee, *No More Secrets for Me* (Viking Kestrel, Penguin, 1985).

Literature for adolescents

Adams, Caren, *No is Not Enough* (London: Impact 1985).
King County Rape Relief, *Top Secret: Information on Sexual Abuse for Teenagers ONLY* (Renton, WA, 1982).
Marsh, Jenny, *Stepping Out: Incest Info for Girls* (Haberfield, NSW: Media Press, 1986).

DATE DUE

DEC 1 6 1999			
OC 23 '01			
APR 2 2002			
OC 23 '02			
SE 1 '05			
OC 26 '06			
GAYLORD			PRINTED IN U.S.A